Gender, Environment, and Development in Kenya

Gender, Environment, and Development in Kenya

A Grassroots Perspective

Barbara Thomas-Slayter
and Dianne Rocheleau

with
Isabella Asamba, Mohamud Jama,
Charity Kabutha, Njoki Mbuthi,
Elizabeth Oduor-Noah, Karen Schofield-Leca,
Betty Wamalwa-Muragori, and Leah Wanjama

LYNNE
RIENNER
PUBLISHERS

BOULDER
LONDON

Published in the United States of America in 1995 by
Lynne Rienner Publishers, Inc.
1800 30th Street, Boulder, Colorado 80301

and in the United Kingdom by
Lynne Rienner Publishers, Inc.
3 Henrietta Street, Covent Garden, London WC2E 8LU

Library of Congress Cataloging-in-Publication Data
Thomas-Slayter, Barbara P.
    Gender, environment, and development in Kenya : a grassroots
  perspective / by Barbara Thomas-Slayter and Dianne Rocheleau with
  Isabella Asamba ... [et al.].
          p.   cm.
    Includes bibliographical references and index.
    ISBN 1-55587-419-3
    1. Women in development—Kenya.   2. Environmental policy—Economic
  aspects—Kenya.   I. Rocheleau, Dianne E.   II. Title.
  HQ1240.5.K4T57   1995
  305.42'096762—dc20   95-3457
                                                                          CIP

British Cataloguing in Publication Data
A Cataloguing in Publication record for this book
is available from the British Library.

Printed and bound in the United States of America

The paper used in this publication meets the requirements
(∞) of the American National Standard for Permanence of
Paper for Printed Library Materials Z39.48-1984.

5 4 3 2 1

To
Julie Anyango Okeyo

We dedicate this volume to Julie Anyango Okeyo, a cherished friend, colleague, and former Clark University student, who passed away in June 1994. Julie graduated from Clark University's Master of Arts Program in International Development in May 1994, launching her career working with women in Kenya and Mali to build more secure livelihoods. She represents for us the many young women all over Africa—especially in Kenya, her home—who are engaged in transforming their lives and their communities. We shall miss her lively humor, her warmth, and her vision of a more just future for the people of Africa.

Contents

List of Illustrations   ix
Acknowledgments   xi

Introduction   1

Part 1 Conceptual and Contextual Frameworks

1   Gender, Resources, and Local Institutions: 7
    New Identities for Kenya's Rural Women
    Barbara Thomas-Slayter and Dianne Rocheleau

2   The African and Kenyan Contexts   23
    Barbara Thomas-Slayter, Betty Wamalwa-Muragori,
    and Dianne Rocheleau

Part 2 The Cases

3   Gender, Ecology, and Agroforestry: 47
    Science and Survival in Kathama
    Dianne Rocheleau, Mohamud Jama,
    and Betty Wamalwa-Muragori

4   Adapting to Resource Constraints in Gikarangu: 75
    New Livelihood Strategies for Women and Men
    Leah Wanjama, Barbara Thomas-Slayter, and Njoki Mbuthi

5   From Cattle to Coffee: 105
    Transformation in Mbusyani and Kyevaluki
    Isabella Asamba and Barbara Thomas-Slayter

6   People, Property, Poverty, and Parks: 133
    A Story of Men, Women, Water, and Trees at Pwani
    Dianne Rocheleau, Karen Schofield-Leca, and Njoki Mbuthi

7   A Pocket of Poverty: Linking Water, Health, and Gender-Based   161
     Responsibilities in South Kamwango
     Elizabeth Oduor-Noah and Barbara Thomas-Slayter

Part 3 Considering Policy

8   Policy Implications and Opportunities for Action   191
     Barbara Thomas-Slayter, Dianne Rocheleau,
     and Charity Kabutha

Glossary   213
List of Acronyms   215
Appendix: Eight Steps to Participatory Rural Appraisal (PRA)   217
Bibliography   219
About the Authors   239
Index   241
About the Book   247

Illustrations

MAPS

1.1 Kenyan Districts and Sublocations Where Research   6
    Was Conducted
3.1 Athi River Basin and Study Area   48
3.2 Machakos District   52
4.1 Murang'a District   76
5.1 Machakos District, Mbusyani and Kyevaluki Sublocations   106
6.1 Nakuru District   134
7.1 Migori District and South Kamwango Sublocation   162

FIGURES

3.1 Topographic Profile with Agroecological Zones   53
3.2 Cropping Calendar   56
3.3 Causal Diagram of Animal Production Problems   60
3.4 Causal Diagram of Food Production Problems   61
3.5 Women's Terraced Croplands with Fruit and Fodder Trees   69
4.1 Percentage of Responses by Landholding Size   84
4.2 Number of Land Parcels per Respondent   85
4.3 Purposes for Which Gikarangu Households Grow Trees   89
4.4 Household Fuelwood Sources According to Size of Landholding   90
4.5 Migration from Gikarangu to Seek Employment   97
5.1 Coffee Bushes as Indicators of Wealth from the Land   114
5.2 Completed Educational Levels for Women   119
    in Mbusyani and Kyevaluki
5.3 Households Acquiring Land by Purchase of Parcels   128
7.1 Primary Source of Household Income in South Kamwango   172
7.2 Births and Child Survival in South Kamwango   181
7.3 South Kamwango Perceptions of Causes   182
    of Mortality of Own Children
    Who Have Died Before the Age of Five
8.1 Gender, Environment, and Development   193

TABLE

3.1 Population and Land Use Distribution for Machakos District,   54
      Mbiuni Location, and Research Area

Acknowledgments

Many people have made invaluable contributions to this volume on gender, resources, and development in the rural livelihood systems of six Kenyan communities. We are grateful for their ideas, energy, and commitment in all the stages of this study.

In particular, we are indebted to the people of Gikarangu, Kathama, Kyevaluki, Mbusyani, Pwani, and South Kamwango who extended courtesy and hospitality and gave us creative ideas along with a generous amount of their time to help with the research project. Residents patiently participated in household interviews, answered survey questions, met in focus groups, and engaged in discussions as leaders of women's groups or sublocation development committees or in their roles as teacher, farmer, government officer, or citizen. We had the valuable assistance of residents from the six communities who served as guides and interpreters and provided useful insights and observations.

We thank the former directors of Kenya's National Environment Secretariat (NES) Amos Kiriro and Wanjiku Mwagiru, who have facilitated this and other collaborative research between the NES and Clark University. Dr. Mwagiru was instrumental in launching our research efforts in Gikarangu Sublocation in Murang'a District. We also thank Dr. Bjorn Lundgren, former director general at the International Center for Research on Agro-Forestry (ICRAF), for his support of the Kathama study.

At each study site numerous government officials and extension officers gave valuable background information and shared useful insights about the communities for which they were responsible. To the assistant chiefs in each of these sublocations, along with the community development officers, agricultural extension agents, and many district, division, and location officials, we express our appreciation.

Colleagues from several institutions have offered valuable support. They include Monica Opole of the Kenya Energy and Environment Non-Governmental Organization (KENGO); Patrick Maundu Munyao and Bernard Muchiri Wanjohi, both of the Kenya National Museums Herbarium; Alex D'ianga and Alison Field-Juma of the African Centre for Technology Studies (ACTS); Calestous Juma, director of the African Centre for Technology Studies; Mary Rojas, then deputy director of international programs at Virginia Polytechnic and State University; Francis Lelo of Egerton University; Nancy Diamond of the U.S. Agency for International Development (USAID); and Louise Fortmann of the University of California.

At Clark University, we are grateful to Gerald Karaska, professor of geography and director of the Systems Approach to Regional Income and Sustainable Resource Assistance (SARSA) project; Richard Ford, professor of history and director of international development research; Elizabeth Owens, who as ID office administrator brings equanimity and order to stressful operations; and colleagues and research assistants Nina Bhatt, Andrea Esser, Thomas Gabrielle, Robert Jacobi, Florence Kariuki, Sara Mierke, Belinda Nicholson, Eileen Reynolds, Laurie Ross, Mary Schmuki, Dale Shields, and Anne-Marie Urban. We are indebted to Genese Sodikoff and Octavia Taylor for their insights and outstanding editorial skills and to Lori Wichhart for her imaginative and tireless efforts in graphics and design of tables and charts. We also thank the Clark University Cartographic Service for maps and charts designed for several of the chapters.

All of our work owes much to prior research by many colleagues working on environmental and/or gender issues in Kenya. They are too numerous to specify, but we would like to recognize especially Louise Buck, Fiona Mackenzie, Luis Malaret, Achola Pala Okeyo, John Raintree, Patricia Stamp, Kathleen Staudt, and Remko Vonk. Most of our research was conducted with funding from USAID through the Office of Women in Development and the Office of Economic and Institutional Development (EID) and through the SARSA Cooperative Agreement. The specific project on Ecology, Community Organization and Gender (ECOGEN) has been carried out jointly by Clark University and Virginia Polytechnic and State University. At Clark, ECOGEN has been housed in the International Development Program.

We are most grateful to Rosalie Huisinga Norem of USAID's Office of Women in Development and Lawrence Abel of USAID's Office of Economic and Institutional Development for their continuing support. In addition, portions of the fieldwork in Kathama were conducted with funding from the Rockefeller Foundation, the Ford Foundation, the National Science Foundation, and the United Nations University.

To all who gave their time and thought toward meeting the objectives of this study, we extend our warmest thanks and appreciation.

Barbara Thomas-Slayter
Dianne Rocheleau

Gender, Environment, and Development in Kenya

Introduction

In this volume, we focus on ways community institutions—specifically women and their groups or organizations—respond to changing resource conditions and on their strategies for regulating access to resources for themselves and others and for gaining control of critical resources such as soils, water, and woodlands. We also examine the impact of these responses on local decisionmaking, changing gender roles, rural stratification, community relations, and other variables within the broader social and political environment. Given the roles of women in managing rural resources and producing food, and given the long-established division of labor by gender in rural Africa, it is critical to determine the relationships among women's roles and elements of effective village-based resource management. These case studies from Kenya provide an opportunity to do so.

The Government of Kenya National Environment Secretariat and Clark University's International Development Program jointly undertook this research. Six rural communities, which we discuss in five case studies, were selected as study sites on the basis of variation in ecological zone, agricultural potential, levels of rural/urban exchange, and performance to date in community-level resource management. These communities are located in four districts: Machakos, Migori, Murang'a, and Nakuru (see Map 1.1). Research took place largely between 1990 and 1993. Each study site is the focus of one of the chapters in Part 2. The authors have extensive research experience, in some instances extending over many years, in the areas under investigation. Thus, we have the opportunity for a longitudinal consideration of gender and resource issues in several areas.

Part 1 of the book sets the conceptual and geographic contexts for the cases that follow. Chapter 1 defines the agenda, clarifying some of the key issues for rural women in Kenya with regard to managing natural resources and livelihoods at household and community levels. It considers the ways Kenyan women are redefining their roles, and it raises questions about gendered space and gendered organizations. It also introduces some of the strategies households adopt for advancing the productivity and welfare of their members and explores the notion that networks and local-level associations are used as both adaptive and innovative mechanisms enabling rural men and women to respond with increased effectiveness to external changes in their environment, as well as to modify social and environmental conditions to meet new aspirations.

Chapter 1 also provides a conceptual overview, identifying key theoretical perspectives from which this volume arises, as well as relevant issues connecting gender, resources, community organization, and development. In communities around the world, women and men are key resource users and managers. They have different roles, responsibilities, opportunities, and constraints in managing natural resources both within the household and in the community. Attention to gender is particularly relevant in the context of natural resource management in many countries because of the close connections among increasing poverty, the feminization of poverty, and the world environmental crisis.

Chapter 2 establishes the broad African arena in which these issues are relevant, as well as the specific Kenyan context under discussion. It introduces a wide range of economic, ecological, and political considerations—such as declining commodity prices and structural adjustment policies—that affect local communities and shape the opportunities and constraints experienced by men and women within them. This chapter explores linkages among population, land use, and food production and also considers how class and gender are crosscutting variables that affect options at the local level. The chapter contextualizes gender within current development trends and issues in Kenya.

Part 2 includes the five case studies. Each of these chapters focuses on a sublocation (Kenya's smallest administrative unit), analyzing specific ecological, gender, community, and resource issues within that community and incorporating the authors' perspectives and insights on the constraints and opportunities that the community faces in the development process. Chapter 3, "Gender, Ecology, and Agroforestry: Science and Survival in Kathama," explores changes in gendered knowledge and practice over time, specifically in a drought situation. It considers the role of wild foods and indigenous plants as poor people's drought and famine reserves. The fact that men actually own most of the private plots and formally control the public lands sets the stage for a gendered struggle for access to resources no less serious for its finesse and skillful manipulation by individual women and women's self-help groups. This chapter also explores the implications of a gender division of labor, which has shifted from complementary tasks and distinct but overlapping domains at farm and community levels to a rural/urban division.

Chapter 4, "Adapting to Resource Constraints in Gikarangu: New Livelihood Strategies for Women and Men," explores the pressures on smallholders in a high-potential setting, located about 90 kilometers from Nairobi in Murang'a District. Fragmentation of the land is severe; households are linked in a variety of ways to the market economy; and small-scale farming activity is slowly shifting from maize, beans, and coffee to include French beans and avocados destined for European markets. Bananas, long considered a women's crop, are increasingly grown for commercial purposes and managed and controlled by men. Economic and ecological pressures, rising unemployment, and a notable increase in the number of single mothers are shaping new gender roles in resource management and livelihood systems. Gikarangu offers insights into communities with high levels of social mobilization and organization, linked in numerous ways with economic, social, and political systems well beyond their borders.

Chapter 5, "From Cattle to Coffee: Transformation in Mbusyani and Kyevaluki," considers environmental and institutional changes occurring in two adjacent communities in Machakos District, located in one of Kenya's semiarid regions. These communities face challenges from a degraded resource base, pressures on the land from a rapidly growing population, water scarcity, inadequate employment opportunities, and a lack of fit between labor needs and labor allocation derived from the gender-based division of labor. Community Participatory Rural Appraisal (PRA) activities in Mbusyani and Kyevaluki revealed some important differences in the ways households and community organizations have responded to resource concerns—in particular to women's roles in these responses. This chapter explores the sources of these differences, examining leadership roles, women's organizations, and institutional linkages in Mbusyani and Kyevaluki.

Chapter 6, "People, Property, Poverty, and Parks: A Story of Men, Women, Water, and Trees at Pwani," focuses on a sublocation on the western edge of Lake Nakuru Park in Nakuru District. It examines a semiarid savanna settlement community to which highland farmers have been moved and in which they must cope not only with a dramatic change in land cover and land use but also with the constraints experienced by park periphery rural communities around the world. The resettlement and the management of resources under these new conditions have affected men and women differently. This chapter explores the convergence of gender, livelihood, resource management, and resettlement issues at Pwani.

Chapter 7, "A Pocket of Poverty: Linking Water, Health, and Gender-Based Responsibilities in South Kamwango," explores gender-based roles in securing a livelihood and sustaining the family within the context of severe problems in environmental sanitation, health, and nutrition, as reflected in statistics on child health and mortality. Located in Migori District (formerly South Nyanza District), South Kamwango Sublocation's climate, soils, water, and vegetation have the potential for strong agricultural production and development. Yet, despite this satisfactory resource base, South Kamwango's levels of production are low; water quality is poor; infant mortality is high; health problems are enormous; and community institutions are fragmented. Exploring issues of local knowledge systems and local political economy, the authors suggest that incorporating a gender perspective increases understanding of complex conditions and choices in rural households. Gender analysis also sheds light on the capacity and motivation of communities to organize and act on issues of environmental degradation, resource management, and health.

In Part 3, Chapter 8, "Policy Implications and Opportunities for Action," considers the implications of the preceding discussions and offers policy options for exploration. It reflects the analyses of the individual communities but synthesizes the material in ways we hope will be relevant to professionals, policymakers, and students of development. In its focus on options appropriate for governments, nongovernmental organizations (NGOs), and international agencies, this chapter circles back to capture the policy implications in the context of the broad analytical framework and questions established in Chapter 1.

These issues are timely, and analyses of gendered roles and resources are extremely important, not only for Eastern Africa but elsewhere as well. The UN Conference on Environment and Development has catapulted these issues into the forefront of our collective international awareness. We hope this book will contribute to the debates on gender and environmental change, as well as to the prospects, especially in Kenya, for people-centered development built on effective and equitable management of resources and secure livelihood systems.

Part 1

Conceptual and Contextual Frameworks

Map 1.1   Kenyan Districts and Sublocations Where Research Was Conducted

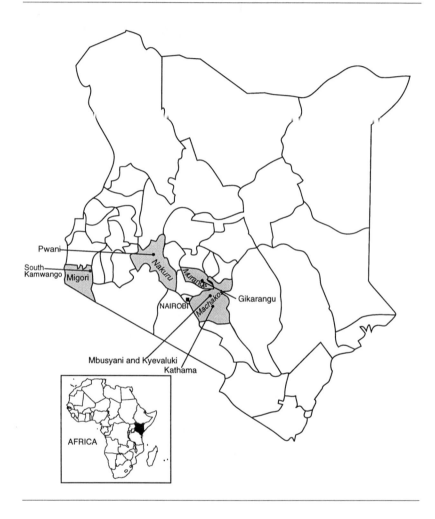

1

Gender, Resources, and Local Institutions: New Identities for Kenya's Rural Women

Barbara Thomas-Slayter, Dianne Rocheleau

KENYA'S RURAL WOMEN REDEFINE THEIR LIVES

Women are beginning to redefine their identities, their roles, and the meaning of gender. The process entails strengthening their sense of human agency, individually and through collective action, with an emphasis on cooperation, struggle, and, sometimes, resistance. Although this is a worldwide phenomenon, it is rooted in specific historical, social, geographic, and environmental conditions. In Kenya, as in other parts of Africa, women are increasingly involved not only in activities to manage and expand resources but in political and social action as well. Such involvement represents a resurgence of traditional institutions and an invention of new formal structures to ensure the survival of families in times of ecological and economic challenges.

Structural changes arising with the growth of capitalism—the increases in wage labor, migration of male family members, a decline in various forms of vertical ties to patrons, and the overall context of declining terms of trade for Kenya—have aggravated the environmental and economic difficulties facing many poor families in the last several decades.[1] Poor households grapple with increased risks and insecurities, which ebb and flow with the seasons and recurring environmental disasters. Environmental degradation, changes in property rights, increased linkages with the cash economy, and the erosion of various traditional rights and patronage systems have either weakened or erased formal entitlements for women in poor households. To sustain themselves, such women have relied on their own skills and efforts and on the social relations of responsibility and reciprocity that persist outside of formal structures.

Resource and gender issues are central to debates about the nature of Kenyan society, the claims that each individual or group can make on this society, and the realities of distributional justice. Decisions affecting resources are inherently political, as are those pertaining to gender relations and redefinitions of gender roles. Access to and control of resources are inextricably linked to the positioning of people by ethnicity, race, class, and gender.

Gender is central to positioning both men and women vis-à-vis institutions that determine access to land and other resources and to the wider economy and polity.[2] Conceptualizing gender is essential for disaggregating and interpreting information about the functioning of households and community organizations in natural resource management. Gender analysis of rights, responsibilities, labor, knowledge, and authority helps to clarify the indefinite boundaries of household and family. It illuminates the complex ways family, household, community, and ecosystem are linked.

In many countries, not only is landlessness among the rural poor increasing but the numbers of women and women-headed households among the poorest are rising as well.[3] There is also a growing awareness that the burdens of natural resource destruction may fall most heavily on women in poor households.[4] In Kenya, for example, where privatization of land is well under way, women rarely have ownership rights to land and hence are not eligible for credit, cooperative membership, or other benefits made possible by land ownership. The inextricable link between land resources and rural livelihoods, along with the increasing role of women as household providers in declining rural economies, stresses the need to consider the gendered terms of access and control of the resource base, particularly in ecologically vulnerable regions.

To these long-term structural changes in poor, rural communities one must add the immediate implications of the structural adjustment policies of the 1980s. Poor women have been severely affected by these policies, and the impact has been detrimental to the welfare of their families.[5] Insufficient food, environmental degradation, rising cost of living, declining services, and eroding economic conditions have encouraged not only protest but also strategies for addressing these issues.

Conceptual Frameworks[6]

Two sets of issues shape this discussion. The first involves an ecological focus on the interaction of the environment and human beings in diverse and complex land use systems. The second involves a focus on a community orientation based on the assertion that strong, viable local institutions and organizations can form a foundation for effective resource management, increased agricultural productivity, and improved livelihood systems.

Ecological perspective.   The key concepts to an ecological approach are those of interdependence and interrelatedness in complex, dynamic systems. Our emphasis is on human interests, values, and activities as they relate to the ecosystem, as well as on sustainable production in the context of specific ecosystems. An ecological approach allows us to see change in land use and technology as a dynamic, interactive process rather than one of incremental and unilinear movement.

Although ecological theories and methods pertaining to resource utilization have dealt primarily with populations of plants and animals, they can be expanded for human ecology to include multiple-resource user groups defined by gender, class, and ethnicity as well as species. Increasingly, some schools of ecology and conservation biology treat people, their resources, and their habitats as parts of a unified whole.[7] This approach is useful because it can incorporate both competing and cooperating groups and their respective uses of space and resources in a given place.

The theories and methods of cultural and political ecology provide a basis for a more inclusive, integrative approach to gender, ecology, and rural community development. Cultural ecology most often focuses on human/environment relations and the resulting land use practices in rural, nonindustrial systems with an emphasis on human adaptations to environmental conditions or human modification of ecosystems. Most political ecologists focus on the uneven distribution of access to and control of resources by class and ethnicity. However, some have expanded their analyses of poverty, powerlessness, and environmental degradation to focus increasingly on gender-based conflicts over natural resources; others have applied an essentially critical and feminist cultural ecology perspective to develop alternative approaches to rural development and resource management.[8] Indeed, cultural and political ecologists treat human decisionmaking and resource allocation as essential factors in environmental quality, and they emphasize the social, political, and economic contexts as determinants of resource policies and practices. Thus, biological, cultural, and political ecology provide a broad array of conceptual approaches to complex interactions among resource users.

Institutional perspective. The institutional perspective is in keeping with the postmodern conceptualizations of situated knowledge and experience, with an emphasis on plurality, difference, locality, and multiple identities[9] and on the value of strong local organizations.[10]

In addition, many see local organizations and grassroots movements as central to effective social change and the empowerment of women.[11] Such organizations and movements may focus on practical needs or strategic long-term interests and often include both in their agenda. They operate in environmental, economic, social, and political arenas. Given the preceding discussion of ecological perspectives, gender, and resources, it is essential to consider how organizations work at the community level and to ascertain the ways they are shaped by gender-defined roles and relations.

Formal associations and organizations may be divided into two broad categories: those based on ascriptive characteristics such as language and ethnicity and those based on a common interest, such as cooperatives, peasant associations, and self-help groups. Membership in the former derives from ascribed characteristics such as religion, ethnicity, gender, clan, and language. Common-interest associations include groups whose origins are in historical, ecological, political, and social structures and material conditions of the particular setting, as well as those that have been introduced recently by outsiders—most typically the state and, occasionally, donor agencies; membership is obtained by joining and may be fully voluntary or may entail pressure from peers, patrons, or authorities.

Informal networks are diverse but fall largely in four categories: patron–client networks involving bonds based on uneven reciprocal obligation and private accountability; familial relationships of an extended family or clan; rural–urban, usually familial, networks; and interhousehold labor and resource exchange networks. These may be quite small and informal, organized on an ad hoc basis, or they may be formally structured collectivities. Involvement in these networks has importance and value well beyond the task at hand.

Examination of individual and household involvement in local networks and associations offers several insights. First, various resource transfers take place among households. Interhousehold exchanges of labor, goods, and/or services are often critical to the viability of the rural household. Second, networks and associations may also be used to gain access to resources of the state or to hold both the state and market at bay.[12] They may coexist with market and state institutions in a complementary way, or they may disintegrate as traditional relationships give way to market relations and the demands of the state.[13] Third, increased levels of formal cooperation may be a consequence of and a response to the intrusion of colonialism, the demands of the market economy, the privatization of once common resources, the need for collective negotiation with the state, or the exigencies of an increase in male out-migration.[14]

Economic and Ecological Struggles

Economic and ecological struggles have important implications everywhere for the meaning of gender and for the nature of men's and women's roles. At the local level in many parts of the world, organizations are beginning to seek more equitable development across classes, ethnic groups, gender, and generations. In some instances, the increased involvement of women is leading to a new sense of agency and empowerment and to new perceptions about women's roles. Increasingly, women are "finding voice," being aided in doing so by their participation in groups and organizations.[15]

These changes are occurring within a broad context of interest in local institutions as change agents. Scholars emphasize new departures for development theory, policy, and practice—among them a developmental role for indigenous, grassroots, intermediary, and nongovernmental organizations that are complementary to each other as well as to the state and market.[16] Yet there is little discussion of the institutional issues gripping Africa that must be addressed in this region of the world, where rural poverty remains widespread. Nor is there recognition that organizations are "gendered" in ways having important implications for their part in development.

For many Kenyan women, both economic and ecological conditions are pressing. They face severe constraints on their livelihood options. Rarely are they integrated into existing mechanisms for seeking redress or assuaging their concerns. Only in the last election (late 1992) did a handful of women step forth to contest parliamentary seats vigorously. Most women are marginalized from existing national-level systems and participate little, if at all, in organized national politics. They have much to gain and little to lose by acting collectively in organizations and networks designed to secure the conditions they need for survival. Their activism usually begins locally on matters critical to their homes and families; it is indicative of the extent to which they are under pressure, disadvantaged by the system, and marginalized economically, politically, and socially. In the last decade the issues they face have become increasingly severe.

The volume focuses on Kenya's rural women and the relevance of community institutions and organizations to the sustainability of productive, "natural," and social systems in six communities. It explores relationships emerging in these communities as rural people examine ways to transform their worlds at the boundaries between state and civil society and the living systems on which both depend. In particular, it considers how women shape responses of community organizations according to environmental and resource issues.

GENDERED SPACE: RESOURCES, LIVELIHOODS, AND THE STATE

Women's involvement in community organization and the changing relations of women to the state are central to this discussion, given the critical roles of women in agricultural processes, rural livelihood systems, and the management of natural resources.[17] Research on gender in Africa has focused on a variety of issues, including the impact of colonialism on African women, women's roles in food production, changing land tenure patterns, the impact of colonial policies on women's rights to land, and the marginalizing impact of commercialization and commodity production on women.[18] Scholars are also exploring the relationships between women and the new, independent African state, the institutional dimensions of male privilege, the impact of the state's extractive and distributive decisions on gender relations, and women's organizations.[19]

The politics of community organization and state–society relations appear differently when viewed from a gender perspective. In general, women have a different relationship with and access to states than do men.[20] Gender is important in state formation, political participation, and resource allocation. Parpart and Staudt suggest that "states are shaped by gender struggle; they carry distinctive gender ideologies through time which guide resource allocation decisions in ways that mold material realities."[21] Others suggest there is an emerging micro politics that relies on temporary and mobile coalitions to deal with specific struggles.[22] Some explore the forms of everyday resistance, providing a gendered reinterpretation of Scott's "weapons of the weak."[23] One reinterpretation suggests that identities and interests are not "given and fixed" but are "forged through political struggle (in its extended sense) on multiple and intersecting sites." Furthermore, "gender is central to understanding the processes through which class identity is produced or undermined."[24]

Women in most African countries have virtually no formal power in state structures. In Kenya, there is no doubt that the state shapes and limits women's use of organizations and networks, even as it promotes and patronizes their formation. Women struggle to find ways to use this "space" to further their own objectives within or vis-à-vis state structures. They face numerous contradictions between what they need to survive and what is possible under current legal codes and traditional social structures. Given their primary and expanding responsibility for agricultural activities and resource management, Kenyan women are greatly—and often adversely—affected by these contradictions with limited (if any) legal control over resources.[25]

Within the last several decades, enormous changes have taken place in many parts of Kenya primarily through the privatization of land. The results have been the transfer of virtually all common lands to state or private owner-ship; a widening rich–poor gap within communities; increasing male migration from many communities; and an increase in the numbers of women functioning as de facto heads of household. These phenomena have enormous implications for resource access, work loads, responsibilities, and levels of deprivation of the poorest households, particularly for the women in them. Such households have relied most heavily on access to common forests, rangelands, and water points for food, fuel, fodder, and water.[26]

With the privatization and increasing subdivision of land, many women see the erosion of their resource base and face a challenge to their social net-works, which historically have been tied to shared access to common property resources. Most have little knowledge of their legal rights to land and its use. Young women from poor households have little hope of obtaining land or of acquiring the skills that could give them good jobs. Many find their way to the plantation work force as a last resort.[27]

For the last two decades, national and international environmental agen-cies addressing the problem of a diminishing natural resource base have sought to involve Kenyan women in a way that fits into their own agendas. The state has defined environmental priorities in rural areas in terms of protecting pro-ductive resources to serve urban and national interests. Soil and water conser-vation took precedence during the late 1970s and early 1980s, when the na-tional government was concerned about protecting hydroelectric dams from sedimentation and conserving soil and water for rural agricultural production. During the 1970s the energy crisis also loomed large in the eyes of national and international planners, and they identified fuelwood supply as a major national problem. Biodiversity and wildlife protection became increasingly important in the late 1980s and continue to command the attention of the state primarily because of the importance of tourism in the economy.[28]

Government responses to each of these concerns relied heavily on the involvement of rural women, both individually and in groups. Women's groups throughout the country were mobilized to construct terraces, repair gullies, construct small dams, and rehabilitate denuded slopes and degraded grazing lands. In many areas soil conservation gave way to reforestation efforts, some geared toward fuelwood, fodder, and fruit on farms and others aimed at community woodlots and protected common areas.[29] Women were also the targets of several energy conservation programs, including alternative cookstove designs to reduce fuelwood consumption. Women's participation in reforestation and cookstove programs was mediated largely by national and international NGOs linked to local and national women's groups on the one hand and to state agencies on the other.

Based on their own perception and prioritization of environmental issues in their home areas, rural women often placed clean water supply first and fuelwood access next, followed by substantial interest in tree planting for fruit, poles, fodder, and medicinal uses. Their efforts to construct terraces and water storage dams have contributed to soil conservation as well as to their own concerns about crop production and domestic water supply. In short, Kenyan women in agrarian landscapes have found common cause with some of the state's environmental priorities, although their own interpretations focus more directly on water and food supply, health, and access to fuelwood, fodder, and fiber at the household and community levels.

Evidence from the cases presented in this volume suggests that in the context of uneven power relations, men's and women's roles continue to be renegotiated, based on a logic of flexible complementarity with frequent instances of overlap and changing boundaries.[30] Yet there is a growing disjuncture between the changing responsibilities and work load for women and their legal status. For example, in Mbusyani and Kathama (Machakos District), cultural, social, and economic practices are being adapted according to the reality of male out-migration and the exigencies that many households face, but the legal system, land tenure, and other regulations have not been modified accordingly. In particular, the woman's livelihood and that of her family depend on the land, yet insecure tenure and lack of rights and control characterize women's legal relationship to the land.[31]

Although responsibilities for men and women are changing, it is evident that women continue to have primary responsibility for meeting the family's basic needs for food, water, and fuel. The husband's responsibility has been to generate sufficient income to pay for school fees and major capital expenditures. Increasingly, in the Machakos sublocations and in Gikarangu (Murang'a District), households are managed by women while their husbands are away working in other towns such as Nairobi or Machakos or perhaps seeking employment outside their communities. This puts an additional burden on the woman, who then has the entire responsibility of running a household on a daily basis.

Related to these changing land use patterns are resource issues linked to environmental problems of soil deterioration and deforestation. Women in many communities have to walk long distances in search of water during the dry season. In many parts of Machakos, for example, the majority of households face water, vegetation, and fuelwood scarcity, while some households have water storage or delivery infrastructure and surplus fuelwood resources. Women and children may spend fifteen hours or more a week, depending on the season, on the two tasks of gathering fuel and obtaining water.[32] No doubt it is because of such demands that poor women are increasingly aware of environmental issues and are willing to sacrifice time to protect their natural resources and, more broadly, the environment in which they live.

HOUSEHOLD, COMMUNITY, AND WOMEN'S ASSOCIATION RESPONSES TO RESOURCE AND LIVELIHOOD CHALLENGES

How do rural households and communities manage ecological change and, at times, crisis? What are their approaches for dealing with the breakdown of traditional systems or perhaps for transforming such systems? How can responses at the local level be made relevant to policymakers at district, national, and international levels? We can identify three basic household and community strategies.

The first involves redeployment of different members of the household. With increasing poverty, declining welfare, and inadequate productivity, many households respond by dividing up responsibilities in new ways. The objective is to diversify sources of income and, in particular, to seek nonfarm work. Usually, the husband leaves and the wife stays behind to manage the farm and the children. There has been an outpouring of men from the countryside seeking wage labor primarily in the cities. As Ngugi wa Thiong'o puts it, the able-bodied men have fled "in search of the golden fleece in cities of metallic promises and no hope."[33] In many parts of Kenya the number of woman-headed rural households is estimated at 27 percent; women-managed households (with migrant husbands) often account for another 47 percent.[34] These figures are not uncommon for other parts of Africa as well. It is in fact commonplace for young men to be flooding into towns and cities seeking jobs. Older men may have spent a working life in the city, returning for visits several times a year; they retire back to the countryside when their days of employment are over. It is equally common for women to manage the farm and care for large families under difficult circumstances without a partner present.

A second strategy for coping with these challenges involves strengthening informal networks comprising kin, friends, and colleagues or patrons and clients. Informal networks are based on reciprocal exchange of goods, services, and information; there is no expectation of a direct return or other kinds of gifts. Rather, such reciprocal exchange is part of a relationship that maintains social ties and identity and provides security or support in times of need, as well as new opportunities and benefits. Households invest in the social relationships that provide them with access to resources—a form of investment as important as ones they might make in productive capacity. Thus, they put effort into maintaining certain entitlements by virtue of kinship, patron–client obligation, or communal loyalty. Economic incentives may be as important in strengthening these relationships as they are in increasing the productive capacity of resources. In fact, the reaction to economic decline may be to diversify and build social networks as a form of safety net and flexible access to new resources.[35] These resources may include fodder, fuelwood, food, water, building materials, and raw material for crafts, as well as economic resources such as informal credit.

Networks have become key elements in individual and household strategies for survival, accumulation, and mobility. For example, in many rural communities poor women are particularly dependent on access to the commons for fuelwood and other forest products.[36] With a decline in common property resources and an increase in privatization, they have been among the first to suffer losses. In the face of this decline, networks and associations are proving valuable instruments for providing poorer households with increased access to productive and exchange resources from private holdings of other members. In addition, networks may enable their constituents to address community problems on an ad hoc basis.

A third strategy involves membership in formal groups and organizations. This strategy differs in important ways from involvement in networks. Networks may solve individual problems, but organized solidarity—a group—is needed to bring about significant changes in any system. Associations may offer a means to deal formally with the political system because they have an explicit structure, sustained and visible membership for political leverage, and a clear purpose and mandate.

In many parts of Kenya, strong and viable women's associations have emerged from traditional group activity originally focused on sharing agricultural labor and helping one another meet critical domestic needs. Today, participation in these associations can be a key household strategy for meeting the challenges of increased involvement in the market and a cash economy. The strategy can either diminish risk or create new opportunities for household members, especially women; it can help to meet goals for maintenance, accumulation, or mobility.

The specific purpose of such a strategy may be improved access to productive assets: land, labor, and capital. For example, women's groups often construct and repair cropland terraces, fences, and sometimes houses or storage structures. Such groups may also generate exchange opportunities (both market and nonmarket) involving cash, goods, services, information, and/or influence. Or, the strategy may be used to obtain access to common property, including resources such as water and communal grazing land, or to institutions and services such as schools and health clinics. Households employ both informal networks and formal associations to enhance their access to productive resources and to exchange opportunities, as well as to enjoy the benefits of common property or, alternatively, to share the use of private property.[37]

Thus, involvement in women's associations can be an important strategy to assist women and their households with access to land, water, cash, labor, and information, five resources on which most African farmers face critical constraints. Women may, in fact, use long-standing and time-honored ways of organizing the factors of production. Drawing on roots in traditional labor exchange mechanisms, both women and the state have formalized and expanded these relationships. For the Kenyan state, encouragement of rural women's groups has a twofold origin. The international women's movement, with its focus on development opportunities for poor rural women, has provided the rationale and impetus for various NGOs and international aid agencies such as SIDA, the Swedish International Development Agency, to provide strong financial support for women's programs through women's groups since the mid-1970s. This effort has coincided very conveniently with both the Kenyatta and the Moi governments' wishes to conserve resources at the center, decentralize development efforts, and return to local communities the initiative for undertaking local development efforts in the spirit of *harambee*, or self-help. Furthermore, a patriarchal ideology has permitted a significant opportunity for administrative officers to control the collective labor of these groups for common purposes, such as building a school or repairing a road. Thus, in many corners of Kenya, the women's groups provide a pool of labor that can be called upon by local officials for public works.[38]

Collective labor is undertaken by women's associations largely for two reasons: to generate income for the group members, both individually and collectively, and to provide needed labor inputs for their own farms at peak times in the agricultural cycle. They may cooperate as a work force seeking wage labor on neighboring farms and plantations. They may also contribute their labor to public works, such as feeder road construction or school repair upon request, as noted earlier.

In addition to provision of labor for each other and the community, women's associations may organize revolving credit schemes for generating cash income, rotating allocation of funds among members. They may establish mechanisms for providing and managing collective goods and services, such as water tanks and delivery systems, nursery schools, literacy lessons, maize mills, meeting halls, and shops. Some groups also provide a means for members to market agricultural produce and handicrafts under more favorable conditions than individual sales.

These groups are particularly useful to poor households and female-headed households. Akamba women, for example, whose husbands are often in Nairobi seeking work and whose forebears engaged in a complex and mobile system of survival under harsh ecological conditions, are organizing themselves to address different environmental problems and implement new resource management approaches. However, many women from the very poorest households, or those with very young children and no child care, may be unable to meet the attendance, contribution, and work requirements of groups and thus are excluded from their benefits.

Resources are at the heart of Africa's food production problems and ultimately need to be managed by local, small-scale, collaborative efforts linked to larger-scale planning and regulatory functions. For example, erosion control is labor intensive—planting trees, terracing hillsides, and damming gullies require a great deal of effort. Activities need to be organized not simply on one household's two or three hectares but across a hill or a valley, perhaps throughout a catchment area. If the measures are to be effective, they cannot be done in isolation. There are economies of scale, and there must be a fit to the particular ecological setting.[39]

These patterns of cooperation, reciprocity, and exchange include both informal networks and formal associations or organizations to which men and women belong to enhance access to resources, to public and private goods and services, and to centers of power and decisionmaking. Such patterns have implications not only for the access of individuals and households to resources but also for stratification patterns within communities. Formal and informal organizations may lead, in some instances, to increased equity or democratization and, in others, to increased social stratification. The consequences are significant for distinct groups of people based on differences in race, ethnicity, age, class, and, of course, gender.

Ultimately, resource issues must be considered in gender-based terms. Throughout most agrarian communities in Kenya, the women have primary responsibility for feeding the family, for carrying water, and for maintaining the homestead. In some areas they manage the farms whether men are present or not. The men are more free to move and to pursue other life options. They do not have the same stake in the viability of the rural community. Yet, women do not often perceive themselves as possessing an organizational capacity to demand accountability from political and administrative officials and from representatives, such as Members of Parliament, who should be responsive to local needs and priorities. They may have succeeded beyond expectation in managing soil or water on their farms as well as in gaining accountability within their groups. Rarely do they have formal institutional capacity to hold leaders at the sublocation, location, or district levels responsible for responding to sublocation needs. They do, however, engage in acts of resistance and mobilize their collective strength to exert influence on local and higher-level politicians through traditional and/or informal channels.

Thus, most women's organizations, strong though they may be in managing particular resources, are fledgling in terms of obtaining access to the national political system. The boundaries of traditional gender relations and public authority are blurred. Given male ascendance in state institutions, rarely do these groups see themselves as having a role in modifying the formal system of resource access and use to benefit the residents of the community. Rather, they focus on transforming daily practice and long-term process on the ground.

Nevertheless, activities that provide access to cash and to extra-household labor and that enable women to participate in collective labor and in decisions about support for community infrastructure inevitably affect a woman's position in terms of decisionmaking and resource allocation vis-à-vis other members of her household. Over time, suggests Ghai, such activities lead to slow but profound changes in the social status and economic position of women.[40] Such changes generated by involvement in women's associations, as well as the emergence of new roles for those associations, constitute part of a far-reaching reassertion and transformation of women's roles in rural Kenya and perhaps in other parts of Africa as well.

GENDER AND DESIGNING THE FUTURE: BUILDING LOCAL CAPACITIES

There is a widely shared concern about the fate of the world's environment and links among declining ecosystems, degraded resources, and increasing poverty. We strive to understand the relationships between resource management and food production, as well as the ecological issues pertaining to water, soils, forests, and land use that have a critical impact on food production and rural livelihood systems. Grasping the role of gender in these local-level processes is more important than ever.

Finding the link between long-term global and regional sustainability and local sustainability of culture, economy, and ecology involves understanding the larger political, cultural, economic, and environmental context, the particular social and biophysical environment, and the details of the local production system. The search necessitates an understanding of the nations and cultures of the North as avid consumers determined to maintain a high level of industrialization and consumerism despite evident social, environmental, and health costs, as well as those of the South enmeshed in growing ecological and economic problems. There must be an understanding of the strategic roles of women— particularly in poor households—in food production, household labor, and family income and as the "daily managers of the living environment."[41]

Many of the resource issues and livelihood problems Kenya faces have been emerging over many decades. One March afternoon ten years ago, a woman in Gitiburi, a rural community about 20 miles from Embu town in Kenya's Eastern Province, lamented, "I have tried all I can to see that there are improvements for my household, but still things are not better. As a result, I believe that problems will be greater in the future than they are now." Her name was Nthara Ngithi. She was a strong woman, middle-aged, resilient yet weary. As we surveyed the landscape outside her doorway, we had to admit that the task of surviving in that environment was extraordinary. In the distance was Mount Kiangombe, a distinctive granite hill rising out of the flatlands. Nearer, the land was rocky and arid with tufts of grass and scrubby vegetation. Her patch of millet plants looked forlorn; a few goats were the only visible asset. There were six or seven children living at home; her husband, Kaguna, was in Nairobi working as a casual laborer. He sent money occasionally; she saw him two or three times a year. Clearly, Mrs. Ngithi was struggling against fierce odds to sustain her family, which, despite her effort and that of her husband, was mired in poverty.

In a nearby community, opportunities and morale, if not the landscape, seemed somewhat different. Muthoni Mwalemba talked enthusiastically about her work as chair of a women's group and the activities the members were pursuing to strengthen their individual households and the services available to the community. The group was building bench terraces to conserve water and soil fertility on members' lands; it managed a tree nursery; and it had constructed a community center. The women's energy and enthusiasm were impressive, even contagious.

Discussions with Nthara Ngithi, Muthoni Mwalemba, and others like them remind us of the underlying socioeconomic, political, and ecological processes affecting their lives, as well as the variation in capacities and opportunities for addressing them. Certainly in Kenya there is a long historical process involving the impact of colonization, the emergence of a settler economy, the introduction of commercial crops for export, the growth of urban areas, and involvement with the cash economy, in which, for the most part, women have been marginalized, having experienced increased responsibilities and diminished control over resources.

Our argument in this book is that specific historical circumstances that create ecological stress and a variety of social problems are placing a heavy burden on the rural Kenyan household—especially on the women in those households. We explore the processes at work, as well as the household and community responses to these changes with particular reference to gender. These responses bear on key issues of local empowerment, local institution building, and peasant–state relations. They affect the capacity of the resource base and the agricultural sector to support local and national economies. They are central to wrestling with these critical questions: Can patterns of environmental degradation be stayed? Can sustainable resource management and livelihoods emerge? Can these systems work for women, or will women simply be mobilized to sustain the resources of others?

Managing local resources is not a matter of technical problems looking for solutions. There are many technical solutions; the critical issues are motivation, organization, equity, and political will. One key lies with the local community. In fact, much of what happens in Kenya, as well as in the rest of Africa, will depend on the choices and activities of thousands of farming households and communities. And given present economic opportunities and conditions, in many communities much will depend on the women who live there.

Increasingly, women like Nthara Ngithi and Muthoni Mwalemba recognize the broad problems that limit their access to resources. In their lifetime, gathering firewood has become much more time-consuming; trips for the family water supply are long and laborious; their security on the land is precarious; and the future of their children is uncertain. The boundaries of their community have expanded in ways that often make life more difficult. The ecological problems are apparent. The economic consequences of continuing ecological deterioration are also evident. The processes of environmental degradation or restoration, of economic decline or development, and of political decay or institution building are long-term, historical processes of change. The human responses are being made here and now, as immediate, pragmatic action. Increasingly, Kenya's rural women are agents of that change.

Gender is not just a women's concern, however. It is a social construct through which all human beings organize their work, rights, responsibilities, and relationships. Its meaning derives from specific historical and material conditions. Understanding gender in particular contexts will enable us to find more effective—and equitable—ways of managing our natural resources for building productive rural livelihood systems.

In the context of ecological and economic struggles and the complex web of resistance and change in which all people live, we argue that rural Kenyan women are characterized by emerging capabilities and a growing sense of urgency on social and environmental issues. Their roles in community organizations and networks are changing as they seek ways to use and expand the "space" they have created. In these processes the relation of women to the environment and to the state is shaped not only by the marginal role women have had in the formal political process but also by their central role in community institutions and their heightened concerns about ecological and social problems. Above all, we assert that local capacities—both men's and women's—constitute a valuable resource for social and environmental change throughout rural Kenya.

NOTES

1. Barker, *Rural Communities Under Stress;* Callaghy, "Debt and Structural Adjustment in Africa"; Kates and Haarman, "Where the Poor Live."

2. Thomas-Slayter, Rocheleau, Shields, and Rojas, *Introducing the ECOGEN Approach.* For a discussion of links among gender, poverty, resource decline, and ecological degradation, see Thomas-Slayter and Rocheleau, "Essential Connections."

3. Folbre, "Women on Their Own"; Paolisso and Yudelman, *Women, Poverty, and the Environment in Latin America;* Stichter and Parpart (eds.), *Patriarchy and Class.*

4. Agarwal, *Structures of Patriarchy;* Fortmann and Rocheleau, "Women and Agroforestry"; Kabeer, "Gender Dimensions of Rural Poverty"; Kates, "Hunger, Poverty, and the Human Environment"; Leonard, *Environment and the Poor.*

5. Gladwin (ed.), *Structural Adjustment and African Women Farmers*; Sen and Grown, *Development, Crises, and Alternative Visions;* Shiva, *Staying Alive.*

6. For a more elaborate discussion of ecological and institutional perspectives shaping our conceptual framework, see Thomas-Slayter and Rocheleau, "Essential Connections," pp. 7–19, and Thomas-Slayter and Rocheleau, "Research Frontiers at the Nexus of Gender, Environment and Development."

7. Haila and Levins, *Humanity and Nature;* Toledo, "Patzquaro's Lesson"; Odum, *Basic Ecology;* Lovelock, *The Ages of Gaia;* Margulis and Lovelock, "Gaia and Geognosy."

8. For the former, see Agarwal, *Cold Hearths and Barren Slopes* and "Neither Sustenance nor Sustainability"; Carney, "Struggles Over Land and Crops"; Talle, *Women at a Loss;* Watts, "Struggles Over Land, Struggles Over Meaning." For the latter, see Fortmann, "The Tree Tenure Factor"; Rocheleau, "A Land User Perspective"; Rocheleau et al., *Farming in the Forest, Gardening with Trees;* Thomas-Slayter, "Politics, Class, and Gender"; Schroeder, "Shady Practice."

9. Rocheleau, Thomas-Slayter, and Wangari, *Toward a Feminist Political Ecology.*

10. Braidotti et al., *Women, the Environment and Sustainable Development;* Bratton, "Farmer Organizations and Food Production"; Bray, "'Defiance' and the Search for Sustainable Small Farmer Organizations"; De Janvry et al., "Introduction to State, Market, and Civil Organizations."

11. Ekins, *A New World Order;* Escobar and Alvarez (eds.), *The Making of Social Movements in Latin America;* Hart, "Engendering Everyday Resistance"; Sen and Grown, *Development, Crises, and Alternative Visions.*

12. For the former, see Berry (ed.), *Access, Control and Use of Resources in African Agriculture;* Holmquist, "Self Help." For the latter, see Glavanis, "Aspects of Non-Capitalist Social Relations in Rural Egypt"; or Hyden, "The Invisible Economy" and *Beyond Ujamaa in Tanzania.*

13. For the former, see Thomas, "Household Strategies." For the latter, see De Janvry et al., "Introduction to State, Market, and Civil Organizations"; or Hecht, "The Transformation of Lineage Production."

14. Collins, "Women and the Environment"; Jiggins, "Women and Seasonality"; Safilios-Rothschild, "The Persistence of Women's Invisibility in Agriculture"; Shields and Thomas-Slayter, *Gender, Class, Ecological Decline and Livelihood Strategies;* Thomas, *Politics, Participation, and Poverty;* Rocheleau, "Gender, Ecology, and the Science of Survival."

15. Ronderos, "Towards an Understanding of Project Impact on Gender Negotiation," p. 81.

16. For a thorough discussion of this topic, see De Janvry et al., "Introduction to State, Market, and Civil Organizations."

17. Jiggins, "Women and Seasonality"; Stichter and Parpart (eds.), *Patriarchy and Class;* Davison (ed.), *Agriculture, Women, and Land;* Charlton et al., *Women, the State, and Development.*

18. Etienne and Leacock (eds.), *Women and Colonization*; Henn, "Feeding the Cities and Feeding the Peasants"; Monson and Kalb (eds.), *Women as Food Producers in Developing Countries;* Davison (ed.), *Agriculture, Women, and Land;* Oboler, *Women, Power, and Economic Change.*

19. Stamp, "Kikuyu Women's Self-Help Groups"; Staudt, "Stratification"; Thomas, "Household Strategies for Adaptation and Change."

20. Chazan, "Gender Perspectives on African States"; Fatton, "Gender, Class, and State in Africa"; Staudt, "Women, Development and the State."

21. Parpart and Staudt, *Women and the State in Africa*, p. 6.

22. Braidotti et al., *Women, the Environment and Sustainable Development*, p. 169.

23. Carney and Watts, "Manufacturing Dissent"; Hart, "Engendering Everyday Resistance"; Kerkvliet, *Everyday Politics in the Philippines;* Scott, *Weapons of the Weak.*

24. Hart, "Engendering Everyday Resistance," p. 117.

25. Davison (ed.), *Agriculture, Women, and Land;* Nzioki, "Effects of Land Tenure Reform"; Rocheleau, "Women, Trees, and Tenure."

26. Pala Okeyo, "Daughters of the Lakes and Rivers"; Rocheleau, "A Land User Perspective"; Rocheleau et al., "The Ukambani Region of Kenya"; Thomas, "Household Strategies for Adaptation and Change"; Wangari, "Effects of Land Registration on Small-Scale Farming in Kenya."

27. Rocheleau et al., "The Ukambani Region of Kenya."

28. Rocheleau et al., "A Hundred Years of Crisis?"

29. Bradley, *Women, Woodfuel, and Woodlots;* Kilewe et al., *Agroforestry Development in Kenya.*

30. The concept of "flexible complementarity" was introduced into the ECOGEN discussions by Dianne Rocheleau as a "central lesson" emerging from her work in Kathama Sublocation over a decade (see Chapter 3). We have found the concept useful in analyzing all our case study sites.

31. Rocheleau, "Gender, Conflict and Complementarity in Sustainable Forestry Development."

32. Thomas-Slayter, "Politics, Class and Gender in African Resource Management."

33. Ngugi wa Thiong'o, *Devil on the Cross*, p. 49.

34. Government of Kenya, Ministry of Culture and Social Services, *The Government Achievements in the Development of Women.*

35. Berry, "Coping with Confusion," p. 269.

36. Agarwal, *Cold Hearths and Barren Slopes;* Hoskins, *Rural Women, Forest Outputs and Forestry Products;* Rocheleau, "Gender, Conflict and Complementarity in Sustainable Forestry Development"; Shiva, *Staying Alive.*

37. For an exploration of these issues in two locations, Weithaga and Mbiri, of Murang'a District, see Thomas, *Household Strategies for Adaptation and Change;* see also Rocheleau, "Gender, Ecology, and the Science of Survival."

38. Rocheleau, "Gender, Conflict and Complementarity in Sustainable Forestry Development"; Thomas-Slayter, "Politics, Class and Gender in African Resource Management."

39. For an exploration of these issues in Katheka Sublocation, Machakos District, see Thomas-Slayter, "Politics, Class and Gender in African Resource Management"; see also Rocheleau and Hoek, "The Application of Ecosystems and Landscape Analysis."

40. Ghai, "Participatory Development," p. 240.

41. Dankelman and Davison, *Women and Environment in the Third World;* Rocheleau and Hoek, "The Application of Ecosystems and Landscape Analysis."

2

The African and Kenyan Contexts

Barbara Thomas-Slayter,
Betty Wamalwa-Muragori, Dianne Rocheleau

The decades between 1975 and 1995 have been difficult for the many African countries struggling with a wide range of political, economic, social, and ecological issues. These concerns arise at global, national, or local levels, from conditions that crosscut and intersect with one another. A thorough exploration of critical issues in Africa must include the dynamics of these interactions and incorporate local, regional, and national perspectives into the current international debates.

Across the continent, the people of many African nations have been troubled by low levels of economic productivity, environmental degradation, inadequate physical and social infrastructure, the exigencies of structural adjustment, and the battering of declining commodity prices. Some have suffered from a variety of natural catastrophes and deteriorating environmental conditions with their toll on human productivity and welfare. Others have endured corrupt governments, which cripple their own economies and subject the populace to a wide range of inappropriate policies. In some instances, political turmoil, exacerbated by ethnic and class rivalries, has led to violence and military conflict. All these circumstances have linkages across local, national, and global dimensions.

Most African nations have become independent states within the last thirty-five years. However, to determine the context in which contemporary politics and economics must be analyzed, one needs to go back one hundred years to the Berlin Conference of 1884, when various European states established their hegemony over Africa. Most African countries became colonies of European states, sustaining an established buildup in orientation of their economies and polities toward the North.

Today a new generation is emerging across Africa, one that has grown up, for the most part, in independent Africa. One might suggest that there is an outgoing cohort of leaders in their sixties and seventies and a new, younger one entering the scene with new perspectives. This generation is searching for ways to meet numerous challenges, including critical economic and ecological concerns, such as widespread competition for resources between governments and their people and among various groups of citizens. Other challenges include those of governance and of accountability of policymakers to all people. They necessitate analysis of the ways ordinary people are made vulnerable by policies serving only a few.

Further, there is the challenge to clarify and counterbalance the ways global circumstances often override local conditions in the uneven power relations between North and South. There is a need to redefine what it means to be a rural or an urban dweller, what it means to be a member of a particular social or ethnic group, and what it will mean to be an African woman or man at the beginning of the twenty-first century. For many, it means seeking opportunities to renegotiate the existing institutional arrangements and the existing compacts, contracts, and understandings by which their lives are defined.

There are, of course, major differences among African nations and the perspectives of people across the continent. Yet some significant commonalities also exist. One of them is noted by Hyden, who states, "Governments and donors alike have tended to ignore the narrow margins of survival that characterize African countries at all levels."[1] These narrow margins provide the context in which our topic—gender, environment, and development—is situated.

THE AFRICAN CONTEXT: DEALING
WITH COMPLEXITIES AND UNCERTAINTIES

Economic Issues

Today, despite political independence, most African nations experience increasing involvement with the global economy, generally on less than favorable terms. And at the level of rural households, one finds increasing involvement with cash and the market, often shaped by global economics. Certain structural orientations in agricultural systems have been inherited from the colonial era and sustained by independent governments. Among these are dependence on one or two agricultural commodities for export earnings. In many countries, export crops have the best land—for example, cotton in Sudan, coffee in Kenya, and cocoa in Ghana. In recent years, real income from export crops has declined, along with African shares in world markets of most commodities. The response to declining prices has been to put more land into the major export crops—thus the economies of many African nations are becoming even more firmly tied to commodities destined for international markets. Nine African countries depend on just one crop for over 70 percent of their foreign exchange. Coffee provides over 90 percent of Burundi's export earnings, and Uganda and Kenya rely on coffee for more than 50 percent of their export earnings. Kenya's coffee production more than doubled in the two decades between the late 1960s and the late 1980s in spite of a decline in the proportion of the world's coffee produced in Africa (from 34 percent in 1970 to 23 percent in 1979).[2]

Despite efforts to produce for the international market, the value of African exports is declining. Over the past seventeen years, many African nations have faced deteriorating terms of trade vis-à-vis the industrialized nations. This relates in part to energy prices, high debt servicing, and major trade deficits, as well as to the fact that most of the value added comes from processing, of which African countries do very little. Overall, per capita income on the continent went from a mean rate of growth of 0.8 percent in the 1970s to –2.2 percent per year in the 1980s.[3] By 1990, import volumes were only 84 percent of the level ten years earlier.[4]

In 1992, developing countries received from the North $60 billion in foreign aid and another $102 billion in private capital, but only 6 percent went to sub-Saharan Africa.[5] Meanwhile, Africa has faced staggering foreign debt problems since the oil crisis in the early 1970s; its foreign debt increased almost tenfold between 1970 and 1982. In 1979, debt servicing costs absorbed 8 percent of foreign exchange earnings; in 1984, debt servicing stood at about 22 percent of those earnings. By 1980, the debt was $55 billion; by 1989, it reached $160 billion, with debt servicing accounting for 25 percent of the continent's exports of goods and services.[6] For Kenya alone, in 1989 the debt service as a percentage of exports of goods and services was 33 percent.[7] In a world of falling commodity prices over which African nations have no control, these countries have great difficulty repaying the debt. Gordon suggests that the debt crisis reinforces the economic crisis in several ways, partially by absorbing a substantial proportion of crucially needed scarce foreign exchange in debt service payments and partially by undermining the imperative for reform through a changing political relationship between debtors and creditors, substituting external pressure and financial resources for domestic leadership and an indigenous process.[8]

In this discussion of economic relationships, problems, and potential in Africa there is a wild card: the new, free, and independent South Africa. South Africa promises to be an economic force not only among the countries of the Southern Africa Development Coordinating Committee (SADCC) but within all of sub-Saharan Africa. At this point, one can only conjecture about the magnitude of South Africa's economic power and impact. However, now that the country's struggle for black governance is over, it has the potential to be a significant influence on the other sub-Saharan African nations.

Although Africa had been producing enough food to feed itself as recently as 1970, in 1984 food imports for the continent took approximately 20 percent of foreign exchange earnings. Africa was feeding the equivalent of the continent's entire urban population on imported grain. While agricultural production increased between 1980 and 1989 at a faster rate than in the 1970s (2.1 percent versus – 0.3 percent), this gain was below the rate of population increase, estimated by the World Bank to be 3.1 percent across the continent. In fact, according to Food and Agriculture Organization (FAO) data, eighteen African nations experienced more than a 10 percent decrease in per capita agricultural production in that decade, and another fourteen experienced a decrease up to 10 percent.[9] Only seven countries, including Kenya, experienced an increase in per capita agricultural production. Even in these more successful cases, that increase often reflects the growth of commercial export production of specialty crops, such as French beans and snow peas for the European market.

In many countries, smallholder agriculture is based primarily on women's labor using simple tools in rain-fed agricultural systems with few inputs and services. Moreover, millions of smallholder households in semiarid lands are raising staple crops unsuited to their environment but promoted by national policy and demanded by urban markets. It seems clear that the household producing its own food in this manner does not readily lend itself to providing the agricultural surplus to feed nations whose populations are growing at 3.1 percent a year and urbanizing, according to World Bank statistics, at the rate of an 8 percent increase per year.[10] Moreover, agricultural policies have generally ignored the responsibilities of rural women. This inattention to women's roles in agriculture has been observed by many scholars.[11] Virtually nowhere in Africa have decisionmakers made the policy linkage between women's roles as food producers, women's roles in managing the environment, and national food security, thereby enabling women to achieve effective participation and performance in national development.[12]

In fact, the 1989 World Bank report on Africa acknowledged that "getting the prices right" was not, in and of itself, an adequate policy for increasing food production, given that the long-term elasticity of aggregate supply for agricultural crops in Africa is approximately 3 percent. That is, for every 10 percent rise in prices, supply will increase around 3 percent, thus generating a modest increase in production.[13] The ecological, social, and institutional aspects of African agriculture have constituted elements beyond the purview of economic myopia.

In many instances, policies of international institutions and African governments have had a detrimental impact on smallholder domestic food production. The crops with an export market have benefited most often from either strong agricultural extension services, well-run marketing boards, effective cooperative strategies, sensitive pricing policies, or generous incentive packages. The "technology packages" promoted (and sometimes even mandated) by state agricultural agencies for cash crop production usually exclude intercropping with food crops and routinely require heavy (and expensive) pesticide applications.[14] Trees are also often cleared from fields to meet the production guidelines of cash crops.[15] The net result is a loss of fuelwood sources, reduction in food supply, contamination of soil and water, increased soil erosion, and disruption of nutrient cycling on agricultural plots. Further, food prices have been deliberately set in favor of the urban areas. Pricing policies have not provided incentives to the rural food producer. In fact, across many agricultural commodities, as prices have declined, they have met a diminishing portion of the farmers' real costs. In some cases the costs of production are higher than the returns, and the farmer is ultimately subsidizing the consumer, often through the unpaid "family labor" of women and children.

Thus, terms of trade are declining. Land devoted to commercial crops for export is increasing. Women's roles as food producers and resource managers are ignored. Populations are growing rapidly. While some families are investing in lucrative cash crop production and increasingly intensive agriculture, other families are moving onto more marginal lands where yields are low.[16] The latter group is likely either to keep bringing into cultivation new areas with poor soils and inadequate moisture or to face declining yields over time. This adds to land degradation, a problem exacerbated by the drought of recent years.

Ecological Issues

Although it is injudicious to venture generalizations about Africa's environment because of such enormous variation, the consensus among many researchers is that much of Africa's physical environment is deteriorating.[17] Changes wrought by colonialism and the move to privatize land have been the most dramatic shifts in land use patterns, but other changes are occurring as well. Pressures to produce—from both state imperatives and rising population—have led to acute problems of ecological degradation: eroding soil, deteriorating rangelands, dwindling forests, and diminishing water resources. Clearing land for agriculture, cutting wood for fuel, and overgrazing of animals all may contribute to these problems.

According to the World Resources Institute, average annual deforestation is taking place in Africa at the rate of 5 million hectares per year out of more than 700 million hectares.[18] For example, in the last thirty years there has been a significant increase in land under cultivation throughout Eastern Africa—as much as 300 percent in Sudan, 200 percent in Uganda, and 50 percent in Tanzania.[19] In many countries, forested areas have been vastly reduced. The World Bank specifies that 3.2 million hectares of forests and woodlands were converted to other uses each year in the 1980s, and the rate of conversion is accelerating.[20]

Deforestation can have a severe impact on agricultural productivity. The population living in the semiarid regions is growing rapidly because of in-migration as well as natural increase, and farmers are now cultivating drier lands. Herders and cultivators compete over use of the land, and migrants, displaced by land concentration elsewhere, displace or "squeeze" established residents. Sometimes, government officials decide to preserve areas for game parks, forest reserves, or other specialized purposes, thus exacerbating the problem. As vegetation is depleted in some regions, families begin to burn crop residues and animal dung as substitutes for wood. With neither fertilizers nor these nutrients, the soil's fertility declines. Though many communities are planting trees for food, fodder, fuel, and timber,[21] the balance in the semiarid lands is still in favor of deforestation.

As one observer put it, "In recent years, Africa's farmers and herders, her soils and forests, have been chasing each other down a vicious spiral of environmental degradation and deepening poverty."[22] Many farmers are caught in a low-level equilibrium in which depleted soils give them low yields and insufficient earnings with which to improve the quality of their soil or invest in alternative methods of farming.

Throughout much of Africa, environmental degradation is arising in large part from these elements—expansion of cultivation onto marginal lands, maintenance of livestock in confined spaces in semiarid lands, deforestation, and inappropriate irrigation, often in response to inappropriate government policies. In Kenya's Meru District, for example, ten years ago the coffee terraces were carefully maintained by small farming households. A government policy forbade farmers either to intercrop or to uproot coffee trees to switch to more remunerative crops. Farmers thus neglected their terraces during the 1980s while coffee prices remained low. Until the 1994 upswing in coffee prices, the terraces remained in poor condition, not because the farmers did not care or did not know better, but because global conditions and national policy made it uneconomical for them to be tended.

Although the facile diagnoses of universal crisis in Africa have been substantially discredited,[23] no doubt many of Kenya's rural farmers currently face overwhelming odds in the struggle to maintain their families and landholdings under current political and economic conditions. The recent turn toward discussions of success and recovery[24] has brought to light the positive reforestation, soil conservation, water development, and agricultural intensification efforts currently in progress.

However, there is not a single wave of land degradation followed by recovery; rather, in various sites degradation and recovery prevail, respectively.[25] For every denuded slope there is a tree planting project, somewhere; and for every degraded farmlot there might be an orchard. But on balance, there is a pronounced downward trend for the poorest third of the population and for the semiarid plains and hills in vast tracts of Kenya. Even in Machakos, where recent studies have heralded economic progress and environmental recovery, land degradation and progressive impoverishment more accurately describe the experiences of the near-landless and of whole communities of displaced upland farmers in semiarid frontier settlements. Also, large numbers of young women and men have migrated to urban areas or frontier towns or to become permanent residents on plantations.[26]

In some cases the displacement of the poor seems to be the price of a stabilized landscape, as poor people are bought out by largeholders who can afford to plant and maintain orchards and to irrigate, terrace, and otherwise "improve" the land. Meanwhile, for every hectare that they sell in their home area, migrants are likely to cut 10 hectares when they relocate to the semiarid frontier. Thus, recovery in one region may be subsidized by degradation in another.[27]

Clearly, many areas within Africa have demonstrated the Boserupian thesis that increased population density can spur intensification, innovation, and greater investments in soil and water management infrastructure and commercial trees.[28] It is unclear, though, how much this intensification, under conditions of free markets for farm produce and unregulated land markets, reflects the expansion of commercial agriculture at the expense of subsistence farming. Also at issue is the extent to which intensification depends on the ability of wealthier residents or immigrants to displace smallholders, with low purchase prices based on the availability of even cheaper land for the sellers in the semi-arid frontiers. Thus many of the commercial successes may be interpreted as displacement of environmental degradation and poverty to the frontiers.[29]

There are also legitimate cases of recovery and even of simple environmental maintenance by smallholders in the face of mounting pressures to produce.[30] We applaud the efforts and successes of the women and men who have worked on so many community-based and household-level conservation and production initiatives, but we would not trivialize the fact that they are doing so out of necessity, given the substantial problems created by previous policies and prior responses to them. We suggest that their heroic efforts should not have been required if the local, national, and international relations of power had not so clearly favored urban and Northern interests for so long. The net result of the recent processes of land use change in Kenya appears to be an increase in sedimentation in the major rivers, a rising tide of environmentally related illnesses (e.g., malnutrition, pesticide poisoning, and disease caused by contaminated water), and the depletion of forests, soil, rangelands, and water resources currently available to the poor.

One element often left out in both the crisis and recovery scenarios is the distribution of access to resources and the extent to which access overrides total supply when viewed in terms of the daily lives of people in the region. A second point concerns the quality of the resources and whether any tree or green cover is as good as any other. In both cases the yardstick of daily subsistence often measures private monocropped tree plots as far less useful to the poor than previously shared common lands as pasture, fallow, or woodland. Finally, largeholders and other local elites may well monopolize control of key resources in the new, more simplified, ecosystem under more intensive land use.

Population, Land Use, and Food Production in a North–South Context

For most African families the major source of livelihood is their land, although they struggle to find other sources of income. In fact, 69 percent of Africa's labor force derives its living from the land. We mention this in the context of an overall decline in per capita food production and a deteriorating standard of living for most rural Africans. While Africa has managed an overall 30 percent increase in food production over the past ten years, its per capita food output has dropped by 5 percent.[31]

Debates often arise about Africa's land use patterns, land degradation, and rate of population growth. These debates have intensified as a consequence of the 1993 UN Conference on Environment and Development (UNCED) in Rio de Janeiro. The lines seem to be drawn generally along a North–South fracture. The South proclaims that the North, with 20 percent of the world's population, consumes 80 percent of the world's resources in blatant overconsumption, whereas the North accuses the South of alarming population growth rates leading to extraordinary pressures for natural resources. One cannot argue with the assertion that "the overdevelopment in the North has been a main culprit in environmental degradation."[32] And one would be hard put to say that African countries are overpopulated; in fact, the continent, overall, is not densely populated. One can argue, however, that given Africa's current dependence on agriculture and the prevailing technologies and conditions of production, the rapidly growing populations will stretch all resources—natural, social, political, economic—during the next several decades.

Questions concerning optimal population size, growth rates, and density occur within certain contexts. In this case, there is a long historical context in which the South, including Africa, has been vulnerable to demands of the North. There is also a contemporary global context, involving a continuing depletion of African resources by outside forces, declining terms of trade, and stringent structural adjustment requirements. In a national context, there must be debate over population, land use, and food production; this context must include discussion of levels of technology, the condition of infrastructure, the nature of educational systems, the efficiency of the manufacturing sector, and the adequacy of water resources for societies that are, today, primarily rural.[33]

The issues are complex. However, given the current levels of economic development, the rate of population growth puts great pressure on governments to provide infrastructure, social services, and employment, as well as on households to care for children and to provide them with the opportunities parents keenly wish their children to have.[34] There are linkages among all these problems. One cannot look at economic constraints, ecological processes, population growth, and declining food production without considering the political and social context in which they are occurring.

Political Issues

There are now forty-six sub-Saharan African nations whose boundaries conform not to the logic of local geography or political community but rather to the lines drawn by the European councils and prime ministers of remote colonial governments of the nineteenth and early twentieth centuries. Some of these boundaries make sense; many do not, severing as they do, for example, the Maasai into Kenyans and Tanzanians, the Oromo into citizens of Ethiopia and Somalia, and the Somali into citizens of Somalia and Kenya. In many ways, the nation-state has been superimposed upon people who previously maintained more flexible and fluid relations between small communities and trading centers in networks operating over vast regions. For example, the visceral wrenching of Somalia or Rwanda may well be more indicative of the interaction of ethnic tensions with the troubled legacy of feudal relations, colonialism, and Cold War politics than of simple ethnic conflict.

In the mid-1990s, however, some inspiring examples may touch all Africans, addressing their own issues of democratization. Among them are South Africa, Zambia, Eritrea, and Malawi, nations that are building multiparty systems and open, democratic processes under challenging circumstances. Other African nations are struggling with what has been called "the second liberation," an opening up of national politics to democratic processes, thirty years after the first liberation in which Africa was freed from direct colonial rule. Some have pointed out that African women welcome the "second liberation of the 1990s . . . with hope, high expectations and determination to use the political space created by pluralism to chart out a women's democratic agenda and to ensure that the fresh efforts at democratization in their countries fully integrate the gender dimension in that process."[35] Women have a long history of struggle against various forms of oppression, whether of race, class, sex, or other forms.[36] It will take women's continuing activism and determination to alter the landscape of their political marginalization in many parts of Africa.

At the 1994 Commonwealth Parliamentary Association meetings in Nairobi, a representative from Mauritius argued that most African countries are worse off now than they were at the time of independence, and he attributed this situation largely to leaders with excessive power.[37] Many African states are trapped in tenuous political situations with near overwhelming economic pressures. On the one hand, they desperately need to mobilize both the political support and the economic resources of their rural people; on the other, they are prevented from fully utilizing these forces by their own fragility and fears of losing control. In fact, even under programs of "decentralization," many governments have actually promoted greater penetration and control, not empowerment of local communities, despite some of the benefits the latter might bring. Discussion of this phenomenon is wide ranging and includes analyses of countries from all corners of the African continent.[38]

This ambivalence underscores the terms by which rural communities are integrated into both market and state. For local communities, this is a key issue because the terms according to which they are incorporated into the larger political and economic systems shape their capacity to act effectively and to demand accountability. For some rural residents there has been a retreat into the kinship support systems of the "economy of affection" documented by Hyden's analysis of the "uncaptured peasantry" in Tanzania.[39] For most, however, this is no longer an option. They cannot "escape" from the reach of market and state, and the terms of incorporation are therefore critical. Their integration into the cash economy and into the political and cultural system of the state is well under way. Their livelihood systems incorporate multiple strategies for gaining access to agricultural produce and cash.

Consequently, there is an intricate process of mutual adaptation as governments and local communities seek ways to work together to meet their divergent and common interests and provide benefits to both. Members of local communities wish to increase family and household welfare, productivity, and income, as well as community viability and well-being. They also want access to the resources of the center. The state seeks a viable rural economy, loyal rural communities, and a local contribution to long-term national growth and productivity.

The risk and danger are that the state will slip into authoritarianism, emphasizing its control functions more than its support functions, with vested interests determining the nature of change.[40] Sometimes state action leans overwhelmingly toward an urban bias, protecting Western life-styles in the capital city. Indeed, the state's intention to appropriate surplus—whether through absolute surplus value extraction or through unequal exchange—may be paramount.[41]

The dynamics of center–locality power relations, specifically the ways rural communities relate to both market and state, are integral to analysis of local organizations and institutions and to issues of gender, resources, and development. At the heart of Africa's development challenge is the way rural institutions engage with the state to effect a transformation of rural livelihood systems that acknowledges and builds the particularities and strengths of the local community.

Growing Marginalization: Gender, Class, and Ethnicity

In a variety of ways, the political and economic systems of many post-independence African nations have led to increasing class formation and to growing disparities of wealth among regions, among households, and along the lines of ethnicity and gender. There has been a tendency to promote high-potential, ecologically favored regions supporting intensive agriculture over low-potential, semiarid lands. Often the more advantaged communities are able to capitalize on the benefits directed toward them by building access to resources at the center. The coffee-growing areas, for example, are more likely to have paved roads, a communitywide water system, or a district-level polytechnic institute. These communities magnify regional differences as they increase agricultural production, invest in household improvements, and build nonfarm trade and business activities.

Across the spectrum of political ideologies and national commitments, specific government policies and programs have often exacerbated rural differentiation among and within households. Frequently there has been an emphasis on large farmers and affluent smallholders in the orientation of rural infrastructure and extension services. In fact, access to physical inputs is often based on politics, clientelism, and wealth rather than on need or the capacity to use inputs effectively. Even within households, differentiation may be observed when men and women have separate purses derived from different sources of income and do not fully share domestic responsibilities. In addition, rural development policies have been directed toward the rural landholder, yet increasingly there are landless families and households with insufficient land to sustain themselves. Agricultural projects simply do not reach many of the poor, including landless and near-landless agricultural laborers or other groups who practice pastoralism or fishing.

This phenomenon of increasing differentiation and marginalization has been well documented across Africa. Watts finds increasing class differences among rural households in Nigeria, a process dramatically exacerbated by the government's inclination to implement large-scale rural development projects.[42] Hecht observes the evolution of rural society in southern Ivory Coast as it has shifted over a sixty-year period from lineage agriculture to small-scale capitalist farm production, in which the share of cultivated land of the wealthiest fifth of households has increased substantially; the share of middle peasants has fallen; and the number of landless has grown.[43] Peters has examined the process of accumulation and increasing privatization of communal lands in Botswana over a fifty-year period following the first establishment of permanent water resources.[44] Ali and O'Brien observe in central Kordofan in Sudan the permanent population of landless families, which has emerged as result of privatization of land ownership.[45]

Among the disparities beyond class, gender, and rural–urban differentials, ethnicity has emerged as a major axis of conflict. In most of the countries under consideration, ethnicity is a salient category. Some have assumed that it will recede as class factors emerge. In fact, observation suggests that class and ethnicity coexist.[46] In the words of one scholar, ethnicity has been the "resilient paradigm" for Africa for the last twenty years, and "to suggest that either modernization or revolution will eliminate one or the other is misguided."[47]

In many African countries there is a convergence between geography and ethnicity within the new confines of the nation-state. Some regions, and therefore some ethnic groups, are better off than others. Where this convergence of place, wealth, political power, and ethnicity exists, it can easily erupt into hostility—as it has in Nigeria, Uganda, Zimbabwe, Rwanda, and Burundi. Communal solidarity, as it is found at varying levels of political and social organization, is a potent force in the process of African institutional and organizational change. In many instances, national-level leadership makes considerable effort to achieve a delicate balance of position, status, and power among ethnic groups. In other instances, it is clear that leaders use ethnicity to organize and augment their power.

There is, suggests Young, "a frayed relationship between state and civil society."[48] Explanations are numerous. Barker laments that "a development-oriented state has yet to appear in Africa. Instead urban bias, personalistic politics, administrative incompetence, and inappropriate international assistance stand in the way of effective government action."[49] De Janvry et al. echo this concern, querying, "How can the state be transformed into a developmental state?"[50] Taylor and Mackenzie assert, "There is no doubt that the quality of life for the majority of Africa's inhabitants has been declining in both absolute and relative terms. In many parts of Africa there is no compelling evidence that 'development,' however defined, is taking place. Increasing degradation would be a better description than 'development' for the current trends."[51]

THE KENYAN CONTEXT: OPPORTUNITIES AND CONSTRAINTS

Politics and the State

Kenya has often been described as one of Africa's most economically prosperous and politically stable nations. It has a modern bureaucracy and a parliamentary system of government, which have functioned continuously since Kenya's independence in 1963, despite an unsuccessful coup attempt in August 1982. Jomo Kenyatta, leader of the independence struggle, established himself as president and head of a patrimonial-style state and governed from 1963 until his death in 1978. He was succeeded by his vice president, Daniel Arap Moi.

In 1982 the Kenyan constitution was amended to include Section 2A, making Kenya a one-party state, and until 1991 the nation was governed by an increasingly centralized political party, the Kenya Africa National Union (KANU), and bureaucracy under the leadership of President Moi. In the late 1980s and early 1990s there was increasing pressure, both internationally and domestically, for the Kenyan government to reinvigorate democratic processes and permit a multiparty system. In December 1991, Section 2A of the constitution was repealed, and in late 1992 many parties, including Forum for Restoration of Democracy (FORD)-Kenya, FORD-Asili, and the Democratic Party, as well as KANU, contested the national elections, the first such elections in independent Kenya in twenty-six years. KANU won this election, and Moi continues as president of Kenya.

Although some people question whether KANU is serious about implementing pluralism through permitting a multiparty political system, the government seems to be moving, albeit reluctantly, to increase the opportunities for public speaking and assembly granted to leaders of the opposition.[52] Indeed, the government of Kenya seems to have been persuaded to accept fledgling plural politics. As this process takes place, many worry about temptations of all politicians to exploit ethnic fears and sensitivities in ways that lead to clashes, retreat, ethnic enclaves, and erosion of national unity.[53] In fact, one analyst suggests, "the fear of civil strife in Kenya is very real, and the seeds for civil war have been sown in the Rift Valley, in particular, and certain parts of western Kenya in general."[54]

Kenya's institutions function within the historical context of a vigorous struggle against colonial rule, which created high expectations among a rural population primed for new political and economic opportunities. Issues of governance continue to be paramount for many Kenyans. These issues go deep, for people are concerned not simply with the winds of change or with multiparty issues but with the nature of the state and its accountability to ordinary citizens.

Increasingly, women perceive that state accountability involves the resource base and their access to resources needed for securing their livelihoods.

The Economy

It is projected that, with a population of 23,590,000 in 1990, Kenya will have 27,890,000 people by 1995.[55] The nation has the third most rapidly growing population in Africa, at 3.5 percent per year, just after Ivory Coast and Djibouti.[56] From the time of independence, Kenya has been committed to a market-friendly economy, private ownership, the concept of comparative advantage, and full engagement with the international economy. Growth rates were at their highest through the 1960s, and into the next decade Kenya flourished, riding the crest of high prices for its most important commodity, coffee, as they surged in the mid-1970s. By the 1980s, declining coffee prices, the long-term impacts of the oil crisis, and various structural adjustment policies were creating a different picture.

Kenya's leadership has continued to emphasize production of coffee and tea not only in the high-potential areas but also in other regions. This policy has remained intact, despite the precipitous decline of coffee prices until the spring of 1994. The government has also been encouraging production of food grains to decrease Kenya's rapidly escalating dependence on food imports. Throughout the 1980s, the producer price of grains has increased significantly, indicating support for increased production and the government's desire to reduce the foreign exchange burden made by grain imports. Perhaps the policy shift acknowledges the administration's interest in political support from the grain farmers of the Rift Valley. Some assert, however, that grain farmers did not benefit widely from the price increases. In fact, according to some analysts, the typical African farmer may have been subsidizing the consumer while a few well-placed politicians benefited.[57]

Between 1965 and 1980, Kenya's economy attained an average annual growth rate of 6.4 percent; in the 1980s, performance averaged only 3.8 percent per year. The growth of GDP fell to .4 percent in 1992 and .1 percent in 1993.[58] Inflation hit a high of 46 percent in 1993 partly in relation to devaluation and partly because 25 billion shillings were pumped into the money supply in 1992. Inflation declined to 28 percent by early 1994. The nation has been in the midst of sectoral adjustment programs—including trade reforms, increased producer incentives in agriculture, and a restructuring of government finance and of public enterprises, along with devaluation of the Kenya shilling (Ksh).

Structural Adjustment Programs (SAPs) are programs of policy and institutional changes undertaken by a government—usually under duress from international banking and development agencies—with the objective of rekindling or increasing the pace of economic growth. Designed to address the fundamental causes of poor economic performance, the process of structural transformation is not easy under the best of circumstances.[59]

Consequences of such policies for Kenya have included a good export performance but a worsening balance of trade situation because there was a sharp increase in the value of imports. The government has expressed much concern about the impact of SAPs on vulnerable groups and has underscored the need to bring down the price of basic commodities by providing some targeted subsidies and safety nets to support such groups. The KANU Governing Council, the supreme decisionmaking body of the governing party, has nevertheless emphasized its commitment to the continuation of reforms.[60] Discussions at the Commonwealth Parliamentary Association meetings hosted in Nairobi in May 1994 concluded that SAPs were a result of mismanagement of resources by African governments and were not in and of themselves the cause of the economic hardships that African nations were currently experiencing.[61]

Kenya's external debt obligations rose by 70 percent through the 1980s, and debt servicing by the end of the 1980s required one-third of the value of goods and services exported.[62] The *Economic Survey* for 1994 shows that the debt service ratio has fallen to a low of 7 percent, partly because of an increase in exports and an accumulation of arrears in external debt service payments.[63] Meanwhile, the value of exports has more than doubled, as a result of both price and volume increases—especially for tea and horticultural items—as well as price increases for coffee.

In agriculture, Kenya has experienced a continuing decline for the third year in a row. Poor performance in maize and wheat production is linked to unfavorable weather conditions, high prices for inputs, and unrest and ethnic conflict in some important grain producing regions of the country. According to recent commentary in the *Daily Nation,* food production in regions known as Kenya's breadbasket has been paralyzed by loss of lives, tremendous destruction of property, and the abandonment of developed farms. These conditions exist in addition to the more typical problems plaguing many farmers: inferior maize seed, high cost of inputs, and delayed payments.[64] The high inflationary trends and rising costs of production have contributed to worsening agricultural terms of trade, thereby further disadvantaging the farmers.[65]

Kenya's structure of production over the last decade reveals agriculture holding constant at about 30 percent, industry declining by 3 percent, manufacturing declining by 3 percent, and services growing by 5 percent. This trend is unsettling in a country with unemployment running high and a population of over 30 million anticipated by the end of the decade. On the bright side, in 1993 the manufacturing sector recorded slight growth, although building and construction activities continued to be depressed.

Sessional Paper No. 1 of 1986 on *Economic Management for Renewed Growth* set the target growth rate in GDP at 5.9 percent per year between 1988 and 2000, yet the country has experienced a rapid deceleration in growth rate, which started in 1989 and continued to 1994. The government predicted that the economy is on a recovery path and that 1994 will see a reversal of the economic decline and a 3 percent growth rate. Such an improvement in the growth rate will be contingent upon satisfactory rains, continued implementation of structural reforms (particularly liberalization and privatization of the economy), full restoration of aid from donors, resolution of debt arrears, and success in bringing down the rate of average annual inflation to single-digit numbers.[66]

Since 1980, the government of Kenya's expenditures have been declining across several social sectors, including health, housing, social security, and welfare. Only education shows an increase in central government expenditure from the early to mid-1980s.[67] Nevertheless, overall human welfare indicators are strong. Life expectancy is currently sixty-three years; fertility rates are beginning to decline, as are mortality rates for children under five. Immunizations are now being administered to approximately 71 percent of the nation's children.[68] Despite these successes, there are critical issues in the area of child health related to the environment and the quality of natural resources, particularly water. Resolution of these issues is central to the lives of rural women.

Ecological Issues

New conceptualizations of the environment—which include the meeting of daily human needs as well as large-scale resource management and protection—are gaining wide acceptance in Kenya. People's welfare is linked to food security and to adequate livelihoods, which in turn are dependent upon a resource base of soils, water, grasslands, forests, and a host of wild and domestic animals. These life support systems are essential not only for the present generation but for future generations as well. Problems associated with the environment are complex and include such seemingly disparate phenomena as poverty, disease, hunger, inadequate energy supply, lack of water, and depletion of genetic resources. Human activities are altering ecological processes through pollution, resource depletion, destruction of biodiversity, and damage to the integrity of ecosystems. The objective must be people-centered development through sustainable use of resources.[69]

From the mid-1960s, the government of Kenya has recognized the importance of its natural resource base, as reflected in Sessional Paper No. 10 of 1965, *African Socialism and Its Application to Planning in Kenya.* By the mid-1970s, both the UN Environment Program (UNEP) and the Environment Liaison Centre International (ELCI) had been located in Nairobi. Nevertheless, the 1980s have been characterized as "a lost development decade," not just for Kenya but for many countries, with unsustainable development, accelerating deforestation, desertification, degradation of soils, depletion of wildlife, reduction of biodiversity, and escalation of industrial pollution.[70]

The focus is now on sustainable development and ways to link sustainable environmental use with socioeconomic development and responsibility of the present generation for the welfare of future generations. Despite the presence of the Ministry of Environment and Natural Resources and its National Environment Secretariat (NES), which carries out environmental research and training, some suggest that Kenya as yet has no clear environmental policy or resource management plan. In fact, "despite past policy rhetoric on the need to conserve the environment the praxis has been that short-term individual, state and corporate economic gains have taken precedence over genuine environmental considerations."[71] Given that environmental degradation and agricultural productivity are closely linked, many Kenyans are beginning to ask critical questions about how to address these issues effectively. The government is preparing a Sessional Paper on Sustainable Development and a National Environmental Action Plan (NEAP). It is hoped that these documents will provide needed guidance and direction.

Current Issues and Debates

Certain problems have arisen from fundamental contradictions and dilemmas in Kenya's political and economic life. These problems can be observed in class and ethnic competition for national resources, a middle class under increasing economic pressures, an overweening bureaucracy, declining terms of trade, increasing international debt, and a political and economic vulnerability to outside forces. In addition, there is growing concern about Kenya's increasingly unbalanced power structure. Even with the repeal of Section 2A of the constitution, the central government and KANU continue to have a wide range of local institutions and political processes within their power.[72] Although this situation is changing, progress remains slow.

There has also been growing public dissatisfaction that only a small minority of Kenyans has been in a position to reap personal advantage from global economic linkages. The UN Development Programme (UNDP) report for 1994 specifies that Kenya has a striking gap between rich and poor, with the poorest 40 percent of the country earning less than 10 percent of GDP, while the richest 20 percent earn more than twenty-two times the income of the poorest.[73] Significant income inequities exist, with the top 20 percent getting 60 percent of the income and the bottom 20 percent receiving 3 percent.[74] Per capita GNP stands at U.S. $350, down from the late 1980s; it is just above that of Equatorial Guinea and below that of The Gambia.[75]

Eighty percent of the population live in rural areas, and most farmers cultivate small plots averaging 2 hectares each. Nevertheless, more than 40 percent of agricultural land is held in large farms averaging 1,000 hectares and numbering less than 1 percent of total farming households.[76] Kenya's 1994 *Economic Survey* specifies the prevalence of absolute rural poverty at 46 percent, with the highest prevalence among subsistence farmers at 52 percent.[77]

The well-being of Kenya's agricultural sector and its rural population are inextricably linked to a number of internal challenges, as well as to the opportunities and constraints of the international political economy. There is an urgent need to address income distribution and equity issues, to stem the rising tide of migration, to support agricultural production by part-time farmers and split households, to improve agricultural production overall, and to generate employment opportunities in the rural areas. Moreover, Kenya's resource base is under stress in virtually all areas of the country. In the semiarid regions there is particular stress on once sustainable traditional production systems in a process of transition to an uncertain future.[78] Women are central to resolution of these environmental and food security concerns in Kenya, as they are elsewhere in sub-Saharan Africa.

Kenya's Women: Factoring in Gender

Although there is no explicit policy on women's development, the *Fourth Development Plan, 1979–1983* highlighted the contribution of women in the agricultural sector, and the *Fifth Development Plan, 1984–1988* and the *Sixth Development Plan, 1989–1993* addressed the disadvantaged situation of women in modern-sector employment, health programs, education, and decisionmaking. The government is moving to introduce a gender and development approach that reflects the different responsibilities of men and women in planning and development activities.[79] Responding to the UN Decade for Women, 1975–1985, and the World Plan of Action adopted at the first World Conference on Women held in Mexico in 1975, the government established the Women's Bureau within the Ministry of Culture and Social Services to mobilize women for development; to orient government services toward women; to facilitate coordination among women's groups, the government, and NGOs; and to carry out research related to women.

A survey administered by the Women's Bureau in 1991 to acquire information about women's groups in Kenya established that there were 23,614 women's groups in the country, both registered and unregistered, with a total membership of 969,941.[80] Though they have their roots in traditional women's associations, most were formally registered (or organized) during the 1970s and 1980s. One common way of addressing local resource management issues has been through involvement in women's groups.

The constitution assures equal political rights for women, but there is a conspicuous absence of women in decisionmaking positions in the government. While the majority of voters are women, few stand for elective positions. However, in the 1992 multiparty elections, women were elected to 6 out of 188 seats in Parliament. Elections were vigorously contested, and, for the first time, a number of women candidates gained national prominence as they participated fully in the electoral process.[81] But among the twelve nominated Members of Parliament (all appointed by the president), there was not one woman.

Education statistics for Kenya as a whole reveal that gender parity has been obtained in primary school enrollment rates, with a male:female ratio of 51:49.[82] These figures, of course, conceal wide geographic variation. National literacy for women is still low at 40 percent, with a male literacy rate of 69 percent and a national average of 59 percent.[83] A decline in female enrollments at university levels from 31 percent of the student body in 1989 to 27 percent in 1992 no doubt reflects the difficult economic times. Male:female ratios at the university level are approximately 3:1. According to Ng'weno, "Girls do not just drop out of school at a higher rate than boys. They are forced out of school. Forced out by . . . tradition-bound parents, forced out by an indifferent, insensitive male-dominated society determined to assign girls, and women in general, a permanently inferior status. . . . The problem has to do with more than just education. It has to do with the position of girls and women in African society—both traditional and present. The combination of traditional African gender discrimination and new forms brought about by colonialism, Christianity, and Islam [has] deepened the problem."[84]

About 75 percent of the total labor force is engaged in the agricultural sector. Women traditionally contribute most of the labor required for cultivation of food crops on family holdings, as well as most of the labor required on small- and medium-size holdings in the production of cash crops. Increasingly they are involved in the management of smallholdings. It is estimated that 27 percent of smallholdings in Kenya are managed solely by women who are also legal heads of households. Another 47 percent of smallholdings are managed by women in the absence of their husbands.[85] Despite these responsibilities, land inheritance patterns continue to favor males, as do patterns of distribution of the various human, financial, and technical resources in the agricultural sector.

Central to women's agricultural and overall livelihood responsibilities are the roles of women in managing resources in rural communities. Water, soils, grasslands, forests, livestock, and wildlife are at the heart of Africa's rural production systems. The effectiveness of their management affects local livelihood systems profoundly. Modes of cooperation and conflict over resource access and use provide a lens for understanding social institutions at the local level. They also facilitate exploration of fundamental social alliances as well as cleavages in the social fabric within local communities or between such communities and the outside world. These alliances and cleavages originate in connections of family, class, ethnicity, race, gender, or religion.

Evidence suggests that consideration of local resource management, as it bears on food production and rural livelihood systems, must incorporate all these variables into the analytical framework. Rural households are vulnerable in crosscutting systems of power relations, particularly those of class and gender. Women bear responsibility for the viability of these households. For poor women, the reality is one of subordination within both of these domains coupled with inadequate access to power in the broader political and socioeconomic arenas.

Kenya is not alone. The specific resource issues may vary, but the interactions of class, ethnicity, and gender in regard to resource management at the local level are pertinent considerations across rural Africa. Those who wish to understand local communities and their production systems cannot ignore the ways these hierarchies affect the equitable access to resources and their effective management. They also cannot ignore the linkages across local, national, and global domains. Choices, opportunities, and constraints for the rural household may be shaped by relations between spouses, by policies at the national level, or by the exigencies of international politics and economics. In most cases, all these combine to influence household livelihood strategies.

Rural communities in Kenya are undergoing transformation across many dimensions. Priorities in international and national development have shifted toward sustainable development, which brings rural women into a new environmental discourse defined by outsiders. There are changing rural–urban dynamics, emerging class relations, new political actors, shifting political and economic boundaries, and new definitions of gender. The cases presented in Part 2 explore these issues of resource management, conflicts, and constraints in the context of these transformations, with particular reference to gender as a critical variable. They investigate the effectiveness of community institutions in local resource management and the ways women and men are served by both. The intent is to illuminate emerging patterns and to pose new questions in relation to gender, resources, livelihood systems, and development in Kenya.

NOTES

1. Hyden, "The Changing Context of Institutional Development in Sub-Saharan Africa," p. 43.
2. Lofchie, "Trading Places," p. 403.
3. Ravenhill, "A Second Decade of Adjustment," p. 18.
4. Ibid., p. 19.
5. UN Development Program, *1994 Human Development Report;* Owuor, "Rich Nations Urged to Scrap Third World Debts."
6. Ravenhill, "A Second Decade of Adjustment," p. 18.
7. World Resources Institute, *World Resources 1994–95*, p. 238.
8. Gordon, "Debt, Conditionality, and Reform," pp. 91–126.
9. Herbst, "The Politics of Sustained Agricultural Reform," p. 335.
10. World Bank, *The Long-Term Perspective Study of Sub-Saharan Africa.*
11. Henn, "Feeding the Cities and Feeding the Peasants"; Guyer, "Women in the Rural Economy"; Dey, "Development Planning in the Gambia."
12. Nzomo, "Policy Impacts on Women and Environment," p. 116.
13. World Bank, *Sub-Saharan Africa.*
14. Anna Kajumulo Tibaijuka, personal communication.
15. Wilson, "Trees in Fields in Southern Zimbabwe."
16. Rocheleau et al., "The Ukambani Region of Kenya."
17. World Bank, "The Population, Agriculture and Environment Nexus," p. 7.
18. World Resources Institute, *World Resources 1994–95.*
19. Berry, "Coping with Confusion"; Clark, *Democratizing Development.*
20. World Bank, "The Population, Agriculture and Environment Nexus," p. 7.
21. Bradley, *Women, Woodfuel, and Woodlots.*
22. Harrison, *The Greening of Africa*, p. 2.

23. Watts, "The Agrarian Crisis in Africa."

24. Tiffen et al., *More People, Less Erosion.*

25. Rocheleau et al., "The Ukambani Region of Kenya."

26. Rocheleau, et al., *Toward a Feminist Political Ecology.*

27. Ibid.

28. Turner et al., *Population Growth and Agricultural Change in Africa;* Tiffen and Mortimore, "Environment, Population Growth and Productivity in Kenya"; Lagemann, *Traditional African Farming Systems.*

29. Rocheleau et al., "The Ukambani Region of Kenya."

30. Blaikie and Brookfield, *Land Degradation and Society.*

31. World Resources Institute, *World Resources 1994–95*, p. 271.

32. Kinuthia-Njenga. "The Population Debate," p. 2.

33. For an excellent discussion of problems Africa must address, see Callaghy and Ravenhill (eds.), *Hemmed In*, p. 48.

34. For a valuable discussion of population questions around the world, see Hartmann, *Reproductive Rights and Wrongs.*

35. Nzomo, "Gender Question and the South African Elections."

36. Sen and Grown, *Development, Crises, and Alternative Visions.*

37. Opala, "CPA Meeting Censures Anti-Democracy Leaders."

38. Holmquist and Ford, "Kenya: Slouching Toward Democracy"; Ndi, "Cameroon: Democracy at Bay"; Sithole, "Is Zimbabwe Poised on a Liberal Path?"; Knight, "Growing Opposition in Zimbabwe."

39. Hyden, *No Shortcuts to Progress* and *Beyond Ujamaa in Tanzania.*

40. This differentiation of support and control functions derives from Leonard and Marshall's (1982) discussion of center–local linkages in which he suggests that there are five types of linkages (finance, regulation, technical and personnel assistance, services, and representation) that can be distinguished by their underlying purposes: control and assistance; see Leonard and Marshall, *Institutions of Rural Development for the Poor*, p. 35.

41. Thomas-Slayter, "Structural Change, Power Politics, and Community Organizations in Africa."

42. Watts, *Silent Violence.*

43. Hecht, "The Transformation of Lineage Production."

44. Peters, "Struggles Over Water, Struggles Over Meaning," p. 45.

45. Ali and O'Brien, "Labor, Community, and Protest," p. 229.

46. Thomas-Slayter, "Class, Ethnicity, and the Kenyan State."

47. Shaw, "Beyond Any New World Order"; see also Chazan et al., *Politics and Society in Contemporary Africa.*

48. Young, "Beyond Patrimonial Autocracy," p. 21.

49. Barker, *Rural Communities Under Stress*, p. 204.

50. De Janvry et al., "Introduction to State, Market, and Civil Organizations," p. 569.

51. Taylor and Mackenzie (eds.), *Development from Within*, p. 215.

52. Kuria, "KANU Not Serious on Multi-Partyism."

53. Mulaa, "Deadly 'Aliens' Syndrome."

54. Opanga, "Are We So Reckless as to Invite a Genocide Here?"

55. World Resources Institute, *World Resources 1994–95*, p. 268.

56. UN Development Program, *1994 Human Development Report.*

57. Bradshaw, "Perpetuating Underdevelopment in Kenya." Bradshaw's theory about policy shifts to gain support of Kalenjin farmers arises from the pork-barrel considerations of democratic politics. Others, closer to the scene, disagree with this analysis.

58. Government of Kenya, Ministry of Planning and National Development, *National Development Plan, 1994–1996*, p. 1; Government of Kenya, Central Bureau of Statistics, *Economic Survey, 1994*, p. 2.

59. Shaw, "Little-Understood SAPs Are Blamed for All Our Failures."

60. *Daily Nation*, "A Most Welcome Sober Approach."

61. Ngugi, "What It Takes for SAPs to Succeed."

62. World Bank, *World Development Report 1989*, p. 253.

63. Government of Kenya, Central Bureau of Statistics, *Economic Survey, 1994*, p. 4.

64. Cege, "The Key to Ensure National Food Security" and "Disasters."

65. Government of Kenya, Central Bureau of Statistics, *Economic Survey, 1994*, p. 5.

66. Nduati, "Kenya's Economic Recovery Real," p. 49.

67. World Bank, *Sub-Saharan Africa*, p. 264.

68. Government of Kenya, Ministry of Planning and National Development, *National Development Plan, 1994–1996*, p. 28.

69. Korten, *People-Centered Development;* Holmberg (ed.), *Making Development Sustainable.*

70. Government of Kenya, Ministry of Planning and National Development, *National Development Plan, 1994–1996*, p. 169.

71. Nzomo, "Policy Impacts on Women and Environment," p. 105.

72. Lofchie, "Trading Places," p. 443; Thomas-Slayter, "Class, Ethnicity, and the Kenyan State."

73. UN Development Program, *1994 Human Development Report;* Redfern, "Kenya Tops in Development."

74. World Bank, *Social Indicators of World Development*, p. 166.

75. World Resources Institute, *World Resources 1994–95*, p. 256.

76. Bradshaw, "Perpetuating Underdevelopment in Kenya," p. 7.

77. Government of Kenya, Central Bureau of Statistics, *Economic Survey, 1994*, p. 41.

78. Cornell University, Institute for African Development, "Development in the Arid and Semi-Arid Areas of Kenya."

79. Government of Kenya, Ministry of Culture and Social Services, *The Government Achievements in the Development of Women (1963–1993)*, p. iii.

80. Ibid., p. 5.

81. Zebralink Communications, *If Women Counted.*

82. Government of Kenya, Ministry of Culture and Social Services, *The Government Achievements in the Development of Women (1963–1993)*, p. 9.

83. Ibid.

84. Ng'weno, "Making Education Meaningful," p. 26.

85. Government of Kenya, Ministry of Culture and Social Services, *The Government Achievements in the Development of Women (1963–1993)*, p. 17.

Part 2

The Cases

3

Gender, Ecology, and Agroforestry: Science and Survival in Kathama

*Dianne Rocheleau, Mohamud Jama,
Betty Wamalwa-Muragori*

In rural landscapes throughout the world, women have increasingly taken responsibility as the "daily managers of the living environment."[1] A steady stream of field research and informal reports, as well as historical research, indicates the gendered nature of ecological science and practice in most cultures.[2] Researchers have documented the changing rights, responsibilities, and tasks of poor rural women and the imbalance of women's rights and responsibilities as resource managers.[3] Yet very little of the literature on sustainability has treated gender as an issue. The implication is that at least half of indigenous ecological science has been obscured by the prevailing "invisibility" of women—their work, their interests, and especially their knowledge—to the international scientific community.

The new wave of enthusiasm for "sustainable" development and the concurrent upwelling of interest in biodiversity and indigenous knowledge warrants a deeper look into the place of rural women's ecological science within this new developmental trend. We can also consider the possible consequences of this new direction for rural women's futures and those of their communities.[4] We speak to both concerns by exploring the gendered nature of rural peoples' own science of survival within the context of a formal research project and the community response to drought and famine in Machakos District, Kenya.

Machakos District, part of the Ukamba region, which is home to the Akamba people, has for over a century been the object of intense scrutiny and intervention by colonial, national, and international agencies concerned with economic development and environmental degradation.[5] European explorers and missionaries spoke of a healthy, prosperous people and verdant landscapes in the mid-1800s, but by the late 1890s all of East Africa was in the throes of human and livestock epidemics caused by contact with European travelers and herds.[6] Coupled with drought, this led to widespread famine of epic proportions throughout the larger region, the decimation of livestock herds, and the death of hun-

Map 3.1   Athi River Basin and Study Area

Study Area

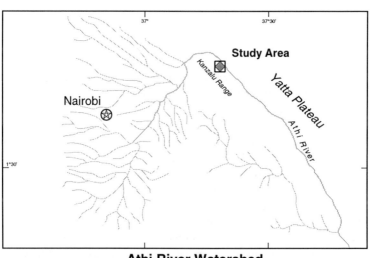

Athi River Watershed

Source: Dianne Rocheleau and A. van den Hoek, "The Application of Ecosystems," ICRAF Working Paper, no. 11.

dreds of thousands of people, with estimates of up to 50 percent of the population in Kitui, adjoining Machakos District.[7]

Since that time, famine has continued to plague the people of Machakos, particularly those in the drylands, even in times of relatively minor droughts. Whereas the most severe droughts would tax the ability of any community to cope, this vulnerability to lesser droughts is due in large part to disruption of traditional mechanisms of mobility between highland homesteads and lowland grazing areas and interference with flexible reliance on both crops and livestock as sources of food.[8] Recurrent famines and the conditions that create them have occurred amid dramatic changes in land use, spawning in turn radical changes in gendered rights, responsibilities, and knowledge within the livelihood systems and landscapes of the region.

In spite of analyses that cite widespread economic and environmental recovery in Machakos,[9] the rural poor of the district—women in particular—continue to experience considerable distress during droughts and recurrent famines. They personally suffer from hunger, malnutrition and related diseases, and the depletion of livestock herds affected by disease and starvation or sold at low prices in times of distress.[10] In addition, their holdings and the region as a whole are further deforested with each drought and crop failure, since most of the poor farmers of Machakos resort either to doing casual labor on plantations or to producing and selling charcoal to purchase food. As men have migrated to urban areas and plantations in search of wage labor, the women have become increasingly responsible for drought response, famine prevention, and, when necessary, famine response and recovery.

The drought of 1984–1985 was a disaster of personal and regional proportions and brought severe hardship to millions of people throughout Kenya. The ensuing famine hit hardest in the semiarid lands, particularly among the rural poor and the women-headed and women-managed households, who depended primarily on their own crop and livestock production for daily subsistence. The ability of the rural poor to survive was due in large part to their mobilization of traditional knowledge and skills, as well as their innovation in ecological, economic, and political domains.

The case of the Kathama market center in Mbiuni Location, Machakos, illustrates the interaction of local tradition and technology innovation with external technical interventions and experiments in a semiarid farming community before, during, and after the drought and famine. Kathama currently serves two sublocations, Ulaani and Katitu, in Mbiuni, which is in Mwala Division. It is an Akamba farming community in a dry forest and savanna zone about 100 kilometers east of Nairobi, nested within the ridge of the Kanzalu Range, the Athi River (which traverses the valley 300 meters below), and the Yatta Plateau (which rises to 60 meters in a gradual slope from the far side of the river) (see Map 3.1). The area covered by the study encompasses just under 50 square kilometers and embodies many of the problems and opportunities of the transition from agropastoral to mixed farming land use systems, a process that has occurred over the past seventy-five years. The current landscape is a densely settled, complex matrix of dry forest, bush, pastures, croplands, and homesteads, criss-crossed by hedges, fencerows, terraces, drainage works, seasonal streams, gullies, footpaths, and roads.

The farmers who live and work in Kathama are primarily women. Over one-third of the households are headed by women; another third are legally headed by absentee men and largely managed by women. Kathama represents a growing trend in rural areas where land is more scarce than labor and where urban employment, at least for the present, provides greater returns for men's labor than alternative, more intensive agricultural systems. The gender division of labor has shifted from complementary tasks and distinct but overlapping domains at farm and community levels to a rural/urban division. Many of Kathama's households have rural roots and urban branches: women are responsible for subsistence and commercial farming while men work for wages in the cities. Women are also increasingly responsible for the care of complex landscapes that sustain livelihoods and life in their community

The objectives of the ongoing research in Kathama are fourfold: (1) to understand connections among gendered work, knowledge, rights, and responsibilities in rural landscapes and in rural peoples' lives; (2) to clarify the relation of gendered work and knowledge to the integration of livelihood and life support in rural life; (3) to identify the points of convergence between ecological science, gender, and development that warrant explicit treatment in research and development agendas; and (4) to explore approaches to support both women's and men's knowledge and vision in shaping future lifeways and landscapes in areas undergoing similar processes of social and environmental change.

THE KATHAMA PROJECT: PEOPLE AND PLACE

In 1981 the International Council for Research in Agroforestry and Wageningen University (The Netherlands) began an exploratory on-farm agroforestry research project in a cluster of five villages in the semiarid farmlands and rangelands of Machakos District. The study site (more than 30 square kilometers) encompassed the area served by the Kathama market center.

The Kathama Agroforestry Project was in itself a very modest effort to develop collaborative research methods for farmer participation in agroforestry research. Rather than a major effort to transform the landscape in Kathama, the project was meant to produce methods to be widely applied elsewhere after initial testing. However, the farmers and community groups involved in the initial project pursued traditional and experimental agroforestry practices in earnest and allowed researchers to document their own independent efforts long after the first project was over.

The account of the formal project and related research efforts, as well as independent local efforts, provides several examples of gendered knowledge, work, rights, and responsibilities in rural land use and resource management at' the household and community levels. The experience of interdisciplinary research teams over several years illustrates the changing terms of the gender division of labor and knowledge, as well as the increasing imbalance between men's and women's rights and responsibilities. However, the story of community responses to drought and famine in 1984 and of the use and expansion of gendered knowledge in that difficult time can teach us much about the resourcefulness of rural women's organizations and the complexity of rural peoples' science of survival—both ecological and political. The application of that knowledge to the continuing process of agroforestry innovation in Kathama illustrates the importance of both men's and women's participation, across class and other groupings, in the research and development process within fields that address rural resource management and production concerns.

The Physical Environment

The climate in Kathama is transitional from subhumid to semiarid, with a mean annual temperature of 21 degrees centigrade (range: 13– 27 degrees). Rainfall is extremely unpredictable both within years and between years; seasonal rainfall can vary between 140 and 730 millimeters.[11] Ecological conditions vary dramatically over short distances, with agricultural potential ranging from coffee growing to ranching, according to planning documents. The 6-kilometer transect from the top of Kanzalu Range, across the Athi River Valley, to the Yatta Plateau spans agroecological zones 3, 4, and 5, as classified by Jaetzold (see Map 3.2 and Figure 3.1). Slopes are gentle (5 percent) over most of the area; however, the upper slopes of the escarpment exceed 50 percent and farmers increasingly cultivate slopes in excess of 30 percent and even 40 percent (Figure 3.1). The lower slopes are densely populated and intensively cultivated relative to the rest of the area. The slopes of the Kanzalu Range and the slopes to the Athi River are valued as homesites because of proximity to permanent water sources (springs and the Athi River, respectively). The same is true for the slight depression at the foot of the Kanzalu Range, where temporary wells are made in the dry riverbeds and permanent open, shallow wells can be found on farmlands (Figure 3.1). Most of the soils are relatively infertile sandy clays, mostly eroded alfisols, and some ultisols,[12] with a strip of pellic vertisols ("Black Cotton soil") in the center of the area.[13]

The diverse landscape is home to a wide variety of plant and animal species. The natural vegetation on the site is described by Fliervoet as *Acacia-Combretum* woodland.[14] The dominant species are *Acacia tortilis, Combretum Zeyheri, Terminalia brownii,* and *Lantana camara.* Large mature trees are rare, particularly in the case of *Acacia tortilis,* which has been felled extensively for charcoal making. Wildlife includes hares, small antelope, wild pigs, baboons, squirrels, and several species of birds, as well as turtles, frogs, toads, lizards, and snakes. Termites are widespread and, along with the hare and antelope,

Map 3.2   Machakos District

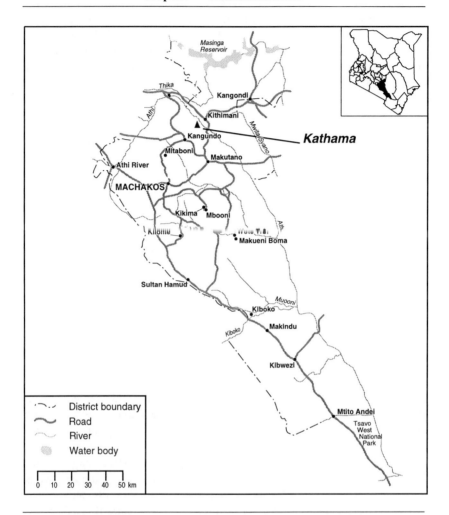

Note: This map represents the boundaries of Machakos at the time of fieldwork. The new district boundaries appear on the map of Kenya (Map 3.1).

Source: Adapted with permission from Jaetzold and Smith.

impose constraints on the species selection and/or management practices for agroforestry systems.

The People

The Akamba people have occupied this region (Machakos and Kitui Districts) for several generations, and although the oral history varies with respect to the area of origin, there is strong evidence that the Akamba migrated to this area roughly four hundred years ago from the plains just south of Mount Kilimanjaro, in Tanzania.[15] The group is in transition from pastoralism with some agriculture (agropastoralism) to permanent cultivation with some animal production (mixed farming). Kathama is on the agricultural end of this spectrum, with a mixed farming system dominated by crop rather than livestock production.

Figure 3.1   Topographic Profile with Agroecological Zones

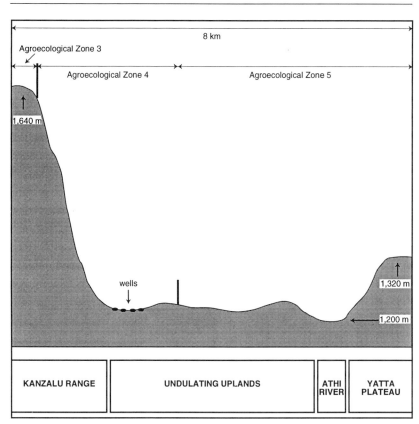

Table 3.1   Population and Land Use Distribution for Machakos District, Mbiuni Location, and Research Area

		District	Agro-ecological Zone 5, Machakos[a]	Agro-ecological Zone 4, Machakos[a]	Zones 4–5, Mbiuni Location	Zones 4–5, Kathama Research Area
Total Area	(km)	14,245	998,000	156,000	144	14
Population		1,109,200	456,000	376,000	19,900	2,415
Population Density	(persons/ km²)	72	47	147	69	172
Cropland	(%)	6	14	19	14	27
Cropland/ Household[b]	(ha)	1.3	1.9	0.4	1.1	1.1
Grazing Land	(%)	80	71	59	72	52
Grazing Land/ Household	(ha)	6.7	9.1	2.4	3.1	2.1
Animal Units[c]/ha Grazing Land		—	—	—	—	3.3
Animal Units/ Household		—	—	—	—	6.9

Sources: Vonk, 1983a; data on Machakos District ecological zones 4 and 5 and Mbiuni from Ecosystems Ltd, *Machakos District—Report for M.I.P.D.;* data on Kathama research area from Gielen, "Report on Agroforestry Survey."

Notes: a. An agroclimatological zone defined by the rainfall potential evapotranspiration ratio; PP:PE zone 2: 66%; zone 3: 52%–67%; zone 4: 37%–52%; zone 5: 22%–37% (Braun, Jaetzold, and Schmidt). b. A household is assumed to comprise an average of six members (Hoekstra, 1984), except for the Kathama area, where households comprise about seven members (Gielen, "Report on Agroforestry Survey"). c. Most households have 10 goats and up to 7 cattle: 1 animal unit = 5 goats, 1 adult cattle, 2 cattle < 1 year, 1.3 cattle 1–3 years (Rukandema et al.).

Within the region occupied by the Akamba, Kathama presents a relatively densely populated site, with 172 persons per square kilometer (see Table 3.1). Access to water along the Kanzalu Range and the Athi River probably accounts for the relatively high concentration of people. Population pressure has already caused some families to leave the area for the more sparsely populated Yatta Plateau and the dry woodlands of Kitui District. Others have moved into more marginal areas within the study site: upslope on the range or out onto the valley and away from the water sources.[16]

The five thousand people who reside continuously in this area are almost all farmers (participating members of farm households), with relatively few people (a mere fifty) engaged in trades or small businesses as their main occupation. Both men and women engage in cultivation, with women responsible for most tasks other than plowing. Most women make sisal baskets and rope for cash income, and many men burn bricks or charcoal for home use and sale.[17] For most households the main source of income other than farming is remittance income from people employed off-farm, usually men residing in cities. Nearly half of the households in Mbiuni Location earn incomes below the national poverty level.[18] The natural rate of increase in Kathama is 4 percent,[19] yet the population growth rate is only 3 percent because of the high rate of emigration. Those who leave are mostly men from twenty to fifty years of age seeking employment in Nairobi or large towns. Increasingly, young families are emigrating to drier zones in search of cheap land, in hopes of maintaining or increasing livestock herds on larger parcels of land. Many men left during drought years.[20] Crop failure due to drought is common (it occurs during at least one season in five), and periodic famines are offset by food relief.

The high rate of natural population increase and the emigration of young men has resulted in a high proportion of women-headed and women-managed households with a very high ratio of dependents to "producers" (children to adults).[21] This subjects the women of the area to double, and often conflicting, pressures to produce more crops than before with less adult labor than was previously available. The average household size is seven persons, with a wide variation in available labor force depending on family composition.

Land Use

The Akamba people who settled Kathama in 1911 were agropastoralists, and each extended family household had 100–200 head of cattle. Most residents now practice permanent cultivation of food crops and have some livestock. Most farmers raise two crops per year for both subsistence and sale of intercropped maize, beans, cowpeas, and pigeon peas. Some fruit crops—such as citrus, mango, banana, papaya, and guava—are grown around the home compound or interspersed with annuals on the cropland. Small quantities of fruit, as well as sunflower seeds and cotton, are sold as cash crops; mango and papaya are the most widespread as small-scale cash crops.[22]

Over 25 percent of the area is in cropland, and more than 50 percent is devoted to grazing. Of the remainder, most is bush regrowth or woodland (including gully and ravine vegetation), which is at least occasionally subjected to grazing and browsing. The woodland serves as a source of fuelwood (usually in the form of cuttings, but sometimes whole trees are used), as well as wood for charcoal and brick burning, which requires whole trees (usually larger hardwoods). The denser woodlands are concentrated in inaccessible areas or on sites extremely unsuitable for cropping or grazing. These sites serve a number of households as sources of stickwood, although most of the land is privately owned. The same is true to a lesser extent of the more open grazed woodlands in the valley.

Figure 3.2   Cropping Calendar

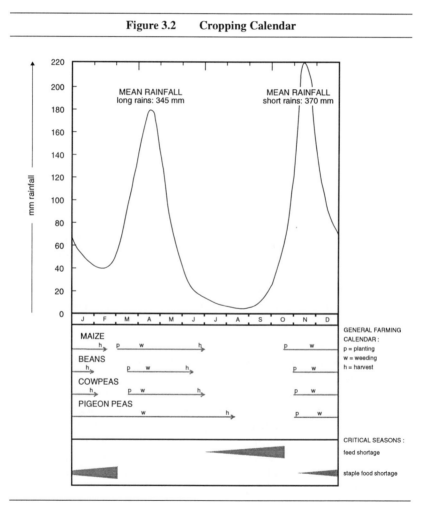

Labor, manure, and seed are the major inputs to cropland; the cost of chemical fertilizer or other agrochemicals limits their use. Almost all the cropland is terraced, even in slightly undulating topography. Most farmers use draft animals for plowing, usually just after the onset of the rains. The cropping calendar shows peak labor demands at planting and weeding times (April/May; October/November) and at harvests (December/January; June/July) (see Figure 3.2). Each household plows and plants concurrently on their respective plots, but self-help groups (rotating labor exchange) often help with weeding, terrace construction and repair, tree crop planting, and fencing on farms of group members. Although groups have changed substantially in response to shifting political conditions, the overall ethic and the practice of self-help work parties continue to operate on the croplands of members.

Cattle and goats are the most important domestic animals in this system (See Table 3.1). Oxen serve as draft animals and as an investment. Some families keep one or two cows for milk. Goats represent smaller, more flexible investments than do cattle, and they provide a periodic source of ready cash, as well as milk and occasional meat for the farm household. Both cattle and goats are confined in corrals at night; farmers collect the manure and apply it to one bench terrace per season, in rotation.[23] Management of grazing and browsing varies from tethering to careful herding to almost free range, depending on landholding. Social pressure to control grazing is strongest when grain crops are vulnerable to attack, but these "social fences" fade during the dry season, when animals are driven long distances to water holes or to the Athi River. Off-farm fodder sources play an important role during this period. Roadside and gully sites provide grass, shrubs, and high-protein acacia tree pods to supplement on-farm fodder. Many larger landholders also grant grazing and browsing rights on private woodlands to several other households, based on kinship or other social ties or in exchange for cash or services.

Land Tenure, Use Rights, and Water Rights

Most of the land in the study site was adjudicated in 1972, with the exception of the woodlands just across the Athi River on the Yatta Plateau and a very limited area of government land on the Kanzalu Range. However, exclusive use by one household is applied only to permanent, terraced cropland, home compounds, and small grazing plots. Woodland and large holdings of wooded grazing land are controlled by single households but are perceived as conditionally available to the larger community or to subgroups thereof. The same plots, now available for restricted common use, are the main source of land for future conversion to cropland, subject to exclusive use by the owners. Since the demand for food is less elastic than the demand for grazing, cropland parcels have tended to remain the same size from one generation to the next, whereas the total grazing and woodland areas have dwindled.

Water rights in the area range from private ownership and exclusive use of open shallow wells on-farm to free public access to hillside springs and flowing rivers. Small ad hoc groups also dig and fence temporary shallow wells in dry riverbeds and may also share water collection and stock watering trips. Access to water is a major determinant of location preference and is reflected in the location of the largest and/or most prosperous landholders (Figure 3.1).

Government Services and Organization

The chief of Mbiuni Location represents the government in the area. He exercises his authority in Kathama through direct decisionmaking and delegation of authority to the subchiefs of sublocations and to village elders with ties to local government. The self-help (*mwethya*) groups at the study site are legally registered NGOs answerable to local authorities. In Kathama, most of the group members are women (80–100 percent), and the organizations are based on traditional labor exchange groups. Leaders may be men or women and span a broad range of income or status. Speaking ability, integrity, and natural leadership qualities are major criteria, and often one or two leaders will also be large landholders. These mutual aid societies have been actively encouraged and registered (i.e., formalized) throughout Kenya since 1981.

The groups in Kathama range from traditional older women's agricultural groups, to mixed men's and women's public works groups, to women's craft and marketing associations. All these are designated as self-help groups and, in Kathama, most engage in public works, such as road and gully repair, one morning per week during the dry season. In 1984 some groups met to work as often as three days per week. A few groups are limited almost exclusively to sisal rope production and sales and to farm-level work.

Churches also provide a strong focus of community organization and service. However, the influence of the churches is often mediated through the self-help groups rather than separate direct-action projects. The churches sometimes channel food aid and construction materials for self-help projects, and the self-help groups often have some religious affiliation in common among members.

The University of Nairobi operates a weekly medical clinic for mothers and young children, which provides infant and maternal health care and family planning. Most residents travel the 10 kilometers to Kabaa or, even farther, to Kangundo for both routine and emergency health care. The clinic at Kathama marketplace has become the focus of a community-based health care and family planning team that constitutes a major influence on daily life in Kathama.[24]

Although Kathama is included in government extension services, the difficulty of transportation to and within the location makes it a low-priority site for overworked extension agents headquartered 7 kilometers away in Mbiuni. Consequently, access to new technologies and social services is rather limited in Kathama.

Marketplace facilities are limited to collection points for charcoal; a small area for vegetable, fruit, and grain sales; a maize mill and storage building; a hide tannery; a tailor's shop; a furniture shop, a few small tea shops; and two shops with a limited selection of household goods. The district-level grain storage and agricultural supply centers are not widely used by Kathama residents. Marketing depends heavily on individual connections with middlemen and haulers and on informal networks among producers within Kathama Sublocation.

Farming System Problems and Potentials

During the course of a rapid appraisal conducted in 1981 to diagnose farming system problems and potentials, residents identified two key points limiting cash income and food production. The dry season fodder gap limited animal production, which was a major source of ready cash (especially when food stores were depleted) and functioned as a bank for savings/investment (see Figure 3.3). Soil fertility, soil moisture, and soil erosion problems limited production on cropland, causing both food and cash shortages (see Figure 3.4).[25]

Several technologies (agroforestry and nonagroforestry) were evaluated for overall feasibility and problem-solving potential. The subsequent farm trials included (1) alley cropping (hedgerow intercropping) with woody perennials in food crop plots and (2) enrichment planting and treatment of existing vegetation in small plots of degraded grazing land.

By late 1983, preliminary results from the grazing land trials indicated a need for improved methods of direct seeding and other low-input methods of plant propagation and establishment.[26] Where nursery seedlings were successfully established, there was a need for low-input pest control technologies and/or more rigorous selection of pest-resistant species. Termites were a major problem at these sites. Better protection and/or preventive design against browsing were also necessary, given the damage sustained in several plots.[27]

The alley cropping trials in croplands had also been established with seedlings after direct seeding failures. In 1982, researchers and farmers planted closely spaced hedgerows of *Leucaena leucocephala* (var. Peru) and *Cassia siamea* trees at 2-meter intervals in plots of intercropped maize (*Zea mays*), pigeon peas (*Cajanas cajan*), cowpeas (*Vigna sinensis*), and red beans (*Phaseolus vulgaris*).[28] The hedgerows were coppiced once each season at 30- and 60-centimeter heights, starting in 1983. The mulch had not shown any discernible effect, but both stickwood and mulch had been harvested and the hedgerows exhibited vigorous growth, considering the dry environment. The growth and vigor of these plants was, however, substantially less than in well-known experimental trials on more favorable sites.[29]

By mid-1983 a team of social and ecological scientists sought to broaden the scope of the research design from agroforestry technology trials on ten farms to include the larger landscape and the community at large. They began by monitoring the original trials of alley cropping, which were intended to produce mulch, nitrogen, and fuelwood in croplands. They soon confronted problems rooted in the gender division of rights, responsibilities, and knowledge at the household and community levels.

Figure 3.3   Causal Diagram of Animal Production Problems

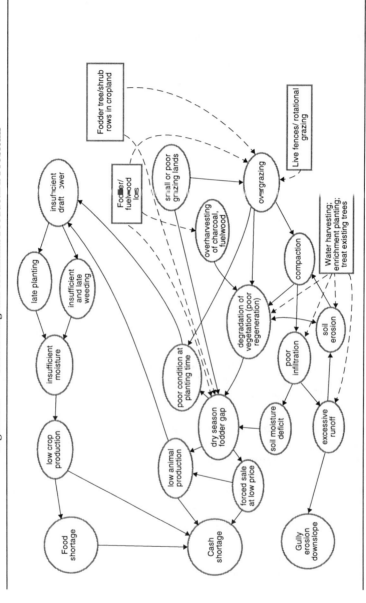

Sources: Adapted/updated from Vonk, *Report on a Methodology and Technology Generating Exercise;* and Raintree, "A Diagnostic Approach."

THE KATHAMA PROJECT: GENDER DIVISION
OF LABOR AND INTERESTS IN AGROFORESTRY

In the ten on-farm trials, nine with male heads of household and one whose household was run by a couple, the project team encountered two key problems that derived from the absence of women in design and management of new technologies. First, some men who wished to expand their alley cropping trials failed in their efforts to grow their own seedlings in home nurseries because of a lack of sufficient water. Although women were responsible for providing water, they had not been consulted about the decision to grow seedlings at the house-

Figure 3.4   Causal Diagram of Food Production Problems

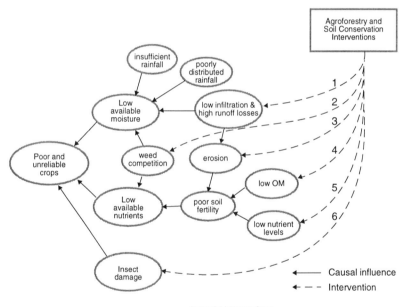

Potential Interventions

1. Improved infiltration, reduced runoff
2. Weed control with reduced labor
3. Reduced splash and runoff erosion
4. Increased organic matter
5. N-fixation and nutrient pump action of deep penetrating roots
6. Use of insect-repellent mulch species

Source: Reprinted with permission from Vonk, *Report on a Methodology and Technology Generating Excercise.*

Note: OM = organic matter.

hold level. As it turned out, they were unwilling to carry extra water on their backs from distant sources over a period of four months.

Second, the proposed agroforestry practice (alley cropping) being tested by men on-farm addressed primarily women's problems with fuelwood supply and soil fertility for staple food production. The women, who had not been directly involved in planning on most of the trials, were unimpressed with the amount and quality of firewood produced by the seasonal pruning of the young tree rows of *L. leucocephala* and *C. siamea*. These compared poorly with *C. cajan,* a woody perennial that produced food and fodder as well as fuelwood and was already well incorporated into the existing system. Men's interests in timber and poles for construction or sale were not addressed at all. This led men to trim the intended "green mulch" and fuelwood trees to produce poles or to allow their goats to browse the trees, both at the expense of the researchers' intended products.

Thus, neither men nor women obtained what they could have from a research design involving both genders as full participants. This experience illustrated that men's and women's labor and interests matter for technology design and testing and that men's and women's domains are distinct at the household level.[30]

"Public Works" and the Proper Work of Women's Groups

Researchers saw the importance of women's self-help groups and their role in community-level soil and water management work. In response to the limitations of the previous farm trials and the presence of the women's groups, they initiated a small participant observation project to introduce agroforestry skills, species, and planting arrangements into the community-based soil conservation work of the women's groups. Researchers and trainees joined the groups in their weekly soil conservation work sessions, devoted mostly to plugging active gullies, and began to raise the possibility of using trees and grasses to stabilize the sites and to provide fuelwood and fodder cuttings.[31]

The groups agreed in principle but seemed uninterested. Researchers tried on numerous occasions to elicit women's groups' preferences for particular species or for particular tree products and services, without suggesting specific options, but met with no success. As foresters had warned, people seemed to have little interest in trees and no strong preference for particular species or tree products.

Finally, as the field team repeated the question for the fourth time in four weeks, some group members asked the team to list exactly what it *could* offer. Once they heard that the range of options included fruit and fodder trees, the participants realized that their choices were not limited to men's timber trees or foreign foresters' woodfuel trees. They asked why anyone would want to waste good trees on such an obviously degraded site as the gully at which they were working. The participants in the soil conservation work requested trees to plant at home and considered themselves to be earning the trees through the group work.[32]

Moreover, the groups gradually revealed themselves as associations of individuals and households, formed as reciprocal work groups and mutual aid networks rather than public works organizations. Although five groups were at one point "mobilized" by local officials to work together at a site chosen by the project, the participating groups prevailed upon the field team to work with them separately in the next season's activities. Based on prior experience, the women noted that the multigroup situations stretched social networks too thin and over too large an area. The individual groups had developed their own means of mutual accommodation and accountability among members and shared an interest in the same geographic space.

Through a series of subsequent discussions, participants explained that their groups each counted from fifty to one hundred official members and usually drew a work force of twenty to thirty women, and sometimes a few men, for any given task. Their "real" work was reciprocal weeding and terrace repair labor on each other's cropland, which was then limited to one day per week, with two days devoted to road and gully repair. They pointed out that in most cases the road and gully work was an onerous duty performed to comply with public service demands from public officials.

Finally, the project's entry into this work coincided with the onset of the drought and subsequent famine of 1984, which began early in the drier parts of Machakos. The self-help groups had acquired greater importance because of the drought, as access to public relief food and/or "food for work" projects was expected to depend on individual wealth and influence or on group membership and participation. The flurry of group soil conservation work at sites chosen by local officials had more to do with drought and famine "insurance" than with specific community priorities for soil and water conservation. Most participants were concerned about soil erosion, damaged roads, and degraded stream channels, but their public work sites and the time, place, and public image of group work did not reflect the group's larger purpose and women's interests.

Changes in Gendered Knowledge and Practice

As the drought set in, the project distributed the first set of fifteen "sample" trees to members from five groups, who subsequently planted the seedlings at their respective homes. For most women, this was a first. Although a few influential men had planted numerous citrus and timber trees in the past and many men had purchased or collected an occasional tree for plot boundaries or home compounds, this was a new activity for women. The project team monitored the placement and performance of the trees and found the women to be undaunted by the poor performance of the mostly exotic trees in the face of drought, hungry cattle, and termites.

When they met to plan the next season's work, the five participating groups requested that researchers abandon the soil conservation sites to devote their efforts to group tree nurseries, with provision of additional seedlings from outside to supplement the groups' first efforts. In effect, the women's primary concern was to get the process of tree domestication into their own hands and their own heads within the context of self-help groups. The project team monitored people's choice of species, their choice of nursery sites, their subsequent construction and management of the nurseries, and group members' planting and management of trees. Through their participation, people taught the research team much about their ability and motivation not only to adopt innovations but to innovate independently and in groups. The participants developed alternatives both to their existing systems and to prepackaged "scientific" agroforestry technologies.

The same process of group tree propagation and individual tree planting also demonstrated the clear gender division of control over land and water, as well as the women's substantial skill in negotiating with men for rights of access and use. Each women's group had to prevail upon a wealthy head of household, usually a group leader's husband or relative and in one case the group leader herself, for secure, long-term access to a site with a reliable water source. All but one of the five groups succeeded in securing a suitable tree nursery site. Likewise, individual women negotiated time and space at the household level for the planting of their own tree seedlings.[33]

After two full seasons of planting trees, some group leaders raised questions about the newly introduced exotic species, especially their performance and management over time and in larger-scale plantings. In spite of misgivings about the advisability of alley cropping, the researchers arranged a visit by group leaders and interested men and women to the most successful of the original ten farm trials, to serve as a focus of discussion. Not only did the group members critique the technology as a package, they also chose specific elements—species, planting arrangement, tree management—that appealed to them. Men and women had somewhat different priorities: timber for men and soil fertility and crop production for women. However, elder women heads of household shared the men's interest in timber for home use and for sale, since they needed cash and building material for their households and would have control over both. Women with nonresident (migrant) husbands also expressed strong interest in fodder trees, since they managed livestock.

Participating group members questioned the field team at length about the rationale and principles of the alley cropping design. Later, some women returned to the project extensionist with examples of local practice and individual innovations that constituted more appropriate application of the same principles to serve the purpose of soil fertility improvement with plant biomass. They reported adding leaves and twigs to cattle pens to "bulk up" the manure supply to fertilize cropland. They collected most of the biomass from fencerow trees (including *Euphorbia terucalli*) and dispersed trees in grazing land (*Combretum* and *Terminalia* species). Subsequent discussions with groups revealed widespread experimentation and experience with these recently developed cattle-pen-composting techniques. Many women used leaves of both exotic and indigenous trees common in the area, all of which were resistant to termites and drought.

Through the farm visits and group discussions, researchers learned that women and men in this farm community have ongoing experiments of their own, including women's exploration of formerly male domains of management. They both have much to gain as well as to contribute by participating in formal research with outsiders. Given the experience of group work in private sites, men and women are most likely to contribute effectively to research activities on individual farms, with group participation.

Farming and Land Use as If Famine Mattered

As the drought wore on, the project team expected a decreasing interest in trees. Many women faced the overwhelming reality of hunger and water and fodder shortages, which threatened the well-being of their families and the survival of their draft animals and small stock. However, the famine and fodder shortage spurred a resurgence of interest in a wide variety of indigenous trees as reserve fodder sources, in tree crops rather than livestock as assets, and in a diversity of wild fruits and vegetables. Wild foods were said to provide nutritious snacks, to combat the effects of malnutrition, and to serve as substitutes for other foods.[34]

Whole extended families took to the woodlands, bushlands, and "in-between" places (fencerows, roadsides, and stream banks) in search of possible fodder sources. Some people tested leaf samples of several tree species on their cattle. The elders in the community made a concerted effort to recall which tree leaves had served in the past as drought reserve fodder. However, unlike the last drought and fodder shortage of similar magnitude, in 1946, there was less grazing land, less flexibility of livestock movement within the region, and in over 60 percent of the households women were responsible for livestock management as supervisors or directly as herders. Women relied heavily on their prior knowledge of wild foods and acquired new knowledge about fodder plants through hearsay and widespread experimentation with trees and shrubs in range and woodlands.

Given the role of wild foods and indigenous plants in general as poor people's drought and famine reserves, researchers approached women's groups with the possibility of protecting and managing some of these plants in situ or domesticating them on-farm within agroforestry systems. Though group members were at first incredulous of outsiders' interest in "primitive practices" and "poor people's food," they gradually rallied around the idea. Moreover, they insisted on including medicinal plants, an unexpected turn for two reasons. Although the project team had associated traditional medical practice with men, there was a well-developed practice by specialized women herbalists, who were midwives and general practitioners; there also was widespread knowledge and practice of basic herbal medicine among women over thirty years of age, "unschooled" and taught by mothers and elder women. In addition, the researchers encountered a widely shared concern about the local disappearance or scarcity of particular medicinal herbs and specific indigenous fruits and vegetables.

The subsequent ethnobotanical survey of men and women in the five villages started with the general public, proceeded to the specialists, and went back again to the women's groups and their children.[35] Together they identified 118 indigenous or naturalized wild plant species used for medicine and 45 used for food. Of these, participants selected five fruit trees, three vegetables, and three medicinal plants for potential domestication in agroforestry systems or small gardens. They also named several fruits, vegetables, and medicinal plants as candidates for special protection in place, although women were quite cynical about their ability to enforce management rules in public and shared lands.

While men's and women's priorities varied, they knew many of the same places, classes of ecosystems, and plant associations. They tended to know and use different species and different products from the same species. Whereas men's widely shared traditional knowledge of indigenous plants had been developed in rangeland food and fodder, their out-migration, sedentarization, and formal schooling had militated against the transmission of this gendered science and practice to the young. Some men knew a great deal about specific classes of wild plants for specialized purposes—such as a charcoal, brick-making fuel; for carving; and as local timber, bee fodder, and medicine—but the knowledge was unevenly dispersed and decreased markedly among the younger men in the community. Among older women there was a widely shared, high level of general knowledge about wild food, crafts, and medicinal plants, but there was an overall reduction in scope and depth of proficiency among younger women. However, the knowledge gap between generations of women was not nearly as pronounced as that for men.

Some members of the community attributed the persistent decline in indigenous knowledge to formal schooling and rejection of "primitive" tradition by the young. Moreover, men's out-migration had removed adult men as tutors and created a labor shortage and double work load for women, leaving little time for traditional education in multigenerational groups of either sex. Women had different rights and responsibilities than in the past and had to acquire and maintain an ever broader range of new knowledge and skills.

The differential erosion of local ecological science among men and women may also reflect their respective rights, responsibilities, and opportunities in farm versus wage labor sectors. Although women maintain livelihoods and retain their rights of access to land through residence and agricultural production, young men can aspire to leave home and to succeed as wage laborers in nearby cities and towns, without fear of sacrificing their long-term access to land. The feminization of famine and drought response and the requisite science of survival reflects the new spatial division of labor between men and women into rural and urban domains. This experience also demonstrates that the boundaries of gendered knowledge are neither fixed nor independent. Content and distribution of gendered knowledge influences and is influenced by the gender division of rights and responsibilities in national, regional, and local contexts.[36]

One Man's Field Becomes a Women's Group Commons

The importance of wild plants during the drought was obvious, as was the increasing responsibility of women to maintain knowledge about them for the community at large. The ethnobotany survey also confirmed that most women normally drew upon fodder, fuelwood, and sometimes wild food sources beyond the boundaries of household land, as did their children. However, those most reliant on resources outside their own land stated that their children were unlikely to enjoy the same facility of access to shared lands in the future.[37] They noted that community-level land tenure, land use, and vegetation changes proceeded on their own momentum, outside the control of individuals and small groups.

Since smallholders and legally landless women relied on the shared use of private lands to make use of wild plants, they had every reason to focus on social strategies to secure and maintain access to wild plants or on alternative ecological strategies for meeting contingencies.[38] Their future access to these resources on shared lands would depend on careful cultivation of social and political networks, as would their influence on soil, plant, and water management decisions made by largeholders and male owners of family plots. Poor women's experience during the drought exemplified the careful interweaving of social and ecological knowledge to survive in the crosscurrents of erratic environmental conditions with uncertain terms of resource use, access, and control.

As the drought persisted, people's terms of access to off-farm lands acquired increasing importance and their domains of use and access became clearer as individuals and groups relied more and more on shared resources as reserves. The map of actual land use and source areas that emerged from their activities bore little resemblance to the formal survey maps that denoted ownership, yet it was in large part circumscribed by these legal boundaries established in 1972.

The term *off-farm lands* as used here denotes any land outside the household property of the user. In Kathama, it includes roadsides (public land), stream banks and riversides (a combination of public and private property), hillslope woodlands (mostly private land), the dry forest across the river (national government land), and, most important, the grazing lands, woodlands, fencerows, and gullies of other farmers (small, medium, and large private holdings). The latter category became increasingly significant as grazing and browsing animals and individual collectors depleted the reserves in less protected areas. Moreover, the private holdings were usually much closer to the users' homes and farmlands, which reduced the long treks for both people and their livestock, when both were already weakened by hunger and malnutrition.

When drought gave way to famine, the women's groups emerged as a critical link to shared use of private lands. As the community tacitly declared a state of emergency, the groups called upon those with greater resource endowments to share an increasing proportion of their resources with others. However, this social pressure applied to the act of sharing, not to the naming of the beneficiaries; in fact, *participants* would be a more apt term because those in need were recognized by largeholders according to long-standing relationships of reciprocity, most often and most predictably in the context of kinship or women's self-help groups.[39]

In effect, the community peeled back the survey map to reveal another map of potential use and users, derived from traditional rules of reciprocity and mutual aid. Yet the power to determine exactly who could use exactly which resources, and where, had shifted from the community and large kin groups to the individuals who controlled the legal boundaries. Thus a third map emerged, which combined traditional norms with new loci of power, at both the community and household levels. The fact that men actually owned most of the private plots and formally controlled the public lands, set the stage for a gendered struggle for access to resources no less serious for its finesse and skillful manipulation by individual women and self-help groups.

Poor women's new and traditional knowledge of ethnobotany was necessary but not sufficient for coping with drought and famine. Poor women also required access to resources controlled by men at the household and community levels. Women's groups and individuals mobilized substantial political skill to legitimize and tap their "social credit" at the household, group, and community levels. The social skills and ethics mobilized to cope with the drought demonstrate the strength and persistence of the moral economy of the community,[40] as cooperation rather than competition intensified during the course of the famine. Expressions of resistance[41] were less apparent during this period, although some groups later used "weapons of the weak" (noncooperation) and directly tabled their grievances with local officials.

The Name of the Famine

All subsequent discussions of species preference, tree management, and land use for the next two years were influenced by the experience of the drought. Not only had people rediscovered trees and wild plants as sources of food, fodder, and medicine, they had observed the diminished but still substantial yield and the survival of one man's citrus orchard in comparison with the death or distress sale of their livestock. Moreover, there was widely shared interest in planting fodder trees and in the introduction of fruit trees for both home use and sale (see Figure 3.5). Many people had acquired a healthy skepticism about overreliance on cash income to offset the effects of famine.

In fact, this last point illustrates an often neglected dimension of indigenous knowledge: the learning, storage, and transmission of knowledge about social, political, economic, and environmental change in the form of oral history, particularly in the naming of events. In the case of Kathama, most men now relate historical events to years (by number) or to the major wars of the twentieth century (World Wars I and II and Kenya's own independence struggle). Women, by contrast, "reckon time in famines, and remember them by name."[42]

Figure 3.5   Women's Terraced Croplands with Fruit and Fodder Trees

---

Source: Reprinted with permission of ICRAF from Rocheleau et al., *Agroforestry in Dryland Africa.*

Although all people in the area formerly used famines and similar events to mark historical periods, the men have increasingly adopted the numbers and categories of outsiders while women retain the more traditional, local categories for recounting the past. The name of the last famine, as reported by an elder women's group leader, captures the painful irony of the changing times: "I shall die with the money in my hand."[43]

Distress sales of major assets—such as teams of oxen, cattle, and small livestock—provided small amounts of cash, which were grossly inadequate in the face of a national-scale food shortage. Poor rural people learned that the terms of the exchange with the national market could fluctuate markedly and unpredictably. The famine name suggests that the people of Machakos District reconsidered the terms of their integration into national markets and came away with renewed resolve to maintain a greater degree of food self-sufficiency.

The codification of knowledge in the form of famine names records the central surprise of the last famine, makes sense of the experience, preempts the surprise of similar incidents in subsequent years, and informs practical, popular planning measures to prevent future famines altogether. As exemplified by the name of the last famine, rural women's indigenous knowledge extends well beyond the confines of botany and agriculture and into the domains of environmental history and practical political economy. Moreover, the knowledge is not guarded exclusively by women but rather is increasingly carried and nurtured by them on behalf of the community at large.

GENDERED KNOWLEDGE AND PRACTICE

Perhaps the most salient feature of ethnoscience research with rural women and men is that it can buy time and create space for each to take stock of the larger-scale processes working against ecological, economic, and cultural diversity in their rural landscapes. If research results in documentation and discussion of gendered ethnoscience at the community level, then rural women and men may make more informed choices about which species, skills, and visions of nature and society to use for shaping their emerging ecological and economic futures. One clear implication for policymakers is the need to recognize and document gendered local science and practice within existing research and development programme as well as in special efforts focused on indigenous knowledge.

The international scientific and development communities have tended to ignore rural people's science or have separated it from the larger context of daily life, labor, and livelihoods. Social scientists and ecologists alike often recast indigenous knowledge as an ethnographic artifact, "unconscious ecological wisdom," or as part of the "environment" for the generation and introduction of new technology. Even these very partial and objectified views of rural people's science often have not been studied and understood as gendered knowledge and practice. We face the double task of reshaping the terms of discourse about popular, local ecological science and introducing women's science and interests into the larger domain.[44]

There is little doubt as to the utility of cataloging some discrete bits of rural women's ecological knowledge. Use of an encyclopedic compendium of wild and cultivated plants can improve the collective ability to survive and flourish in Kathama and our contributions to "sustainable" and equitable development elsewhere. Even extractive documentation and conservation of such knowledge is preferable to complete loss of the information. However, there is even more to be gained by an ethnoscience research approach based on empowerment of rural people rather than simple extraction of their knowledge.

For example, an action research program might facilitate the discussion and transfer of knowledge among men, women, and children as their roles, responsibilities, and interests change.[45] This process could result in renegotiation of the division of rights and responsibilities as well as domains of knowledge and skill, though not without substantial struggle over conflicting interests at the household, community, and larger levels of organization. The mere recognition and documentation of survival as a gendered science in harsh and unpredictable environments—political, economic, and ecological—could also effect change at the local and national levels. Such a process could serve to legitimize and strengthen rural women's and men's separate, shared, and interlocking knowledge as tools to shape their own futures.

In summary, the interests of both women and men in sustainable land use practices can best be served by the adoption of a user-focused approach to technology design and land use planning, with special attention to the gender division of resources, knowledge, work, and benefits. Once the existing gender division of land use and interests is understood, fieldworkers and policymakers alike may build upon this to reinforce complementarity, to resolve conflicts, and to restore the balance between men's and women's shared rights and responsibilities in traditional, evolving, or experimental land use systems. Such an explicit and flexible treatment of the gender division of land use could help to reconcile the objectives of environmental sustainability, social equity, and economic productivity from the individual to the national level.

NOTES

Parts of this chapter have been reprinted with permission from *Agriculture and Human Values*. See Rocheleau, "Gender, Ecology, and the Science of Survival."

1. Dankelman and Davidson, *Women and Environment in the Third World.*
2. Chavangi, "Cultural Aspects of Fuelwood Procurement in Kakamega District"; Hoskins, *Rural Women, Forest Outputs and Forestry Products*; Moore and Vaughan, "Cutting Down Trees"; Meyerhoff, "The Socio-economic and Ritual Roles of Pokot Women"; Rocheleau, "Criteria for Re-appraisal and Re-design," "A Land User Perspective," "Women, Trees and Tenure," and "The Gender Division of Work, Resources and Rewards"; Merchant, *The Death of Nature* and *Ecological Revolutions*; Fleuret, "Methods for Evaluation of the Role of Fruits and Wild Greens in Shambaa Diet"; Murphy and Murphy, *Women of the Forest*; Fernandez, "Technological Domains of Women in Mixed Farming Systems"; King, "The Ecology of Feminism"; Shiva, *Staying Alive.*
3. Agarwal, "Engendering the Environment Debate."
4. Redclift, *Sustainable Development.*
5. Rocheleau et al., "A Hundred Years of Crisis?"; Tiffin, "Productivity and Environmental Conservation."
6. Krapf, *Travels, Researches, and Missionary Labors.*
7. Hardinge, "Report on the British East Africa Protectorate for the Year 1897–1898."
8. Bernard and Thom, "Population Pressure and Human Carrying Capacity"; Bernard et al., "Carrying Capacity of the Eastern Ecological Gradient."
9. Tiffen, "Productivity and Environmental Conservation."
10. Downing et al. (eds.), *Coping with Drought in Kenya.*
11. Vonk, *Report on a Methodology and Technology Generating Exercise.*
12. Collinson, "Research Planning Study."
13. Vonk, *Report on a Methodology and Technology Generating Exercise.*
14. Fliervoet, "An Inventory of Trees and Shrubs in the Northern Division of Machakos District, Kenya."
15. Although academics most often use the name Kamba, the people of the region prefer the name Akamba to identify their ethnic group; see Muthiani, *Akamba from Within.*
16. Rocheleau et al., "Environment, Development, Crisis and Crusade: Ukambani, Kenya 1890–1990," *World Development.* Forthcoming.

17. Wijngaarden, "Patterns of Fuel Gathering and Use"; Jill Cantor, personal communication.

18. Vonk, *Report on a Methodology and Technology Generating Exercise.*

19. Ginneken, "Second Progress Report."

20. Ginneken and Muller, *Maternal and Child Health in Rural Kenya*; Gielen, "Report on an Agroforestry Survey"; Vonk, *Report on a Methodology and Technology Generating Exercise.*

21. Though children do participate in herding, gathering, and other tasks, the small children have limited capabilities and the older ones are in school.

22. Charcoal is widely used during the rainy season and is a minor but strategically timed source of cash at the end of the dry season; it also assumes more importance as a cash crop when crops fail. Vonk, *Report on a Methodology and Technology Generating Exercise*; Rocheleau and Hoek, "The Application of Ecosystems and Landscape Analysis"; Jama and Malaret, "Farmer/Researcher Collaborative Approach to Rural Development."

23. Nijssen, "Nutrient Cycle Study of the Cultivated Area"; Vonk, *Report on a Methodology and Technology Generating Exercise.*

24. Ginneken and Muller, *Maternal and Child Health in Rural Kenya.*

25. Raintree, "A Diagnostic Approach to Agroforestry Design."

26. Vonk, *Report on a Methodology and Technology Generating Exercise.*

27. Ibid.

28. Vonk, "A Study of Possible Agroforestry Tree Species"; Raintree, "A Diagnostic Approach to Agroforestry Design."

29. Kang and Wilson, "The Development of Alley Cropping."

30. Rocheleau, "Gender, Ecology, and the Science of Survival," "Participatory Research in Agroforestry," and "Criteria for Re-appraisal and Re-design."

31. Rocheleau and Hoek, "The Application of Ecosystems and Landscape Analysis."

32. Rocheleau, "Criteria for Re-appraisal and Re-design."

33. Rocheleau, "Gender, Ecology, and the Science of Survival" and "Participatory Research in Agroforestry."

34. Rocheleau et al., "Women's Use of Off-Farm Lands"; Wachira, "Women's Use of Off-Farm and Boundary Lands."

35. Rocheleau et al., "Criteria for Re-appraisal and Re-design" and "The Gender Division of Work, Resources and Rewards"; Wanjohi, "Women's Groups' Gathered Plants and Their Potentials"; Munyao, "The Importance of Gathered Food and Medicinal Plant Species"; Wachira, "Women's Use of Off-Farm and Boundary Lands."

36. Rocheleau, "Participatory Research in Agroforestry" and "Gender, Conflict and Complementarity."

37. The term *shared lands* is used as an alternative to *common land* because the formal definition of the latter (see Bromley, "The Common Property Challenge") excludes the complex pattern of use, access, and control described here.

38. Rocheleau, "The Gender Division of Work, Resources and Rewards"; Rocheleau and Fortmann, "Women's Spaces and Women's Places."

39. Rocheleau, "Participatory Research in Agroforestry" and "Gender, Conflict and Complementarity."

40. Scott, *The Moral Economy of the Peasant.*

41. Scott, *Weapons of the Weak: Everyday Forms of Peasant Resistance.*

42. Alice Mwau, personal communication, 1989.

43. Alice Mwau, personal communication, 1989; Rocheleau and Jama, "Annual Report of Farming Systems and Ethnoecology Research Project."

44. Thrupp, "Legitimizing Local Knowledge"; Bebbington, "Farmer Knowledge, Institutional Resources and Sustainable Agricultural Strategies."

45. For a separate discussion of the methods used in the fieldwork and those appropriate for further action research, see Chambers et al., *Farmer First*; Institute for Low External Input Agriculture, "Participative Technology Development"; Jiggins, "Problems of Understanding and Communication"; Rocheleau and Fortmann, "Women's Spaces and Women's Places."

4

Adapting to Resource Constraints in Gikarangu: New Livelihood Strategies for Women and Men

Leah Wanjama, Barbara Thomas-Slayter, Njoki Mbuthi

In recent years, major economic problems have adversely affected many communities throughout Kenya. Structural adjustment policies, adverse conditions in the international primary commodity markets, the high inflation rate accelerated by depreciation of the Kenya shilling against major currencies, the balance-of-payments gap, and the cutback on donor aid have slowed the economy and diminished agricultural productivity. These circumstances have challenged Kenyan men and women in their struggles to secure their livelihoods.

The results of these conditions are particularly evident in Gikarangu Sublocation, the site of this study, located in Murang'a District, Central Province, and inhabited primarily by the Kikuyu people. Gikarangu, like most sublocations in the district, is linked to urban centers through a colonial past, which transformed its farmers into producers of export commodities for nearby cities and international markets. This colonial link is central to the economic and political issues facing Gikarangu today. A century ago, in the fertile, gently sloping hills of Central Province, European settlers began growing coffee destined for international markets. They launched a process of integrating Kenya's high-potential agricultural lands into the world economy under terms of trade based on agricultural commodities. Coffee, tea, sisal, and pyrethrum became Kenya's key agricultural exports during the colonial period.

Kenya, like many nations in Africa, has been independent for more than thirty years. Central Province remains a source of export commodities and a key to the national government's efforts to secure foreign exchange. Despite the depressed status of coffee prices throughout most of the 1980s and early 1990s, coffee, the major agricultural crop in Central Province, continues to be one of Kenya's foremost earners of foreign exchange, ranking third after tourism and tea. Murang'a is one of five districts in Central Province and is one of the leading districts in the production of coffee.

The time is apt to probe the relationships among international markets, ecological changes, household livelihood systems, gender roles, and commu-

Map 4.1   Murang'a District

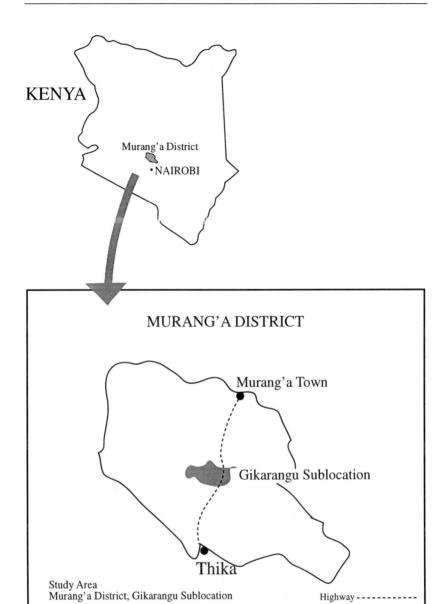

nity welfare in Central Province. The rural people of Gikarangu Sublocation have become commodity producers for the international market. This chapter considers how their changing livelihood strategies are reshaping gender roles and responsibilities. It investigates these environmental and economic challenges and the responses of rural households and communities to them, assessing the implications for both men's and women's access to and control over resources. We focus on the following ecological and economic issues:

First, livelihood options of Gikarangu residents are affected by external forces far beyond their borders. Families, therefore, struggle for livelihood security under conditions well beyond their control.

Second, Gikarangu is primarily an agricultural community functioning under patterns of land ownership and inheritance in which extreme parcelization and fragmentation have occurred. Most families can no longer sustain themselves solely on the basis of the productivity of minuscule pieces of land, particularly when coffee prices have declined dramatically throughout the last fifteen years.

Third, as a consequence of declining coffee prices, livelihood strategies have changed. Initially, these strategies involved considerable out-migration of men seeking employment while women engaged in small-scale, local trading. However, the current situation is one of increasing pressure on the land in Central Province, along with increasing unemployment throughout Kenya. In addition, Kikuyu men face marginalization within the current political context and declining employment opportunities outside Central Province. Thus, many families are increasingly dependent on the livelihood skills of the women, such as small-scale trading efforts.

Such pressures also intensify the urgency with which young Kikuyu men wish to protect the customary rights dictating that only sons inherit land from their parents. Because of changing times, some young women would like access to parental lands, yet most do not know their rights to inheritance under statutory law. In increasing numbers, young women are leaving the sublocation to seek trading or other opportunities outside their home community.

Fourth, within the household, the gender-based division of labor is becoming increasingly flexible as both men and women undertake productive and household responsibilities as need arises. Control over resources, however, is becoming less flexible. Men tend to control the resources, while women, in the case of land, work on it. As competition increases for the scarce resources of land and income-earning opportunities, the poorer women, such as the banana sellers, are most hard pressed. Moreover, some resources, traditionally belonging to women, are becoming more valuable commercially and are thus being taken over by men.

Fifth, the rural women and men of Gikarangu are adapting to these changes, transforming their environments, and modifying their lives, not without difficulty and often with extraordinary energy and determination. They continue to rely on informal social networks as safety nets of support while strengthening the capacity of community institutions to address the problems confronting them.

Gikarangu presents an opportunity to examine socioeconomic and ecological transformations in a rural area within the economic, physical, and political orbit of a major urban center. Located in the central part of Murang'a District, the sublocation lies 90 kilometers north of Nairobi, adjacent to the highway linking Nairobi, Thika, and Murang'a Town. (see Map 4.1). Its residents are drawn into urban life as workers, consumers, and suppliers of agricultural products. Greatly affected by its proximity to the nation's capital, Nairobi, and its accessibility to the wider world, Gikarangu is well integrated into the cash economy not only of nearby towns and cities but also of Kenya and beyond.

Methods for investigating the patterns of change in Gikarangu included household interviews, focus group discussions, key informants, and a survey questionnaire. The questionnaire drew on a random sample of 106 Gikarangu residents and was administered in August and September 1993. Analysis blends an interpretation of the macro-level structures shaping economic and political relations taking into account the relevant social history and the agency of individuals and groups at the grassroots level.[1] Thus, this chapter permits exploration of the gender-based impacts of resource management and changing livelihood systems in a high-potential agroecological zone where both opportunities and pressures are shaped by markets and polities well beyond its borders. It considers how economic and ecological changes in a small, central highland community are affecting issues of resource tenure, use, and access for men and women at the household and community levels, and it explores how women and men are adjusting their livelihood strategies to cope with, adapt to, and transform the resource base and the options it presents.

According to the 1989 census statistics, Murang'a is one of the most densely populated districts in Kenya, with 858,063 residents at that time, a population density of 468 per square kilometer; population projections for 1993 were 991,000 people.[2] Gikarangu Sublocation lies in Muthithi Location of Kigumo Division in Murang'a District, covers 22 square kilometers, and has a population of approximately 10,285 people in 1,945 households. It comprises seventeen hamlets and is headed by an assistant chief. Governance is carried out by the local administration, including the assistant chief, representatives of some government departments, and the sublocational development committee made up largely of local notables. Most of these positions are occupied by men.

With its deep volcanic soils, relatively high rainfall, wide fertile valley bottoms, undulating landscape, and crisscrossing rivers and streams, Gikarangu Sublocation falls within a medium-high potential agroecological zone, the third best of the six land use classifications for the nation. Two perennial rivers, the Sabasaba and Kamiguta, traverse the sublocation, as do numerous small streams, which dry up seasonally. Rivers and streams in the sublocation are subject to heavy siltation during the rainy season as a result of soil erosion, which has been accelerated by the intensive farming.

The favorable ecological conditions found in Gikarangu have nurtured a lush vegetation; trees and shrubs grow in abundance. One can observe careful management and utilization of space in local farmsteads. Both women and men plant numerous indigenous and exotic trees for poles, building materials, fodder, medicinal uses, and firewood, as well as for the general aesthetic improvement of their homesteads and compounds. Many landholdings in Gikarangu contain a permanent woodlot. For the most part, people no longer allow their cattle and goats to graze freely. Instead, livestock are tethered and fodder is collected twice a day (morning and evening), which protects the land from destructive overbrowsing and overgrazing (especially from goats).

Inhabitants of Gikarangu enjoy relatively easy access to clean water, as rivers and streams provide plentiful sources and groundwater lies close to the surface. Indeed, the longest distance a person must walk for water is 1 kilometer. Several communities have sunk boreholes at the valley bottoms to supply water for local residents. Women's groups have purchased the materials and installed most of the local water tanks at members' households on a rotating basis. Through local self-help efforts, the communities have provided water tanks for the schools, for use by both the pupils and staff. Although water is not a major concern, community members expressed disappointment that the Kigumo Water Project, begun in the late 1960s and intended to supply piped water to all of Kigumo Division, lost momentum and remains incomplete.

Like most communities in Murang'a District, Gikarangu is well endowed with educational facilities, including five primary schools, one secondary school, one girls' training center, and two village polytechnics. With the early educational activities of the missionaries, the Independent Schools Movement, and the subsequent emphasis by the government of Kenya on primary education, literacy rates and overall academic achievement in Central Province, including Gikarangu, are high. According to data from the 1989 census, 80 percent of the adult population of Murang'a is literate, divided almost equally between men and women.[3]

Unlike the educational infrastructure, health facilities in Gikarangu are inadequate. Only one government health center serves the whole sublocation. The only other medical facility, a private clinic, is rarely open.

Gikarangu is well served by a good communication network and is easily accessible via the all-weather Nairobi–Thika–Murang'a highway, which passes along its southern boundary. At the junction of the Nairobi–Murang'a and Kigumo Roads is an active banana selling center, Kaharati, where women of all ages, as well as young men, spend the day selling their fruit to passers-by.

Gikarangu's proximity to Nairobi makes it possible to trace the latest fashions in Nairobi to the heart of Gikarangu. It also facilitates adoption of the technological innovations from Nairobi by Gikarangu's *jua kali*, or informal sector. On the negative side, certain behavioral patterns that are growing in Nairobi are also found in Gikarangu. For example, according to the assistant chief, drug use is spreading. In addition, more young people are dropping out of high school to take up trading, marginal livelihoods in the informal sector, and, occasionally, prostitution in the city.

THE LAND: PAST AND PRESENT
ISSUES OF ACCESS AND CONTROL

The History of Land in Murang'a

Access to land in Murang'a has a long past and remains the most critical resource issue. Okoth-Ogendo describes the land tenure system emerging in precolonial Kikuyu society as one in which there were "interlocking individual and corporate rights and interests of access and control which were mediated through the subclan. There was not outright ownership but rather a complex set of rights embedded in a particular social, political and cultural context."[4] Clan land, known as the *githaka*, was controlled by the extended family or the subclan. From *githaka*, members were entitled to access land.

Undoubtedly, the most profound and far-reaching impact of colonialism in the rural areas of Kenya was the introduction of Western forms of individual land ownership. The British colonial government proclaimed that rural Kenya's prosperity depended on sound agricultural practices, which in turn depended on individual land ownership. From the early years, the colonial government appropriated land for European settlers and various foreign-owned companies.

For the Kikuyu in Murang'a the alienation of land seriously aggravated a concern about the ratio of population to cultivable land. The late nineteenth and early twentieth centuries saw population pressures, increasing land fragmentation, and growing numbers of landless or near-landless for the Kikuyu Native Reserves. Encircled as they were by the White Highlands, which effectively cut off possibilities of finding new land or migrating, the Kikuyu experienced mounting tensions in the community.

Throughout the 1920s, landless and near-landless people became squatters, laboring for white settlers and residing on their land with limited farming and grazing rights. This process alleviated community land pressures somewhat. By 1930, there was little or no communal land in the Kikuyu areas. In addition, the depression of the 1930s brought wage cuts, unemployment, and a diminishing squatter system. Meanwhile on the crowded Kikuyu reserves, the *mbari* holdings (communal property) were being subdivided into minuscule, frequently badly eroded holdings. Between 1925 and 1940, the land shortage forced the Kikuyu to freeze clan and tribal boundaries. By the early 1950s, land tenure had become the norm, and in little over fifty years the traditional pattern of land entitlements had been destroyed. The breakdown of the indigenous system of land tenure, land degradation, the increasing number of landless, and seizure of vast tracts by colonial settlers led to the confrontation between the Kikuyu and the colonial government in the 1950s and the "Emergency" (1952–

1953), when the colonial government attempted to suppress the independence struggle.[5]

During the Emergency, the government passed a Forfeiture of Lands Act, which permitted the confiscation of land individually owned by "terrorists." Eventually, the government took the *mbari* lands of "terrorists" as well. By 1956, 868 households from Murang'a District had seen their land confiscated and set aside for public purposes such as markets and schools.[6] Forfeiture was closely followed by a "villagization" policy, which forced all members of the Kikuyu and Embu communities into fortified villages and allotted degrees of punishment or privilege depending on the amount of aid a particular group had supplied the so-called terrorists. Next followed a massive land consolidation program, which condensed fragmented holdings into single units registered under freehold title. Those with a substantial claim to *mbari* land could gain by the formalization of a freehold title, whereas those with a tenuous claim stood to lose the various informal use rights granted to all community members. In this process, women lost all their rights to land.

At independence, the new government passed the Registered Land Act, granting individual titles to land. Titles were given to the heads of households, who were all men. This was considered a prerequisite to effective land development, but it has disrupted customary laws. Land can now be acquired through individual ownership by means of inheritance or purchase; trusteeship, in which one acts as guardian of young members of the family; tenancy, involving user rights of another person's land; and communal ownership, in which two or more individuals or families jointly own the land. Ultimately, however, the state owns all land.

Women and land in Murang'a.   The introduction of freehold title resulted in increased individualized, male control over land. Patrilineal custom dictated that each male offspring had the right to inherit an equal share of land, no matter how small the parcel. With the introduction of individual titles, the clan lost its right to allocate land based on a broad set of interests. These changes have upset the traditional delineation of male/female rights, shifting the rights of access in men's favor. Today, Murang'a grapples with two land tenure systems—one of customary law and the other of statutory law. Men have tenure rights over land and seek to control the products of women's labor, specifically with respect to coffee, tea, and other cash crops.[7] As Mackenzie notes, "The struggles over land and labor illuminate the contradiction between women as producer/non-owners and men as non-producer/owners."[8]

Although the law has not denied women the right to own land, custom largely does. Women gain access to land through marriage. Title is in the name of the senior male household member, who may use the land as collateral to acquire credit. Although women routinely manage the land, it offers them no security. In 1990, the government endeavored to rectify women's handicapped position concerning access to land by issuing an administrative directive to deal with land acquisition, inheritance, and disposal. It decreed that a man cannot sell the land to which he has title without the consent of his wife and children. The first child acts as the representative of all the children and must consent to the sale. Although sons have an upper hand in this process, daughters have a right to stop any transactions pertaining to the parents' land. The assistant chief and the chief, having jurisdiction over that piece of land, must certify either that the man has obtained the required family consent or that he has no family at all.

Furthermore, daughters have a right to inherit a share of their parents' land. Daughters may now legally own and construct on inherited land. The family and the clan are under obligation to cooperate with the local administrators, particularly the assistant chief and the chief, to ensure that any woman desiring a share of her parents' land is rightfully granted it. Men and women are aware of this directive and know that not only a son's, but also a daughter's consent must be obtained before the parents sell or transfer land.

Additionally, an individual seeking a loan against a land title must gain consent from the spouse and the oldest male child or, if there is no male child, a female child. Thus, adult offspring have considerable power. Parents can jointly decide to give their title deeds as security to their children, male or female. In sum, the directive has significantly empowered women on paper, but it is still too early to determine whether it is having an impact on local practice. In fact, challenging male privilege in land inheritance and ownership is likely to be a real struggle for women.

According to Bradley's data (1991), less than 10 percent of women in Murang'a own land.[9] The ECOGEN survey revealed that in 9 percent of the households responding, women have title to land. Approximately one-third of these women are in the poorest category, indicating an effort on the part of independent women to invest in property on their own behalf. These are mainly widows or, occasionally, single mothers who have managed to buy a piece of land. Nearly half the women who have titles are from more affluent households, where an additional parcel of land is occasionally put in the name of a wife or grown daughter (usually unmarried or divorced) in the household. Even in households where women have title, it is unusual for them to take advantage of land ownership to acquire loans to improve their status and the productivity of their land. Many fear that they might not be able to repay the loan and would lose what little land they possess. Often people can point to instances in the past when family members have lost the collateral they placed against loans. In addition, the elaborate requirements for obtaining loans discourage women from seeking them.

The customary land tenure system leads to continuous fragmentation of land through the generations, often resulting in uneconomic parcels with declining productivity. On the one hand, this system provides a minimal assurance of security for a household; on the other, it forces most to seek alternative approaches for securing a livelihood because the landholding is too small to support the family. It deeply affects women's access to a vital resource.

Besides inheritance issues, other aspects of changing land access and use affect women. Land pressure has transformed the practice of cattle rearing to zero grazing, a system where cattle are fed in sheds rather than allowed to graze freely. Traditionally, men took charge of livestock, but the shift to zero grazing has transferred most of the responsibility to women, who must now fetch fodder and water for the penned or tethered animals. Many households own one or two cows and goats, which provide milk and a source of cash when the household needs it (e.g., for school fees). This relatively new strategy for livestock management is unavoidable in a densely populated region where people work the land intensively. The responsibilities weigh most heavily on women, although men do help with fodder collection for the animals.

Land Tenure and Social Stratification in Gikarangu

Gikarangu has been shaped by its history of land access and ownership; fragmentation and parcelization of land have reached a critical stage. Figure 4.1 reveals that 66 percent of the households surveyed have less than 4 acres of land; 38 percent of the population have less than 2 acres of land; only one respondent out of 106 has more than 10 acres of land.

Sixty-three percent of the households cultivate land in several different parcels. Figure 4.2 shows the levels of fragmentation occurring in Gikarangu. While 38 percent of the households have only one parcel (including their place of residence), 37 percent have two parcels; 16 percent have three; 9 percent have four; and only 1 percent has five pieces of land. Data reveal that parcelization is commonplace among those who have less than 2 acres and who seek small pieces to own or rent for purposes of cultivation. Of those with access to less than 2 acres, 68 percent have land in two to four parcels. Of those with 2 or 3 acres, 57 percent are cultivating two to five parcels.

For purposes of this analysis, households are grouped into four broad economic categories. The criteria used for this purpose are the size of the landholding, the material and size of the house, and the educational level of the occupants. Land is the most important indicator of a Gikarangu household's economic status; it represents wealth, power, prestige, and security. Most households derive their livelihoods from a combination of the land and off-farm trade or employment. Land size, the management of land, and the economic benefits it supplies, however, largely indicate the owner's economic status.

The wealthiest residents.   Seventeen percent of the residents of Gikarangu have 6 or more acres of land and are the sublocation's wealthiest residents. Many in this category are above fifty years of age and have taken advantage of missionary education and Central Province's independent schools in their early years, which later led to employment opportunities. The wealthiest households in this category usually own holdings of 10–12 well-managed acres. They cultivate predominantly coffee and bananas, and their holdings include woodlots and tree groves with various scattered fruit trees. A flowering hedge often surrounds

---

Figure 4.1   Percentage of Responses by Landholding Size

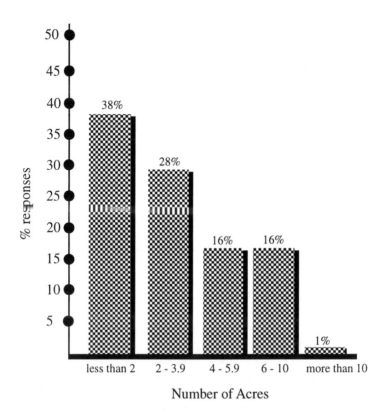

Note: N = 106.

---

a well-tended compound, and a cluster of trees shades the large, main house. The house is built with stone and corrugated iron or tile roofing and consists of a main living/dining room and two to four bedrooms. Typically, there is a large cement water tank. Households in this category may also have a shop or own rental property in a nearby town. Though the farm is the main source of income, external sources of income are often available from employed adult family members, who may provide an important source of cash. Usually both parents are literate, and the adult sons and daughters may be well educated.

The middle class.   A broad middle category exists in Gikarangu, divided for this discussion into an upper middle class and a lower middle class. Those with 4 or more acres but less than 6 are considered upper middle, whereas those with

Figure 4.2   Number of Land Parcels per Respondent (including place of residence with residential farm size in acres)

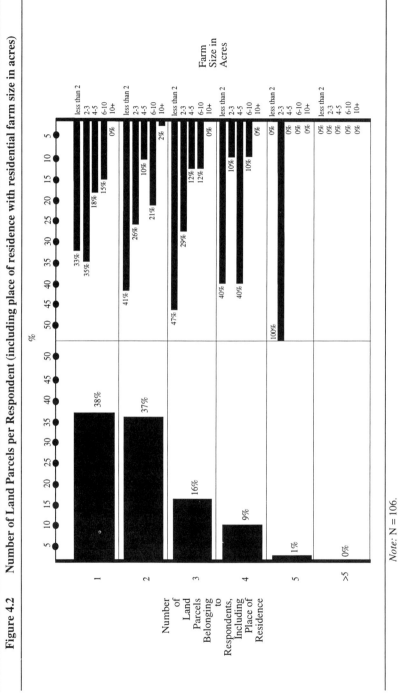

Note: N = 106.

more than 2 acres but less than 4 are categorized as lower middle. The survey indicates that the upper middle category contains 16 percent of the households, whereas the lower middle category contains 28 percent.

The majority of household heads with 4 to 5 acres of land are over thirty-five years of age. Overall educational levels are not high in this group, although most are literate. Usually, the household head has had some formal employment and either works off-farm currently or has recently retired. Most cultivate coffee, with stands ranging from a few coffee trees to over five hundred. Their homes are smaller than those of wealthy residents, constructed of stone or plastered walls, with corrugated iron roofing. Most of these households educate their children, some of whom successfully obtain formal employment. And most have acquired a water tank, either through participation in a women's group or from their own savings. In lower-middle-class households, it is common for children to drop out of school and remain unemployed.

Low-income households. As mentioned, approximately 38 percent of Gikarangu's households have less than 2 acres of land, holdings vary from a mere fraction of an acre up to 2 acres. In many instances, people in this category have inherited land from their parents within the last ten to fifteen years, and their holdings exemplify the problem of increasing land fragmentation throughout the district. Most of these households cultivate mainly subsistence crops on their land, but crop yields do not meet household consumption needs. These residents thus seek supplemental income through casual labor, growing French beans on rented pieces of land or engaging in small businesses, such as buying and selling bananas at shopping centers or at the roadside. These households constantly struggle to eke out enough extra income to purchase the necessary food their land cannot provide and to pay school fees.

The majority can achieve self-sufficiency in this high-potential region. Nevertheless, there remain those in the lowest economic stratum struggling to survive. This is especially true for single mothers, some widows who have access to few resources, and those in particularly difficult circumstances. Women, the primary food producers, are forced to find alternative means of securing food for the family. Some opt to rent land, but often these rented plots lie far off, requiring them to walk long distances to work the land. Men who are not involved with commercial crops seek employment elsewhere and are often unwilling to work on rented land. These circumstances increase problems of securing livelihoods in a region where land is fully privatized, agriculture is the primary source of income, and employment opportunities in industry, trade, or manufacturing are minimal.

NO FORESTS BUT PLENTY OF TREES

Trees and Their History in Murang'a

Gikarangu is green and tree covered; most of the trees grow on privately owned lands. There are no remaining forests; therefore, access to trees for all purposes is linked to socioeconomic status and land ownership. Even Murang'a's trees must be viewed in the context of the district's changing history and political economy. In the 1930s exotic trees were introduced as commercial trees by the British in Murang'a District. Prior to this time, one saw indigenous trees such as *muu* (*Markhamia hildebrandtii*), *mukoigo* (*Bridelia micrantha*), *muhuti* (*Erythrina abyssinica*), *mugumo* (*Ficus natalensis*), and *muringa* (*Cordia abyssinica*). They grew on the slopes and hillsides, as people farmed the wide valley bottoms.

Diverse economic, political, and demographic factors have contributed to the eradication of many of these indigenous trees from the area. During the Emergency of 1952, many trees were felled, under orders of the colonial government, to build settlement villages or to provide firewood for the police posts scattered throughout Central Province. In addition, the government cleared large tracts of land to eliminate the hideouts of the "Mau Mau" fighters.

After the Emergency, land demarcation, intensive cultivation, and demand for more construction led people to continue clearing trees. But perhaps the most devastating cause of deforestation was the move for privatization in the 1950s, which altered local social relations governing access to trees. Land reform ended the communal property regime, including rights of commonality to forest products.[10] Privatization created a landless and impoverished population, disinherited from access to trees for fuelwood, fodder, and other purposes and bereft of income. The Registered Land Act of 1963 granted access to resources affixed to the land solely to the registered land owner (the male head of the family), thereby denying resource access to women and those relying on *mbari* lands. Poor women suffered particularly. As Dewees summarizes, "Land reform increased the security of tree tenure to those with well-established rights to cultivate land, but greatly reduced—indeed, largely eliminated—rights of use and access to trees on communal lands which might have been guaranteed to households or individuals with less secure rights of cultivation."[11]

In focus group discussions, community members narrated the history of the decline of forested areas, indicating that as time progressed, demands for firewood and wood for construction drastically reduced the number of trees. After 1963, there remained remarkably few trees; by 1965, people were buying trees for construction.[12]

The trees that one sees today are a result of an aggressive tree planting campaign undertaken in the 1970s by government officials, several churches, and NGOs. This campaign encouraged mainly "environmentally friendly trees" such as *Grevillea robusta*, which community members like for its rapid growth and relative immunity to insect infestation and other tree-related diseases.

Current Uses of Trees

Favorable climatic and agroecological conditions found in Gikarangu have permitted households to continue growing trees to meet domestic needs, particularly for fuelwood. This effort, launched in the 1970s, has been adopted by almost all landowning households. Women and men have taken advantage of the fertile environment to plant numerous and diverse indigenous and exotic trees. Rights to existing trees depend on plot ownership, but planted trees belong to the person who planted them.[13] On private farms in many parts of Kenya, for example, planting a tree may be visible evidence of a claim to land. If any person or member of the household does not have the right to land, tree planting can be denied. Louise Fortmann notes that individuals may be denied tree planting privileges on the basis of gender, birth order, or intrafamily status.[14]

Although not enforced, there is a law that requires two trees to be planted for every one tree felled. Women and men, nevertheless, plant trees often. Respondents were asked whether they had participated in any community tree planting activities. Fifteen percent responded that they had done so largely through projects of the Greenbelt Movement, a grassroots environmental organization run largely by women, through school projects, or through the chief's special efforts. Most, however, frequently plant trees on their own property.

A tree's function determines who has use rights to it. A major distinction is whether the tree has commercial or subsistence value; typically, men have rights to commercial trees. People generally use the indigenous trees for firewood, as many of these species are slow growing and produce good-quality fuelwood.

The permanent woodlots on many of Gikarangu's landholdings provide firewood, building materials (poles and roof trussing), fodder for livestock, medicinal herbs, and (though losing importance) animal slaughter sites during special occasions such as weddings, dowry exchanges, and childbirth. In his analysis of tree planting and household decisionmaking, Dewees suggests that trees offer smallholders an important land use option, particularly when there are household labor constraints. He notes that changes in land use, such as the establishment of a woodlot, are linked to temporal changes in household composition and labor availability.[15]

Data from Gikarangu support the evidence provided by Dewees and others that woodlots constitute an important use of land, even on very small holdings. However, the Gikarangu evidence suggests that use is primarily for home consumption. Only 38 percent of persons keeping woodlots indicated doing so for the cash income they provide. More important is their function as a source of fuel, fruit, poles, and home building materials. In addition, they constitute a capital investment available for future needs, equivalent to "money in the bank." Figure 4.3 shows the purposes for which Gikarangu residents indicate they grow trees on their land. Fuelwood (97 percent) and building material (96 percent) ranked as the most important purposes.

Murang'a is one of the districts in the high-potential areas where tree planting has increased with population growth. Dewees notes that woodlots account for most of the tree planting in the district.[16] Farmers in Gikarangu make optimal use of land at low opportunity cost by planting trees along field boundaries, in wind rows, and in hedges around homesteads, in addition to creating woodlots. Rarely do people clearcut or fell entire trees for firewood. Rather, they use various lopping and coppicing techniques. Gikarangu's smallholders obtain most fuelwood by the traditional Kikuyu practice of pruning both trees and shrubs. This method of fuelwood collection allows trees to stand in the landscape, which can also help to stabilize soils (or hillslopes).

Many households obtain much of their fuelwood from their own land. However, increasing numbers of households find that their smallholding provides an inadequate supply. The absence of common lands for fuelwood collection means that fuelwood must be purchased. The fuelwood shortage existing in Gikarangu since the early 1960s has been mitigated by the opportunity for women to collect firewood from a neighboring estate, Samar Estate Ltd. However, respondents indicated that this estate has been sold and subdivided into private parcels and will soon no longer be accessible. Thus they anticipate a crisis of fuelwood availability in the near future and problems in providing for

Figure 4.3   Purposes for Which Gikarangu Households Grow Trees

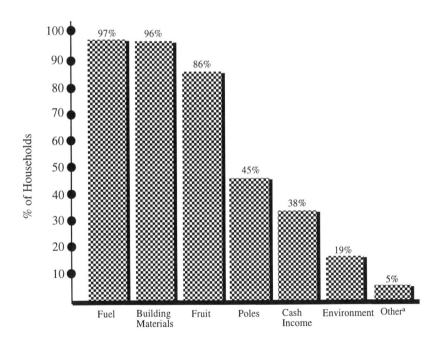

Note: a. Medicinal uses, dyes, fiber, etc.

their families in the face of a diminishing, essential resource. Figure 4.4 shows
the current sources of fuelwood for residents of Gikarangu.

Methods for dealing with fuelwood needs vary substantially across households with different sizes of landholdings. As one might anticipate, those with
less than 2 acres depend almost equally on obtaining fuelwood from their own
land, searching outside the farm for fuelwood, and purchasing fuel. Those with
2–4 acres depend primarily on their own sources; they also purchase and do
very little searching. Seventy percent of those who have 4–10 acres are self-
sufficient in fuelwood. Most who purchase fuelwood need to do so for only one
to three months of the year.

Figure 4.4   Household Fuelwood Sources According to Size of Landholding

---

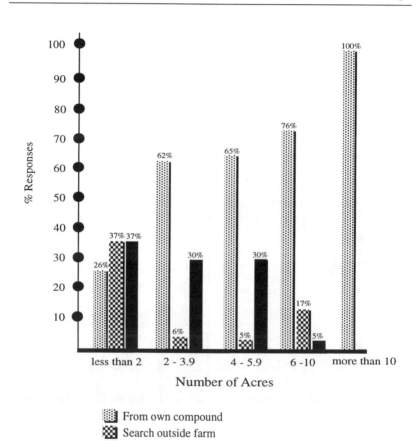

Access and reliability of renewable sources of energy are significant and growing concerns in Gikarangu. A rural, agricultural population is heavily dependent on trees for many purposes. In the context of increasing social differentiation and land scarcity, those who have access to and control over trees have a distinct advantage. Fetching firewood is the responsibility of women. However, the control of the tree is an undisputed male right. This clear distinction—another illustration of the labor/ownership dichotomy—has both gender and class implications. Households constantly work to increase access to trees for fuelwood, fodder, and many other purposes. For those residents of Gikarangu who have little or no access to land, however, this point is irrelevant. They must rely on new livelihood strategies to gain income to enable themselves to purchase tree products.

CHANGING LIVELIHOOD STRATEGIES

Division of Rights, Roles, and Responsibilities within the Household

In Kenya, women are responsible for over 80 percent of the food crop production and provide labor in commercial crop farming, especially on small-scale farms producing such commodities as coffee and tea. This labor is largely unaccounted for in statistical analyses of the Kenyan economy; the labor input of women has always remained "invisible." Only women's involvement in household activities is recognized.

Discussions with groups of men and women in Gikarangu confirmed that women are responsible for household activities, such as home care, child rearing, cooking, washing, cleaning utensils, and fetching water and firewood. Daughters also have a large burden of domestic duties, assisting their mothers with most domestic responsibilities; sons help their mothers if the household has no female children. Sons may occasionally be called upon to help their sisters, but they are usually exempt from domestic activities. All agree that these duties are essential for maintenance of human life. During discussions with a male focus group, it was found that men will take on domestic chores only when absolutely necessary, such as when the wife is ill or away on a marketing trip.[17] One respondent indicated that if he undertook such chores, he kept it a secret to avoid ridicule by other men.

Productive activities are carried out by both women and men on their own farms or for pay in cash or kind. In Gikarangu, the productive realm includes the following: (1) agriculture—clearing, preparing land, digging, planting, weeding, cultivating, fertilizing, pruning, spraying, harvesting crops, tree management, transportation, marketing; (2) animal husbandry—herding, collecting fodder, watering, milking, overall animal care; and (3) trading and small enterprise, such as tailoring, sandal making, bicycle repairing, owning a *duka*, or selling bananas.

A high degree of complementarity exists between men's and women's productive activities in Gikarangu. Most discussants held that it is becoming more common for men and women to undertake necessary tasks in agriculture or animal husbandry without considering whether they fall into the realm of men's or women's responsibilities. The current economic hardships and trends have necessitated joint efforts to support the family and its livestock. Although women are generally responsible for bringing fodder and water to the animals, men will carry out these responsibilities if needed.

Key Trends in Gikarangu's Agriculture
and Their Impact on Gender Roles

The decline of coffee.   Coffee remains the major commercial crop, although bananas, French beans, avocados, papaya, and macadamia nuts are becoming significant cash earners. After a high point in the mid-1970s, coffee prices declined drastically, and, as mentioned earlier, only in the spring of 1994 did they start to build up again. In 1989, coffee was at its lowest price in forty years, bringing in returns below the cost of production. Participants in the focus groups said that the smallholders who relied on coffee as a sole income source desperately tried to abandon coffee altogether or to reduce their dependence on a livelihood that was fast pushing them to bankruptcy.[18]

Meanwhile, the government forbade farmers from uprooting their coffee, in the persistent hope that prices would improve. With such insufficient returns, many farmers chose to neglect their household's coffee stands, since they could not be legally destroyed. This course of action was readily observed by the research team between 1991 and 1993. Thus, smallholders were in effect underutilizing the most valuable and fertile land in the sublocation to comply with the law, a clear illustration of resistance of local people to outside control. Only when prices began to rise were farmers encouraged to care for their coffee again.

Traditionally, coffee has been managed and tended by both men and women, but men control the income generated from it, notwithstanding inadequate returns. Instead of acting on their own judgment, women must ask permission to use coffee acreage when they wish to plant crops such as beans or potatoes. In focus group discussions, men and women commented that where women have cultivated beans amid the coffee, they have derived a comparatively high yield per acre. The assistant chief confirmed these observations.[19]

Meanwhile, to compensate for loss of coffee income, men in some households have been gradually appropriating the women-controlled food crops, including bananas and surplus maize and beans. Through focus group discussions it emerged that these crops, which women traditionally control for domestic purposes, are slowly becoming alternative sources of income to meet school fees and other customary, male responsibilities or cash needs.[20]

Co-opting the banana.   The banana has been women's most valued food crop besides maize and beans; it matures quickly and fetches ready income at the market. Most farms, big and small, possess banana groves. Lately, bananas have become big business in Gikarangu, and men have become more interested in their commercialization. There is evidence that control of this crop is beginning to shift from women to men. This shift relates in part to the unreliability of coffee for cash income. It probably also relates to the European Community's official shift to Africa (its former colonies) for bananas and away from Latin America.

Men and women sell bananas in approximately 10 percent of the surveyed households. In some instances women must consult with their husbands when they want to sell bananas. Group discussions revealed that men feel no discomfiture in having become banana vendors, although responsibility for producing and marketing the crop originally rested in the women's domain. Men say this change is acceptable because they use the income earned to pay school fees, customarily a man's concern. This gendered shift in control bodes poorly for some women, as bananas have been their foremost source of income.

The rise of the French bean.   The French bean has recently started to gain popularity as a commercial crop in Gikarangu. French beans grow primarily in the valley bottoms, where irrigation is possible. They are cultivated mostly by young men, but sometimes by young married couples, women, and unemployed youth working together on rented plots (rental charges vary greatly and depend on negotiations). Involvement in French bean cultivation is increasing most vigorously among those who have the smallest landholdings. More than two-thirds of those involved in French bean cultivation and marketing have tiny landholdings and rent land suitable for this purpose. They hope to find a new and profitable way to supplement their incomes from a small piece of intensively cultivated, rented land.

French beans not only require intensive care but also have an initial capital input for the seeds, herbicides, and insecticides. A kilogram of French bean seeds costs Ksh 50 (Ksh 1 = U.S. $.02; U.S. $1 = Ksh 50); Ksh 200 are required for fertilizer and Ksh 150 for herbicides and insecticide for spraying the French beans. Total expenditures for inputs (as of 1994) are Ksh 400. It takes about six weeks for the plants to mature. An estimate of returns suggests that on a one-half-acre plot, it is possible to harvest an average of twenty-four cartons per week. A carton of French beans sells for approximately Ksh 60. Therefore, in one week it is possible to earn Ksh 1,440. The season lasts for three weeks, so returns per season are approximately Ksh 4,350. French beans are planted twice a year, yielding approximately Ksh 8,700 per year.

Felicita Wanjeri Mwaganu has been growing French beans for three years. She and her husband have only 1.5 acres of land recently inherited from Felicita's husband's father, who subdivided his land equally among all his sons. Neither she nor her husband are employed, and the land is insufficient to support the family. Observing the success of a neighbor who was cultivating French beans, Felicita rented a half-acre plot about half a kilometer from her home in a valley bottom, where water is permanently available. She obtains two crops of French beans per year and at other times plants kale, cabbages, and tomatoes on the plot. With the latter items she feeds the family and sells any surplus; the French beans are for commercial purposes only. Felicita declares that her household has been greatly assisted by growing French beans. She intends to continue and even to expand cultivation if she can obtain more land.

Trading and Small Business

Trading and small businesses play a major role in supplementing farm produce, and women far outnumber men in this activity. They trade mostly in bananas, maize, beans, mangoes, and other food crops. Discussions with focus groups of men and women revealed that increasing numbers of women in Gikarangu rely on trading. The woman who typically earns a living selling fruits and vegetables comes from a household with landholdings too small to derive an adequate livelihood. Bananas are the mainstay of many such small-scale entrepreneurs. Sixty-six percent of women in the poorest households sell bananas. Some sell them alongside the road, as does Flora Njoki, who for the past ten years has been a regular banana seller at Kaharati.

Flora started selling bananas in 1981 to supplement the meager returns from her 1-acre *shamba* (farm), inadequate for her family's needs. Her husband is not employed regularly but works as a casual laborer. The returns obtained from the sale of bananas are used to meet basic household needs, purchase clothing, and pay school fees. Flora's husband does not ask her for the money, as he knows that the banana selling business is for supplementing what they get from the farm.

Reflecting on the banana trade in recent years, Flora says people are buying fewer bananas now than they were two to three years ago. Times are hard: she used to get at least Ksh 500 or more per week, whereas now she is getting less than Ksh 200. This is due to declining sales as well as the increasing cost of unripe bananas, which she purchases to sell. Nonetheless, her profits have been sufficient.

Commenting on the future of the banana business, Flora fears that young men will soon take over the trade and may push her out of business. The entrance of young men and teenage boys into the banana trade because of a lack of jobs elsewhere has created stiff competition. The men are quick and agile; they are able to run to the buyers and sell faster than the women. Since most have no families, the money they earn is spent largely on their own amusement.

As women feel the threat of losing their business, those who are able and permitted by their husbands are opting to venture into Nairobi in hopes of expanding their banana trade. Flora said that she has not been allowed by her husband to try her luck in Nairobi. Sometimes women who take their bananas to Nairobi spend two to three days there; according to Flora, some husbands (like hers) have not yet come to terms with the changing times and the need for women traders to travel independently.

Flora imagines that five years from now she will still be selling bananas at Kaharati as she has done for the last thirteen years, unless she is forced out of business. In that case, she will seek work as a casual laborer for neighboring farms in Gikarangu. Maybe by then her husband will allow her to sell bananas in Nairobi, although she may not have the financial means to get the business started.

Flora's account describes women's participation in an emerging long-distance banana trade alongside small-scale business within Gikarangu Sublocation. The long-distance traders extend their reach to such places as Kangari, Murang'a Town, Maragua, Sabasaba, Thika, and Nairobi, sometimes requiring their absence from home for a couple of days. Some women are now purchasing large quantities of bananas for the Nairobi market. This has inevitably led men to assume domestic duties when their wives are away. In poorer households most men do not hesitate to take over the roles of their wives in their absence, as the earnings are extremely valuable. For example, trading may be the only source of income to pay school fees.

Wanjiku Wainana, a long-distance banana trader, can make a profit of Ksh 2,500 per month. She has full responsibility for the money earned from the bananas. Her husband recognizes that she uses the profits to buy more bananas for the next sales, as well as to pay school fees and meet household needs. Additionally, returns go toward women's group contributions. Wanjiku belongs to three such groups, and each month she gives at least Ksh 250 to the three groups, which are among the unregistered, very informal women's groups. These groups act as her savings bank, and when her turn for the "merry-go-round" contribution comes, she has a lump sum to meet school fees or other major expenses. She observed that going to a commercial bank involves a lot of work and said that she prefers the savings plan of the informal women's groups.

Wanjiku noted that in the last five years the number of women from Gikarangu getting involved in the sale of bananas in the Nairobi market has increased markedly. In her view, the banana business is more profitable than any other agricultural business for women. Asked to rank the most profitable crops in the area, she specified coffee, bananas, and French beans (in that order). But women do not control coffee returns, and not many people grow French beans because of their high demand for water.

The banana business has aided many women in their struggle to survive. With the decline of coffee returns and the steady erosion of earnings by inflation, more and more men, as well as women, are entering this market. This process is having a significant impact on gendered rights and responsibilities. The banana's rising importance in the outside market has provoked the loss of some women's control of the crop and the attendant income and decisionmaking power.

Out-migration

Out-migration of men from Gikarangu to urban areas such as Murang'a, Nairobi, Thika, and Mombasa is commonplace. As noted earlier, this phenomenon is changing in light of Kenya's economic adversity, high rates of unemployment, and the increasing marginalization of Kikuyus. Gikarangu residents observe that men from their community are having a more difficult time obtaining employment outside the locality than in the past. They see increasing discouragement on the part of male members of their households about prospective employment elsewhere. Young men are returning home, sometimes to remain idle and other times to compete with women for the small returns from such activities as selling bananas.

Although men's absence adds to women's work load, women recognize that their families cannot subsist off the small farms year-round, and they welcome the extra income earned by a family member laboring elsewhere. In general, most men earning a wage remit a substantial part of their earnings to their families to help with meeting school fees and other home expenses. However, some respondents were quick to note that not all men send remittances to their families; these men could assist their families more tangibly with their physical presence. At the time of the survey, 53 percent of the households had a male member involved with the urban economy, and 25 percent of the households had a female member working outside the community. For men, both Murang'a Town and Nairobi were important destinations; for women, more than half were in Murang'a Town. (See Figure 4.5.)

Like men, women regularly leave home to seek employment elsewhere. However, the circumstances are often quite different from those sending men to the cities. In general, male migrants who obtain employment are better educated than female migrants who do so. Among men who migrate, a portion seek and obtain employment in business or professional life, not simply low-paying jobs as casual laborers or menial workers. Women, on the other hand, most often seek employment as housemaids; some single mothers are entrepreneurs in the marketplaces of Murang'a Town, barely managing to earn a living.

COMMUNITY RESPONSES TO OPPORTUNITIES AND STRESS

One of the most striking attributes of Gikarangu is its array of local institutions: government affiliates, churches, women's groups, coffee producer societies, a training center for girls, a dispensary, and various projects initiated by the church and women's organizations. In the face of economic difficulties and various

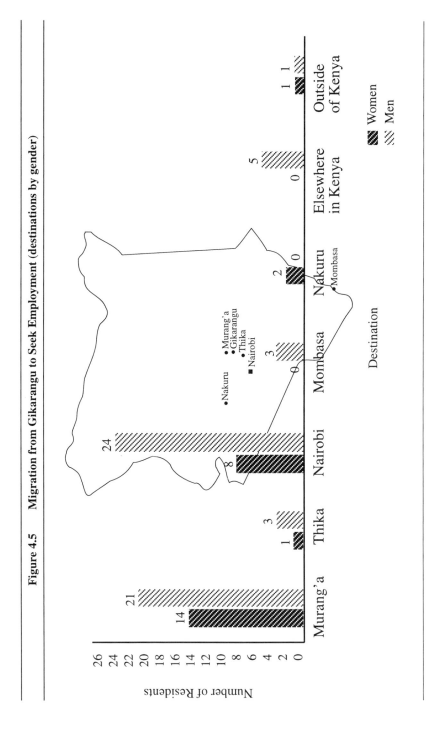

Figure 4.5   Migration from Gikarangu to Seek Employment (destinations by gender)

social problems, Gikarangu's institutional infrastructure appears to be growing stronger. It is useful to consider the reasons for this institutional durability in light of economic and ecological pressures on this community.

Underlying Explanations for
Institutional Diversity and Strength in Gikarangu

Among the characteristics of traditional Kikuyu social and political structures were a sense of communal solidarity and a high level of territorial loyalty.[21] Women's overall status was subordinate to men's, but egalitarian structures existed among men within military and political domains and among women within agricultural and domestic domains. These features have helped shape the nature and role of local organization and the building of institutions for contemporary Kikuyu society, such as the formation of strong women's groups characteristic of the Kikuyu areas.[22]

The colonial government focused on establishing a system of control to maintain law and order, regulate labor, collect taxes, and foster profitable settler farming. In implementing its objectives, it virtually dismantled the traditional systems of governance. The colonial government also established new councils and committees on agriculture, education, and other matters. Contrary to the government's intent, some of these early activities fortified Kikuyu organizational skills and encouraged a drive for political independence.

The flagrant inequity of the dual agricultural economy between settlers and the Kikuyu fueled discontent during the 1940s and 1950s. The government's tactics involved preventing competition by Kikuyu farmers in the sisal and coffee markets while assuring a supply of labor for the settler farms. Prohibited from growing cash crops, the Kikuyu were impelled to seek wage labor for cash needed to buy desired goods and services. These circumstances intensified the spirit of political activism among the Kikuyu.

For the people of Gikarangu Sublocation, the colonial epoch wrought immense social upheaval and change. It introduced a system for the production of export commodities, relegated Africans to poor-quality "reserve" lands, promoted male out-migration to work on plantations or in cities and towns, created urban centers, introduced formal education, and focused agricultural extension and the "upgrading" of agricultural skills on men rather than women. While colonialism and the settler economy displaced the Kikuyu and weakened their traditional political structures, it also encouraged high levels of social mobilization and political organization, motivating the Kikuyu to lead the struggle for independence. Murang'a was at the heart of the resistance, and Gikarangu's history was forged in the crucible of this struggle.

At independence, the Kikuyu organizational skills manifested themselves not only in politics but also in self-help community development efforts. Gikarangu is a microcosm wherein these political and organizational skills can be observed today. Gikarangu's women's groups, some of which are linked to churches (which are also strong institutions in Gikarangu), offer a forum through which women residents confront some of the challenges facing their community.

Women's Organizations: Responses to Livelihood and Community Issues

Women's informal groups and networks have been in existence throughout Kikuyu history. However, a large number of Murang'a's formal women's groups emerged in the 1960s, when they were established to address specific practical household needs or problems of the members. Women's groups have played an important and active role in household and community development in Gikarangu since independence.

Approximately 20 percent of the women in Murang'a belong to women's groups,[23] which enable their households to respond more effectively to problems and needs in the social and physical environment. Specifically, women's groups aim to improve women's access to the factors of production and to common property. They help women cope with insufficient household labor resources, assist with loans to meet urgent household needs, and provide social support and solidarity to members.

Many women's groups were formed to improve roofing on houses by changing the traditional grass thatch to corrugated iron sheets. In fact, this motive for forming groups was so commonplace that women's groups were dubbed *mabati* (corrugated iron) groups. Presently, eight formally registered women's groups exist in Gikarangu, one of which had one hundred members when it began in the 1960s. This particular group has provided labor for its individual members, rotating from one farm to another to work the fields. In addition, the group has provided casual, paid gang labor on land belonging to wealthier farmers and then used the earnings to buy corrugated iron roofing for the members. Within four years they succeeded in buying iron sheets and roofing for all members' houses.

After roofing needs were satisfied, some of these *mabati* groups dissolved. Others pursued new goals, such as purchasing water tanks. Still others organized rotating credit schemes among group members, wherein each member contributes a monthly fee, the sum of which is used as credit to one or more members. Usually women use these loans to meet school fees or other major household expenditures.

The eight Gikarangu groups of today have shifted largely from labor sharing and fulfilling practical needs to long-term investment opportunities, although they still help members buy water tanks, kitchenware, and grade cattle (high-yielding breeds) and to pay school fees. The Rwatumu Group, for example, has bought a plot in Maragua Town (about 20 kilometers away) and has started building rental rooms. The Nyawira Women's Group has set up a canteen, which it rents to a private operator. It also operates a tree nursery, which sells seedlings, and it currently plans to build shops and rental rooms on a plot it owns in

Maragua Town with money it is saving from various small projects. One group manages a small-scale pig operation, one raises and sells goats, and another purchases grade cattle. Still others are involved with small-scale horticulture—growing and selling beans, onions, potatoes, cabbages, and greens.

Women perceive group activities and membership as a way to increase their access to new technologies and new forms of capital investment. Under present circumstances, acquiring new land is virtually impossible, and men typically do not allot women a portion of their commercial crop earnings. Thus, women have little income to spend on improving food crop production or to invest in other enterprises. Membership in women's groups allows women to meet some livelihood needs and to explore new economic options. Unquestionably, these benefits can gradually improve their status and augment their power and effectiveness within both the household and the community.

Apart from opening up income opportunities for women, women's groups are beginning to address long-term social issues within their communities. There has been a recent increase in drug and alcohol abuse, as well as prostitution. The community attributes these social ills to a breakdown in traditional relationships. Men migrate; women take on greater work loads; parents have less time to devote to guiding their children. People report an increasing incidence of early pregnancies and single motherhood, as well as increased beer drinking among young men. Some young women who have suffered early pregnancies, poverty, and discrimination have turned desperately to prostitution.

The Irigiro Training Center for Girls, initiated by women members of the Presbyterian Church of East Africa (PCEA), is one response to some of these problems. Mrs. Mereka, the vibrant chairperson of the project, has played an important role in inspiring the Irigiro Training Center. A trained teacher, she has been involved in church work since 1963, when she was appointed the coordinator of the women's wing of the PCEA. Her vision, leadership, creativity, and tireless energy have helped establish the Irigiro project.

Other women like Mrs. Mereka are emerging in Gikarangu and are beginning to make their mark. These women tend to be in their forties, educated to upper primary or lower secondary school level, and at the higher end of the economic spectrum. Dynamic and energetic, they eagerly seek outside support and information; where they lack capital and some skills, they have ample motivation and drive.

Indeed, some women in Gikarangu are assuming nontraditional responsibilities, both in the household and in the community. These responsibilities may include handling arrangements with the coffee cooperative, hiring laborers for their farms, or becoming involved with a project such as Irigiro. Similarly, some men are assuming domestic responsibilities when their wives become traders traveling to other communities. The exigencies of daily life simply demand that both women and men deal with new situations and new problems as they arise. Changing patterns in household labor allocation and organization reflect the social and economic changes taking place in the central highlands of Kenya.

It is therefore not surprising that women are major contributors with multiple roles in building community infrastructure.[24] In the productive sphere, women engage in activities that improve community resource access and use and provide new benefits to the households within the community. In their domestic roles, which encompass not only bearing children but perpetuating social institutions and mores, women actively form organizations that serve to strengthen the institutional fabric of the local community.

As community managers—in the broadest sense—these women contribute to building Gikarangu. Empowering local organizations may require scaling up to strengthen capabilities for local action and to deal more effectively with external demands. In Gikarangu, with the support of the social development officer (SDO), the women's groups have established an informal link with each other. Thirteen groups (including five from a neighboring sublocation) have come together to share ideas and exchange views on how to strengthen their roles in the community. These groups visit each other once a month on a rotational basis and contribute Ksh 250 per month to support various development activities. This fee is in addition to the usual monthly dues for individual group members. Group visits may occur when an urgent need or a social event arises. These emerging linkages reflect an expansive outlook that recognizes common concerns among communities. In sum, the women's groups increasingly provide forums for women to test and encourage their public voices within their respective communities. In these ways, women are asserting themselves in the male-dominated power structures.

CONCLUDING OBSERVATIONS

Gikarangu is a vibrant community buoyed by the opportunities arising from its proximity to an urban center and from its strong infrastructure. Yet many residents face persistent cash shortages, land scarcity, ecological stress, the uncertainty of shifting livelihoods, and eroding social structures. The impact of these concerns varies according to the age, class, and gender of Gikarangu's residents. All are pulled and pushed by economic and social forces. What they must do to survive may contradict rules defined by current legal codes and traditional social structures. Poor women, who bear primary responsibility for their livelihoods and for the care of their children, feel these contradictory pressures most severely.

Throughout the course of this research, team members observed pressures on local residents seeking subsistence and cash under conditions of land scarcity and rapid population growth. These pressures have led to agricultural intensification, as well as to a frantic search for income opportunities within and beyond the community. There are several consequences. First, food crops, which women traditionally managed, are increasingly coming under the sphere of male regulation and control. Second, while demands on women's labor have increased, many women are experiencing declining independence and authority in the productive sphere and decreased control over resources. Third, people in Gikarangu are shifting from coffee production toward commercialization of horticultural crops and fruit. Fourth, there is significant short-term male out-migration, as well as an increase in the migration of young women. The migration of young men in search of employment often fails, given the state of the current economy.

Issues of male and female access to and control over resources are more important than ever. Many young women witness the erosion of their social networks, which are tied to land and resource access, as land is carved into smaller and smaller parcels to which they do not have access. Some young women from poorer households realize they will never obtain land or acquire marketable job skills. Instead, they resort to selling bananas at the crossroads or travelling to Thika or Nairobi for small scale trade. Sometimes they choose early marriage and pregnancy or are forced into prostitution.

Despite the obvious underlying structural causes, such problems are widely regarded as "women's issues," arising from what has been described as a failure to educate girls and young women properly. Meanwhile, women's groups are beginning to mobilize to support individual members and to respond to the educational and social concerns of the community. In the face of a number of social issues arising from the pressures on this community, the women's associations constitute a critical strength. They resist the marginalization of young women and help build security for older ones. The groups assist women to secure their basic needs and invest in their futures while providing a sense of strength through unity. However, these women and their households remain vulnerable to the vagaries of international markets, national decisions, and traditional land policies.

In short, residents of Gikarangu are enmeshed in a complex web of social, economic, and ecological problems. This chapter has unraveled some of these complex problems and considered the ways the dynamic interactions of household, community, and resources—shaped from within and beyond the community—are transforming the lives of Gikarangu's women and men.

NOTES

1. Hetherington, "Explaining the Crisis of Capitalism in Kenya"; Mackenzie, "Local Initiatives and National Policy"; Nyong'o, "State and Society in Kenya"; Stamp, "Local Government in Kenya."
2. Government of Kenya, Central Bureau of Statistics, *1989 Census*.
3. Ibid., p. 254.
4. Okoth-Ogendo, "Some Issues of Theory," p. 12.

5. Thomas, *Politics, Participation and Poverty*.

6. Lamb, *Peasant Politics*, p. 11.

7. Mackenzie, "Gender and Land Rights," p. 635.

8. Ibid., p. 624.

9. Bradley, *Women, Woodfuel, and Woodlots*.

10. Castro, "Indigenous Kikuyu Agroforestry," p. 15.

11. Dewees, "Trees, Farm Boundaries, and Land Tenure," p. 11.

12. Focus group discussions in Gikarangu, August 1993.

13. Dewees, "Tree Planting and Household Decision Making."

14. Fortmann, "The Tree Tenure Factor."

15. Dewees, "Tree Planting and Household Decision Making," p. 33.

16. Dewees, "Trees, Farm Boundaries, and Land Tenure" and "Tree Planting and Household Decision Making."

17. Focus group discussions on this and related topics were held in Gikarangu in August and September 1993.

18. Focus group discussion, August 1993.

19. Discussions with focus groups in Gikarangu, as well as with the assistant chief, August 1993.

20. Focus group discussions, Gikarangu, August and September, 1993.

21. Lambert, *Kikuyu Social and Political Institutions*; Muriuki, *A History of the Kikuyu, 1500–1900*; Rosberg and Nottingham, *The Myth of Mau Mau*.

22. For a more detailed discussion of the precolonial and colonial structures shaping contemporary political life, see Thomas, *Politics, Participation and Poverty*, pp. 23–61.

23. Mackenzie, "Gender and Land Rights," p. 636.

24. Caroline Moser, in "Gender Planning in the Third World," p. 1, discusses women's "triple role": productive, reproductive, and community management.

5

From Cattle to Coffee: Transformation in Mbusyani and Kyevaluki

Isabella Asamba, Barbara Thomas-Slayter

Visitors to Machakos District in the 1990s find two scenarios awaiting them. One is of a prospering district, an exemplar of the Boserupian model demonstrating that population growth can lead to revegetation of barren hillslopes and intensification of production. With the right boost of economic policies, increased productivity and income follow. The other scenario is the reverse, a district suffering from environmental degradation, exploitation by nearby urban dwellers, growing inequities, and increasing poverty. This story is one in which increased male out-migration (males leaving to seek wage labor) divides families and leaves women managing farms without access to the resources they need to do so effectively. Which scenario is accurate? Both have elements of truth and accuracy, and both have elements of oversight and misrepresentation. At the center of both stories are the women of Machakos—involved in agricultural intensification but also bearing the brunt of increasing poverty and marginalization.

This chapter focuses on two adjacent communities, Mbusyani and Kyevaluki, in a largely semiarid region of Machakos. These communities offer an opportunity to consider the implications of both sides of the Machakos reality and to reflect more broadly on the findings. They also offer an opportunity to review the specific gender dimensions of these livelihood systems, which are currently undergoing a transformation from cattle to coffee and beyond.

TWO SIDES

Increasing Productivity and Environmental Recovery

A strong note of optimism regarding Machakos District has emerged during the last several years from a long-term study (1930–1990) sponsored by the University of Nairobi, Kenya's Ministry of Reclamation and Development of Arid, Semi-Arid Areas and Wastelands, and the British Overseas Development Institute.[1] The findings from this research are presented in articles in the *Develop-*

Map 5.1   Machakos District, Mbusyani and Kyevaluki Sublocations

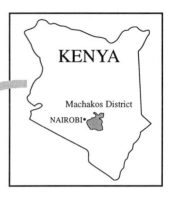

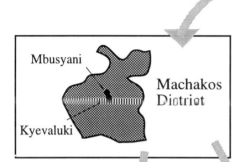

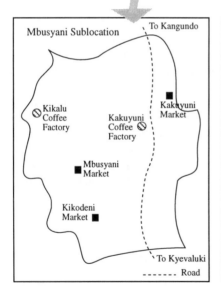

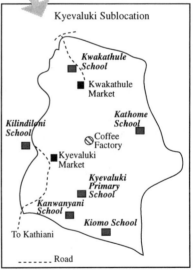

ment Policy Review (1992) and *Journal of International Development* (1993), an ODI Working Paper (No. 62), and a book, *More People, Less Erosion: Environmental Recovery in Kenya* (1994), by Mary Tiffen, Michael Mortimore, and Francis Gichuki. These researchers suggest that Machakos offers remarkable testimony to the Boserupian thesis that population increase is compatible with environmental recovery, provided that market developments make farming profitable.[2]

Research findings of Tiffen and Mortimore indicate that between 1930 and 1990 there have been approximately threefold and tenfold increases in the value of output per capita and per hectare, respectively, in Machakos District.[3] Tiffen argues that the mutually reinforcing effects of capital investment and new technology adoption have led to output rising much faster than population, outweighing any negative effects of population growth.[4] Examining changes between 1930 and 1990, Tiffen and Mortimore see impressive increases in productivity and in the capacity to deal with environmental problems.[5] According to the argument, if the policies are right, Machakos will continue to prosper and its experience should be replicable elsewhere in Kenya.[6]

Declining Resources and Marginalized People

Others state that the district faces fuelwood shortages, soil erosion, deforestation, and periodic famines. O'Keefe and Wisner observed the spatial marginalization of the rural poor into semiarid lands.[7] Mung'ala and Openshaw documented the districtwide fuelwood deficit and deforestation rates.[8] Mbithi and Barnes, as well as Mbithi and Wisner, long ago chronicled the pervasive poverty and land shortage in the region.[9] Others cite land shortage, population pressure, physical resource base deterioration, water scarcity, the vagaries of an erratic climate, inadequate employment opportunities, and a lack of fit between labor needs and labor allocation derived from the gender-based division of labor.[10]

While Machakos has long served as a focal point of land degradation debates in Kenya, the balance has now tipped in favor of the "recovery narrative" as the dominant view of the region and of the larger process of agricultural intensification in the country.[11] Rocheleau, Benjamin, and Diang'a suggest that neither of these one-dimensional stories represents the complexity of life in Machakos. They further characterize Ukambani (Machakos and Kitui Districts) as an "endangered region" undergoing a variety of processes that make the land and people of the region "more vulnerable to economic and ecological stress, or more dependent on external market forces and the state."[12] However, according to their perspective, there is striking variability in the conditions within the region, and land degradation in newly opened sections and in neighboring Kitui District has outstripped the undeniably positive countereffects of intensive resource management in the more densely settled regions.[13]

According to Ondiege, rain-fed farming by smallholders is difficult in more than 75 percent of the district.[14] He specifies that 60 percent of the holdings in

Machakos are made up of less than 6 acres. Many of these small landholdings are insufficient in land quality, labor availability, or capitalization to support household production. Moreover, over 90 percent of the district's labor force is employed in farm and nonfarm activities in the rural areas, predominantly in smallholding farming and pastoralism.[15]

Ondiege suggests that despite increased yields and productivity, most Machakos residents have marginal livelihoods and continuing economic and ecological difficulties. Rocheleau, Benjamin, and Diang'a share Ondiege's concerns about increasing stratification in Machakos District with the "displacement of many of the poorest (or the next poorest group, the near-landless-but-still-mobile) people to the rangelands and sparsely populated farmlands of frontier areas in Machakos and Kitui," with skewed distribution of land, income, and access to resources.[16]

Bringing the Marginalized into the Discussion

While Tiffen, Mortimore, and Gichuki tell a story of accomplishment as Machakos moves into the wider economy of Kenya and the international community, Ondiege as well as Rocheleau et al. express concern about the poor 20–30 percent who are vulnerable in both ecological and economic dimensions. They accept Downing's assertion that "ecocatastrophe is not immanent," yet they suggest that "fear of ecotragedy is not unrealistic" when catastrophe implies substantial universal suffering and tragedy refers to the suffering of a minority.[17] Several considerations expand discussion of the ecological, economic, and gender dimensions of the debate.

First, use of districtwide data—particularly per capita indicators for productivity—masks what appears to be increasing differentiation within Machakos District. Data that do not reveal significant variation may misrepresent the reality with which most people live. It is therefore valuable to examine the specific conditions shaping people's lives, including both the historical and the present contexts.

Second, we need insights into the lives of the 36 percent of the district's population that lives in agroecological zones 5 and 6, Kenya's poorest land classifications. It is essential to understand conditions faced by marginalized groups, whether in Machakos District or elsewhere. Aggregated statistics may disguise both class and geographic differences.

Finally, we need to clarify what is happening to women in Machakos District. The data available do not address entitlement questions for the poor generally and for women specifically. Using Sen's conceptualization of "exchange entitlements," commodity specialization as it is occurring in Machakos today does not provide a mechanism for preventing the unfavorable entitlements of the poor from becoming even more unfavorable.[18] Nor does the emphasis on pricing policies and market strategies encourage discussion of the structural disadvantages for women under current definitions of property rights, the designation of labor along gender lines, and other gender-based asymmetries and restrictions affecting access to and control over resources.

In this exploration of conditions in two sublocations in Machakos District, we argue that the interconnections between social processes and economic and environmental change are central to a discussion of Machakos's story. We explore two less affluent communities in Machakos to find out what is happening to people's lives and particularly to gender-based rights and responsibilities in the context of significant economic and environmental challenges.

Evidence from these communities, and from other studies as well, suggests that over time the Akamba have adopted numerous ecological, social, and economic strategies to cope with economic and ecological problems. These include various environmental strategies such as bench terracing, tree planting, dam construction, afforestation, and water conservation. Economic strategies include household decisions to produce untried commodities, perhaps coffee or tobacco, and a variety of different household and interhousehold income-generating activities. They also include an extraordinary capacity to build viable local institutions.[19]

In this study of Mbusyani and Kyevaluki we focus on (1) the impact of changing economic and environmental conditions on the social construction of gender; (2) the ways gender roles and gender-based responsibilities shape rural livelihood systems and affect the sustainable management of natural resources at the household and community levels; and (3) the similarities and differences in these two communities as they affect the activities of the women's organizations.

We hope that a close consideration of the political, cultural, and historical conditions in Mbusyani and Kyevaluki will enable us to understand more clearly the variations in struggle, vulnerability, and poverty, as well as in agency, initiative, and successful management of resources in rural Machakos.

THE CONTEXT

Machakos District

Machakos is a predominantly semiarid area of approximately 14,250 square kilometers. It is characterized by inadequate and unpredictable rainfall, along with shallow soils, steep slopes, and unstable surface soil structures.[20] Approximately 56 percent of the land is categorized as low in agroecological potential; 38 percent has medium potential (zone 3), and 5 percent has high potential. Poor soils and the arid climate contribute to low agricultural potential.

One hundred years ago, the region was sparsely settled. The 1890s brought major changes in land use among the Akamba, a Bantu-speaking agropastoral people who had lived there for several generations.[21] A two-year drought and a simultaneous epidemic of rinderpest devastated the Akamba's traditional pastoral life-style. Then in the early 1900s, colonial settlers arrived and established coffee and sisal plantations. The immediate effect was displacement of a few *shambas* (smallholding farms) and reduction of the total amount of grazing lands in the region by 20–30 percent. The longer-term impact was more severe—the coffee estates not only reduced available land but also served as a magnet to attract local labor. Migrations into the area began in the 1900s.

As the amount of grazing lands decreased and human population increased, deeply rooted attitudes toward cattle accumulation heightened. By the late 1930s and 1940s, the area was suffering from severe overgrazing, with large numbers of livestock contributing directly to resource degradation. Furthermore, the colonial administration had decimated the authority of local leadership and therefore successfully eliminated any authority or capacity at the village level to deal with overgrazing. During the next several decades the colonial government enforced severe destocking as well as massive conservation measures.[22] Such policies left a legacy of resentment against the government, hostility toward conservation, and a population abandoning livestock and taking up agriculture. Since independence, reliance on agriculture has increased, while cattle raising has declined.

Today, the Akamba of Machakos District are concentrated in the higher-potential areas where there are high population growth rates and increased densities. Most people are employed in agriculture and in piecing together a livelihood from multiple sources. Those in the formal sector earning wages constitute less than 10 percent.[23]

Mbusyani and Kyevaluki

Like many neighboring sublocations, Mbusyani and Kyevaluki have much in common, but there are also some key differences. The two communities are located approximately 90 kilometers east of Nairobi in Kakuyuni Location of Kangundo Division. The population of Mbusyani is approximately 7,000, with 800 households; Kyevaluki's population, as of 1989, was 6,915, with 794 households. Mbusyani is 15 square kilometers (5.7 square miles), and Kyevaluki is nearly twice as large. The terrain is stony, the climate is dry, and the land is gently sloping to hilly. A tarmac road leads from Nairobi to just beyond Tala, where it becomes a dirt road stretching the remaining 20 kilometers to Mbusyani and Kyevaluki. The road occasionally traverses a stream or a dry, rocky streambed.

Mbusyani and Kyevaluki Sublocations lie in upper-midland agroecological zones 3 and 4. Zone 3 is characterized as a marginal coffee zone suitable also for maize, beans, and pigeon peas; zone 4 is suitable for oil seeds, sorghum, and millet.[24] Mbusyani is more favorably endowed, with most of its terrain in zone

3, whereas the greater portion of Kyevaluki lies in zone 4. Fragile soils, eroded hillsides, and marginally productive land are characteristic of many parts of both Mbusyani and Kyevaluki, particularly the latter. Rainfall is low and unreliable, with drought occurring in approximately one out of four years. Normal annual rainfall averages 600 millimeters in Mbusyani and somewhat less in Kyevaluki.[25]

At one time these lands were considered suitable for cattle and were grazed by large herds belonging to the resident Akamba.[26] Decades of government regulations have limited the land available for herds, enforced destocking, and privatized land that had previously been common grazing land. The people of these communities can no longer afford to keep large numbers of cattle. Today they gain their livelihoods largely through farming, but the land available to them is inappropriate for intensive cultivation.[27] Because of their desperate need for cash and because of government encouragement to do so, farmers are struggling to grow coffee even though the land is particularly ill suited for high-yielding coffee production.

The Dynamics of Rural Transformation

The magnitude and rapidity of change in Mbusyani and Kyevaluki are extraordinary. Though appearances may suggest otherwise, the reality is that life has been transformed in the course of a generation along every dimension imaginable. At the core of these changes lie new livelihood patterns. The title of this chapter suggests one pattern. No longer do farming families keep large herds of cattle; rather, almost all struggle to earn a cash income from coffee grown on land only marginally suitable for its production. The privatization of land, the loss of communal lands, the increasing number of land sales, the pressures to get jobs and earn money, and a growing gap between rich and poor are all aspects of this transformation. It entails significant modifications in responsibilities for both men and women as they struggle to secure a living for their families.

Mbusyani and Kyevaluki are at different points on a spectrum in regard to these changes. Mbusyani is probably a generation ahead of Kyevaluki in its transformation from a cattle-keeping, agropastoral society to one of agriculturalists heavily reliant on a commercial crop and well integrated into the cash economy. The different levels of activity among community organizations, as well as divergent leadership styles, reflect the conditions existing within each of these sublocations. These subtle yet critical variations in leadership and in the functioning of community organizations shape and direct differing momentum and outcomes for resource management and development activities within these two communities.

Probably the most notable trend for these sublocations is the inexorable way they are being drawn into and affected by the broader political and economic systems. No longer are these relatively isolated and self-contained communities able to feed themselves and manage their own affairs without concern about the outside world. Government intrusion began in the colonial era. Economic as well as political intrusion now comes from far beyond the capital city. Ironically, as they move from cattle to coffee, many households are being integrated into those larger systems on disadvantageous terms. The struggle to diversify sources of income under unequal terms of rural–urban exchange and little local employment can be very difficult indeed.

Methods

The team, comprising researchers from the government of Kenya's National Environment Secretariat (NES) and Clark University, drew on the Participatory Rural Appraisals (PRAs) conducted in these sublocations in 1988 and 1989 by Egerton University, the NES, and Clark University. (See the Appendix for an outline of the steps in conducting a Participatory Rural Appraisal.) The PRAs required a variety of data gathering techniques, including spatial methods (village transects or farm maps); time-related methods (establishing time lines or preparing seasonal calendars); methods focusing on social data, such as household interviews; and group meetings to discuss the institutions within the community.[28] Technical data regarding water sites and materials needed for construction were gathered with the assistance of technical officers.

These PRAs did not have a specific gender focus, so in 1990 the ECOGEN research team compensated for this orientation in choice of methods. First, we used in-depth household surveys based on a stratified random sample from each of the sublocations, interviewing 4 percent of the households in Mbusyani and 5 percent of the households in Kyevaluki. In all cases, we interviewed an adult female in the household. Although life histories, as such, were not collected, we endeavored to capture the central elements of the respondent's life, as well as changes over time for her and her household.

Second, we interviewed key informants, among them community leaders within both sublocations. These included people such as teachers, headmasters, ministers, women's group leaders, and government administrators; questions pertaining to gender issues were asked of all informants.

Third, we administered a short, highly focused random survey to one hundred men and women from different households within each of the two sublocations (11 percent of Mbusyani's and 12 percent of Kyevaluki's households). The survey addressed critical observations from the key informant and household interviews. Its purpose was to determine the nature, variability, and spread of some of our findings. In addition, both authors followed up with visits and other communication through June 1994. These methods are not exhaustive, but they give a clear picture of the changing resource, economic, and social conditions within Mbusyani and Kyevaluki. In particular, questions have been focused to direct inquiry to gender-related rights, roles, and responsibilities in managing natural resources and livelihood systems.

STRATIFICATION AND
EVOLVING HOUSEHOLD CIRCUMSTANCES

Mbusyani and Kyevaluki, perhaps more than many parts of Kenya, reflect the unyielding draw of Nairobi's city life. The "up side" and the "down side" are experienced in a myriad of ways by households in these communities. Buoyed by resources from family members working outside, some households prosper. Others, unable to gain a toehold in the cash economy, find the merest household expenditure an overwhelming burden. These households must deal on a daily basis with the exigencies of desperate poverty in an economy that increasingly functions through the medium of cash. Local residents may become, on the one hand, creative at finding solutions to problems and, on the other, mired in low-level and often ineffective patterns of economic activity.

Particularly evident in these two sublocations is the growing differentiation among households. No longer is it possible to generalize about the nature of landholdings, the numbers of cattle, the magnitude of earnings from commercial crops, or the likelihood that households will manage to feed their members in times of drought. Households vary substantially in the constraints they face and in the opportunities they perceive. These differences bear close attention, for they constitute the framework in which the issues facing these communities must be addressed. It is possible to group the households in these communities into four broad categories: affluent (in the context of semiarid rural Kenya), average, medium poor, and poor.

The Wealthiest Households

In general, the more affluent households in both sublocations share two characteristics. First, they have outside, off-farm sources of income. These monies are most often from employment outside the local community in areas such as Nairobi, Machakos, or Mombasa. Sometimes, however, the source may be locally based, such as ownership of a *duka* (small shop) or a teaching position in a nearby school. The employment generates significant income for capital purchases largely to increase agricultural productivity and to invest in educational opportunities.

Second, the affluent have sufficient land to allocate to commercial and subsistence crops. Indicators of prosperity are found in the size of the holding, the size of the home, the use of iron sheets for roofing material, the number of coffee trees, the capacity to hire laborers, the existence of a rooftop water catchment tank, and children who are being educated outside the community. In addition, in Mbusyani, two or three, stall-fed cows indicate wealth, whereas

Figure 5.1   Coffee Bushes as Indicators of Wealth from the Land

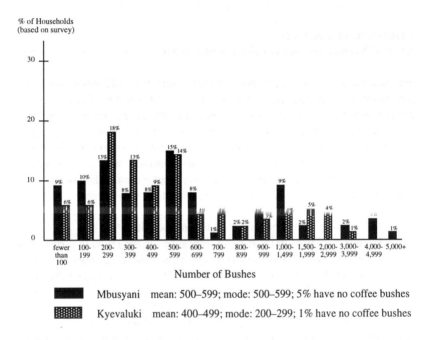

% of Households
(based on survey)

Number of Bushes

Mbusyani   mean: 500–599; mode: 500–599; 5% have no coffee bushes

Kyevaluki   mean: 400–499; mode: 200–299; 1% have no coffee bushes

Note: N = 200 (100 each sublocation).

in Kyevaluki, a more prosperous household might keep eight or ten head of cattle tethered for grazing.

The Middle Range

The average household derives its livelihood from the land. Households experiencing average levels of well-being always have enough land—at least for the time being—to support their families and to provide both subsistence and commercial crops. Typically, these households have between four hundred and seven hundred coffee bushes, bringing into the household (using 1990 figures; 1 Ksh = U.S. $.05) Ksh 6,000 (U.S. $300), the low estimate for Kyevaluki, to Ksh 14,700 (U.S. $735), the high estimate for Mbusyani. Figure 5.1 reveals the wide range of wealth from the land, based on the use of coffee bushes as indicators of cash income. Most households have no regular salary income. Some have occasional outside income or remittances from a relative who provides some support as it is needed or, more likely, as some surplus is available to him or her.

It is useful to make comparisons about typical household expenditures for which coffee returns and other cash income would be used. Most households consider school fees for their children to be a top priority. School is free through Standard 8, except for books, uniforms, and some building fund contributions. Secondary school is not free. For a government or *harambee* day school in an area such as rural Machakos, fees per year have been as high as Ksh 2,400. Fees for boarding schools have ranged from Ksh 4,000 to as high as Ksh 10,000 for private schools, depending on the location and quality of the school. The Ministry of Education is standardizing fees for secondary schools at Ksh 1,620 for day schools and Ksh 2,460 for boarding schools (1990 figures). Even so, the average rural household in either Mbusyani or Kyevaluki would have a tough time educating several youngsters beyond primary school.

The Poorer Households

The medium-poor households function with 4 or 5 acres of land, little in the way of a commercial crop, and little cash income, which is usually based on the casual labor of household members. Typically, they have between two hundred and four hundred coffee bushes and feel constant pressure to transform more land into coffee production to increase their cash resources.

The poorest households often comprise partial or fragmented families—for example, widows, divorced women and their children, or young unmarried mothers and their children. The luckier ones manage on a half to 2 acres of land. They may nod in the direction of a commercial crop, but the returns are negligible. Others are virtually landless families. As one resident described it, "We have sold all the land around our house and now own only the house we live in." Rarely do these households have relatives who are providing even occasional financial support. They rely heavily on the returns from casual labor, which average Ksh 20 (U.S. $1) per day. The work is, of course, seasonal, and their incomes are highly unpredictable.

A glimpse of one household may be the best way to understand what it means to be poor in Kyevaluki. Beatrice Kathui has five surviving children, the eldest of whom is now twenty. Her biggest problem is obtaining funds for school fees. For income, they have sixteen coffee trees and hope to plant one hundred, but so far, these yield little cash. In any case, the household has less than 2 acres, providing little opportunity to extend the fields. Mr. Kathui, who is unemployed, living at home, and in poor health, does not seek casual labor.

Mrs. Kathui engages in four kinds of activities to secure cash income in addition to the meager earnings from the coffee. First, she sells bananas. She takes approximately twenty bunches per year to market to sell by herself or to a trader, for returns of Ksh 30 per bunch. Second, she makes baskets. She can make one per week, for which she earns Ksh 25, with costs of Ksh 4 per basket. Her earnings from baskets are roughly Ksh 80. Third, she works as a casual laborer cultivating other people's farms for Ksh 15 per day. In the dry season she works only four or five times per month, unlike her schedule during the rainy season, when she works daily. Finally, she cuts firewood to sell, bringing in Ksh 10 per bundle. The household has neither a cow nor goats; it has only chickens.

Mrs. Kathui worries because the parcel of land is small for her four sons, who are entitled to inherit it. The prohibitively high school fees (about Ksh 5,000 per student each year), prevent her from paying for her sons' secondary school education. Thus there is no opportunity for them to learn new income-earning skills. She feels acutely the pressures of insufficient land, the inability to educate her children, and inadequate employment opportunities.

GENDER AND LIVELIHOOD SYSTEMS

Evidence from both Mbusyani and Kyevaluki suggests that men's and women's responsibilities in the livelihood system are changing in the direction of greater flexibility and complementarity. The changes are linked with the pragmatic requirements of daily life related to both economic and environmental constraints; new technologies; and the level of women's education. Men are being pulled out of the community by pressures to earn a wage; therefore, by default, more burdens and responsibilities are placed on the women. These circumstances have ramifications within both the household and the community.

Within the Household

Though responsibilities for men and women are changing, women continue to have primary responsibility for meeting the family's basic needs for food, water, and fuel. The husband's responsibility is to provide the home and to generate sufficient income to pay for school fees and major capital expenditures.

The woman is the main producer of food for household consumption in Mbusyani and Kyevaluki, as in most of Kenya. Apart from these agricultural responsibilities, she also attends to her traditional tasks of caring for the children, housekeeping, fetching water, and gathering fuelwood. In Mbusyani about half of the households are managed by women whose husbands are away seeking employment or working in other towns such as Nairobi or Machakos. This situation adds to the woman's burden, as it leaves her with the entire responsibility of daily management of household and farm.

These responsibilities are complicated by the fact that many households have more than one parcel of land scattered within the sublocation. This is an important strategy for diversifying risk, yet the time spent to reach these parcels, which are often tiny, has a negative impact on labor allocation for food production. Some plots are as much as 30–45 minutes away from the homestead.

Moreover, the women work with rudimentary tools on modestly productive land. Very few households have sufficient land for using fallowing techniques. Although aware of the benefits, they can no longer afford to let the land lay fallow because of the small size of holdings. They do, however, rotate crops to improve productivity, and they use animal fertilizers, although they have access to relatively little. Commercial fertilizer is purchased from the coffee cooperative primarily for coffee trees, not food crops.

Most households do not produce enough food to sustain themselves fully and must purchase food for some portion of the year. Coffee returns are scant, and the majority of households have limited outside sources of income. In fact, only 42 percent of the respondents in Mbusyani and 26 percent of those in Kyevaluki indicated that their households benefited from a major monthly cash contribution to household expenses. Food purchases and school fees are the two major household expenditures.

Small, scattered holdings, insufficient agricultural yields for the family, and poor returns on coffee force many women and men to seek employment as casual agricultural laborers. In Mbusyani and Kyevaluki about 40 percent of the men seek such work; among women, 40 percent in Kyevaluki and 24 percent in Mbusyani do so.

In the past, the households of Mbusyani and Kyevaluki had larger holdings, practiced patterns of shifting cultivation, and kept many more animals to provide milk and meat for the diet, as well as fertilizer to increase soil productivity. Population pressures and the privatization of land no longer permit this system to function. One consequence of these changing land use patterns is a food and water crisis directly linked to soil deterioration and deforestation. Women in both communities must walk long distances in search of water during the dry season. With little natural vegetation and little afforestation practiced in the past, a shortage of fuelwood is now a problem faced by most homesteads.

Men who possess sufficient land and have no regular employment outside the farm concentrate their efforts on coffee cultivation. Those with small parcels and no employment seek casual labor—for example, building terraces on other people's land. Both men and women constitute the labor force revolving around coffee production—manuring, pruning, picking, and transporting to the factory. It is unusual for men to work on food production or soil conservation; women, who make up the main labor force in soil conservation, work on the family's land.

Some women are assuming entirely new responsibilities because their husbands work outside the community. They may, for example, handle the arrangements with the coffee cooperative, including collecting coffee payments, and they may hire and manage laborers for their farms. Management of cattle is another arena of transition. In the past, men in this region took care of the cattle herds. With the increasing pressure for land and the concomitant shift to settled agriculture, with its emphasis on coffee production, the men who do not migrate are no longer as actively involved in livestock raising. The cattle are increasingly being managed by women.

In addition, technology is altering the customary allocation of responsibilities. Men have rarely engaged in fetching water, a responsibility that has traditionally been relegated to women and children, who carry water containers on their heads or backs. Today, in Kyevaluki, where water sources are distant, one can occasionally see men loading water for the household into donkey carts.

Finally, the process of decisionmaking is similarly undergoing noticeable change. One woman remarked, "In the past, women had no say in what decisions were made, but now I play a role even if it is only consultation." The range of women's decisionmaking power in this community varies greatly, however. Many women must ask their husbands for permission if they wish to cut down a tree, sell a goat, or undertake any noticeable change on the farm, no matter how mundane. Yet others have considerable authority to make decisions concerning household resources.

Household interviews suggest that these changes are linked to the level of the woman's education. The more highly educated the woman, the more likely she is to participate in major decisions affecting the household. For the most part, women who had completed Form 3 or Form 4 expressed self-confidence about their roles within the home and the strategies for collaborative decisionmaking between husband and wife. For Mbusyani this figure represents 8 percent of households; for Kyevaluki, 2 percent. Some women who completed Form 2 also have growing self-confidence. See Figure 5.2 for a comparison of completed educational levels for women in households surveyed in Mbusyani and Kyevaluki.

Changing Rights, Access, and Control in Regard to Land

The woman's livelihood and that of her family depend on the land, yet insecure land tenure and lack of entitlements, including rights and control of land, characterize their legal relationship to the land.[29] Historically, women have had use rights guaranteed to them by community tradition, but with the privatization of land and the introduction of registration and land titles, these informal arrangements have no legal binding.[30] Land is held in the name of the head of the household, and in all but a few cases this is the husband. If the husband is deceased, his widow(s) may hold the title, but this situation is normally regarded as temporary until the widow's sons come of age. As Staudt observes, "Many indigenous norms legitimize women's control over aspects of their work. The additional layer of male authority represented in the modern state redefined women's relationship to men such that resources were channeled to men and men were overwhelmingly provided the voice in authoritative decisionmaking. The state has institutionalized—even subsidized—men's more privileged access to capital and land."[31] Few women own land registered under their own names. Those who do are usually widowed. Divorced women are not granted land as part of a settlement.

Nzioki describes this situation starkly: "The new land reform has reduced the women to a state of dependency on those who control the land (the men)

Figure 5.2   Completed Educational Levels for Women in Mbusyani and Kyevaluki

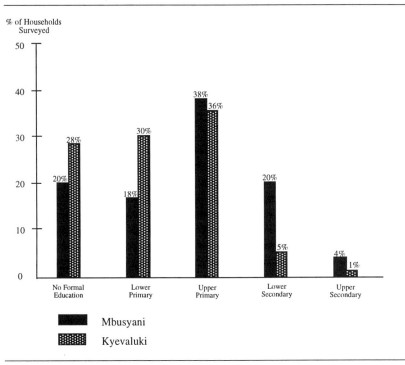

Note: N = 200 (100 each sublocation).

---

and this is very unfortunate particularly taking into consideration that they provide the bulk of agricultural labour in the country."[32] Without ownership, women are unable to obtain credit for tools, equipment, and other inputs necessary to increase food production. Land is the only major resource, and without land to serve as security in acquiring loans under current arrangements, women will have difficulty improving their agricultural output.

For the most part, women in Mbusyani and Kyevaluki do not perceive that their customary rights are legally and formally nonexistent. They have confidence in their status as wives in the household and in their husbands' fairness concerning land issues. Only occasionally, as in the case of divorce or conflicts with co-wives, do women indicate an instance of unfair land allocation. They generally have confidence in the justice of an administrative system that protects them should they need to approach the assistant chief for adjudication of a household land dispute. Most believe that their husbands would consult them before the sale of land. In cases where the wife is not consulted, the present-day law allows the woman to request the chief of the area to stop the sale.

As mentioned, in the past women never had control of land; they merely had management responsibilities for small portions allocated to them for production of food for the household. Now, however, many women are in charge of managing the farm. Ironically, the same woman manager rarely has control of the returns from commercial crop production. Profits from the sale of coffee and cattle remain largely in the hands of men. Most women make decisions regarding small amounts of cash on a regular basis; the decisions on larger sums are usually made by the husband but are increasingly made jointly by husband and wife. Ultimately, ownership and control over land and its resources continues to reside in male hands.

COMMUNITY RESPONSES TO
CHANGING RESOURCE CONDITIONS

The institutions of Mbusyani and Kyevaluki reflect the changes taking place in this region as well as the subtle differences between the two sublocations. Within the last three decades, enormous changes have occurred in both these communities primarily through the privatization of land. As referred to earlier, these changes include (1) the transfer of virtually all common lands to private ownership; (2) a widening rich–poor gap within the community; (3) increasing male out-migration; and (4) an increase in the numbers of women functioning as de facto heads of household.

It is therefore not surprising that women are playing key roles in building community infrastructure. Specifically, to use Moser's terminology, the women have a triple role—in production, reproduction, and community management.[33] They are engaged in activities that improve community resource access and use and provide new benefits to the households within the community.

More than that, women are building community organizations, some of which are becoming institutionalized and strengthening the institutional fabric of the local community. Although such organizations are present in both communities, under the circumstances of less pressure on land and less male out-migration in Kyevaluki, they tend to be not as widespread as in Mbusyani.

These are important changes, central to issues of sustainable development at the local level. Until now, development planners and NGOs have not fully incorporated them into their planning strategies. True, they have taken note of specific activities and have offered support for specific projects, but the overall scope and relevance of institutional change has not been grasped.

Local Institutions

The household interviews, key informant interviews, and the survey reveal a range of institutions and organizations operating within both communities. These included the Kenya Africa National Union (KANU), Kenya's political party, which has become increasingly important throughout Kenya at the local level; the Coffee Cooperative, which is the sole institution through which farmers are able to process and sell coffee beans and to obtain the necessary inputs for production; the 4-K Club, active in some of the schools; and the KANU Youth Wing, which plays a role with teenagers and young adults.

Of particular importance to community resource management are the *mwethya* groups, which in recent years have become key actors on resource issues. Results of the survey carried out in Mbusyani and Kyevaluki show that in 60 percent of the households one person or more belongs to a *mwethya* group.

For many generations, the Akamba people had used *mwethya* groups, consisting of men and women organized along clan or family lines, to provide emergency assistance or perform special needed functions such as house building or clearing new fields. The custom of *mwethya* had slipped away during the colonial era and was replaced with a more formal system of work groups and conscripted labor units such as those coerced into soil conservation programs.[34]

Beginning in the mid-1970s, the *mwethya* tradition has been reinvigorated and transformed. In some communities, such as Mbusyani, the groups have become the backbone of resource management initiatives. Each group consists of approximately twenty to forty villagers (mostly women), usually from the same cluster of *shambas* within a village. Today they are not necessarily organized along clan lines but instead as households with a common interest.

Factors Shaping Levels of Group Activity

Community organizations in Mbusyani are noticeably more active than those in Kyevaluki. Close examination of the two communities suggests six explanatory factors for the difference. Three of these factors are contextual circumstances characteristic of Mbusyani, conditions that will likely affect Kyevaluki in another decade or two. The remaining three are instrumental factors that help explain the greater involvement in local institutions and the greater effectiveness of these groups in one location than in the other.

Background factors.   First, the impact of commodity production on land rights is greater in Mbusyani than in Kyevaluki. Farm sizes are larger in Kyevaluki than in Mbusyani. Survey data reveal that the average landholding size around the homestead is 15 acres, and many households have other pieces of land within and outside Kyevaluki.[35] The fragmentation of land in Mbusyani has proceeded at a more rapid pace than in Kyevaluki. The quality of land is somewhat better in the former than in the latter, and it has attracted more buyers from outside. Thus, the whole process of privatization and subdivision of holdings is moving along more rapidly in Mbusyani than in Kyevaluki, despite their proximity one to another.

In addition, there is greater stratification in Mbusyani than in Kyevaluki, with 7 percent of the sample having more than three thousand coffee trees, whereas the survey revealed that only 1 percent of the Kyevaluki sample was in that category. The mode for number of trees per household in Kyevaluki is 200–300, which brings paltry returns with current prices. In Mbusyani, the typical farmer does somewhat better, with 500–600 trees, grown also under better conditions and therefore giving higher yields. In both communities, farming households struggle to increase income from commodity production. Yet their returns are limited, and their expenses both for production and for household maintenance, including education, loom large.

One might suggest that Kyevaluki represents the "last of the old," with some traditional options regarding extensive agriculture and cattle not foreclosed to all. Mbusyani is the "first generation of the new," with dependence on a cash crop and intensive agriculture along with high levels of integration into the cash economy. This process affects women's rights to land. It means that women, as the chief food producers, need to think about ways to improve yields under conditions of intensive, as opposed to extensive, agricultural production. This is particularly the case in Mbusyani. Women perceive group activities and group ownership as a way to increase their access to new technologies and new forms of capital investment. Under present circumstances, acquiring new land is virtually impossible, and there is little or no transfer of earnings from the coffee crop into improving food crop production or into other investments that can provide the household, particularly the women, with spendable income.

Second, many of the households have precarious livelihoods, operating under circumstances that keep them perched on the edge of serious deprivation. Of the households chosen randomly for the interviews, over 50 percent were characterized as poor or medium poor in Kyevaluki, and 40 percent were in the same categories in Mbusyani.

More often in Mbusyani than in Kyevaluki, women are managing the farms while their husbands are elsewhere. These women have learned how to increase their access to the factors of production by sharing the only element over which they have control—their labor. They have taken some extremely arduous jobs, such as digging bench terraces, and execute them in ways that soften the work load through group effort and permit the accomplishment of major work responsibilities at the time of peak seasonal labor requirements.

Third, educational levels and general awareness of new opportunities are, overall, greater in Mbusyani than in Kyevaluki. Mbusyani has had a day secondary school offering all four forms since 1975. Kyevaluki is just now introducing Form 3 into the sublocation. The survey revealed that twice as many young people are leaving Mbusyani for educational opportunities outside the sublocation than are leaving Kyevaluki. In Mbusyani, 45 percent of male respondents had completed some secondary school; in Kyevaluki, 32 percent had done so. Forty-one percent of women had attended some secondary school in Mbusyani, whereas only 8 percent had done so in Kyevaluki.

Instrumental factors. Attributes of political and administrative leadership are of great importance. Leadership styles reflect the different socioeconomic circumstances and resulting attitudes existing within the two sublocations. The combinations of ecology, population pressure, and new arrivals in Mbusyani have led to a more modern community, one with different expectations from a more traditional one. The leadership in Mbusyani reflects these new values and assumptions. The process, of course, is interactive. Leadership may reflect community attitudes; it also plays a key role in shaping the effectiveness of local institutions. In Mbusyani, promoting development is a priority. The assistant chief for the past ten years is hardworking, dedicated to the welfare of his community, and highly respected and appreciated by the residents. His interest in promoting development within his community is unquestionable.

The leadership style of the assistant chief in Mbusyani reflects the people's interest in development and change. He perceives his role as promoting development by listening, mobilizing, generating ideas, responding to the interests expressed within the community, and working closely with the people. Moreover, the assistant chief is regular and attentive in his availability to members of his community. His open-door policy extends to all, and there is evidence of easy, informal communication. Chairwomen of the groups in that sublocation feel comfortable entering his office to talk over problems of the groups or activities or plans. The assistant chief also makes a point of attending activities and events related to these groups. He is quite prepared to set aside an afternoon to visit a group working at an erosion control site, to welcome guests at a formal meeting, or to sit with a group to work out the details of writing a proposal for funding. He is, as one respondent observed, "in one hand with the people."

Circumstances shaping leadership styles in Kyevaluki are quite different. Within a more traditional context, the assistant chief is expected to be an authority figure. His job is not so much to listen, to shape, and to mobilize but to inform and to maintain discipline and control. Earning the confidence and respect of the people in the community and mobilizing them for development activities is perceived as less important than establishing authority.

The assistant chief in Kyevaluki has been in the position for only three years. Within this more traditional context, he is clearly interested in fostering development for the sublocation. For example, he recently established an award ceremony for effective teaching and for high marks in the national examinations. He is very much aware that Kyevaluki has been lagging in comparison with the other sublocations in the division, and he wants to move the community forward.

Aspects of this process are made more difficult in Kyevaluki by friction among some of the village headmen who reflect a somewhat authoritarian set of expectations. There are difficulties in moving a community from expecting an assistant chief to serve as an authority figure to anticipating leadership that emerges from and works with the people. Under such circumstances it is difficult to achieve unity and a sense of common purpose.

In sum, the people of Mbusyani are demanding enthusiasm, commitment, and accessibility. They want—and receive—vigorous participation in the activities of organizations within the community. The people of Kyevaluki are more prepared to accept traditional styles of leadership. In important ways, these varying responses relate to gender roles in the two communities and the emergence of women as active participants in the public sphere in Mbusyani.

Group leadership is a second important instrumental factor. Leadership from the community is a significant factor in the effectiveness of local organizations. In Mbusyani, women leaders play a vital role in community groups. These women tend to be in their forties, educated to upper primary or lower secondary school, and at the higher end of the economic spectrum. They have ideas and energy. They are not shy about seeking outside support and information. They lack capital and some skills, but they are hardworking and eager to seize new opportunities.

In Mbusyani, thirteen groups engage in a wide variety of activities, including agricultural tasks such as growing and selling beans, onions, potatoes, cabbages, and greens and commercial activities such as making and selling honey, paraffin, bricks, and baskets. Some manage a maize mill; others have built a social hall. Almost all groups undertake resource management activities, including bench terracing and tree planting. In Kyevaluki there are six such *mwethya* groups. All share agricultural work on each other's farms. One group, Ivuuwo, has been involved in tree planting and has bought a plot for a meeting place and to put up a shop. More typical is Kwakathule Women's Group, which started in 1977, has sixty members, raises money by hiring out collectively as an agricultural labor force, and offers traditional dancing for special occasions. The Kyevaluki groups differ in number, scope, and breadth of activities from those in Mbusyani.

The third instrumental factor involves the institutional linkages emerging in Mbusyani. They can be observed in the Mwangano Women's Group, which brings together the thirteen different *mwethya* groups to manage the maize grinding mill. Some of the activities of churches in conjunction with *mwethya* groups also reveal these linkages. In one instance, the Catholic diocese established a scheme for matching funds for *mwethya* groups. If the group raised Ksh 10,000 for a project, the diocese would match it with an additional Ksh 10,000. One group used the funds to purchase Ksh 20,000 worth of maize, which it then resold at a small profit. Members rented a shop in Mbusyani for this purpose. With the profits, they are now engaged in building their own shop.

Most denominations are not involved in resource management activities, nor do they have any sort of coherent development policy for the areas in which they work. However, there is potential for constructive collaboration based on a growing institutional infrastructure. The *mwethya* groups are beginning to recognize and take advantage of this opportunity.

TRENDS IN MBUSYANI AND KYEVALUKI

Links to and Dependence on the Outside World

Four observations are especially pertinent to resource management, gender, and community organization in these two communities as they head toward the next century. Probably the most notable trend for both sublocations is the unalterable way their linkages with the broader political and economic systems are growing. One facet of these linkages is the increasing need for and reliance on cash as rural residents get drawn into and become dependent on the cash economy, a phenomenon more widespread in Mbusyani than in Kyevaluki. The vast majority of households in Mbusyani and Kyevaluki struggle to grow coffee to pay school fees and meet other requirements of modern life. The price per kilo that each farmer in Mbusyani or Kyevaluki obtains for his or her coffee is determined not by markets at Kakuyuni or even Nairobi but in London or Washington. The welfare of those households is shaped by, for example, the drought in Brazil or strife in Colombia. Returns on their most significant commercial crop vary according to events taking place far away and well beyond their control.

The impact of other international factors, such as structural adjustment, can be felt even in the households of Kyevaluki and Mbusyani. Pressures on countries such as Kenya to reduce social services and keep expenditures down affect the adequacy of educational opportunities and health services in rural communities around the world. The majority of residents in Mbusyani and Kyevaluki note that their purchasing power has dropped drastically in the past few years. Most of the respondents observed that they do not have enough income to meet their basic requirements and pay school fees for their children. The decline in value of their currency and the drop in world coffee prices have made life difficult for residents of these two communities, most of whom rely on coffee as their main source of cash income.

Population Pressures on Degraded Landscapes

Population in these communities has been increasing steadily since independence. The natural growth rate is over 3 percent annually and seems likely to continue at or near this rate in the immediate future. Families are large, often with six to eight surviving children. The average age of marriage for women and for bearing the first child has been declining. At the same time, the period of time between having children has narrowed since the mid-1950s. Thus, typically, more children are born to each family today than in the past. These children, of course, provide options for the household in terms of a labor pool and diversified livelihood strategy, which the small household does not have. There are, however, important consequences in terms of both customary inheritance patterns and communitywide deterioration of the resource base.

The population increase relates to in-migration and to the combination of high birth rates and low death rates. In the early 1960s, there was substantial in-migration, reflected in a marked increase in land sales and purchases during that period. People have continued to seek new opportunities to purchase land, even in areas of marginal agricultural value such as Mbusyani and Kyevaluki. This has resulted in an increase in human pressure on the natural resource base. Particularly in Mbusyani, the pressures of population growth on smallholdings are apparent in fragmentation and in diminished size of holdings.

Population growth is a serious issue when viewed in the light of finite land and water resources. Fragile soils and eroded hillsides characterize land that is only marginally productive. Vegetation is increasingly destroyed because of the growing population's need for firewood. Intensive cultivation, under current land use practices, along with deforestation, encourages further degradation. There is, for many, a vicious circle of low levels of productivity, low yields, low levels of capital to improve agricultural inputs or technology, and continuing poverty. The immediate consequence of population growth and the degraded landscape can be increased poverty and an allocation of resources for immediate benefits and needs, which quickly exhausts the capacity of the soils, vegetation, and water. In Mbusyani and Kyevaluki, however, people are not unaware of land degradation issues. Through their groups, the women in these communities carry out a variety of projects such as bench terracing and dam rehabilitation to sustain their livelihoods and their landscape. Thus, the picture of population, resources, use, and abuse is complex. Evidence from these two sublocations suggests that community interventions are providing important benefits to all.

A Depressed Economy

A depressed economy affects all households. Most grow coffee, and even the smallest farms allocate a sliver of land to this crop. Yet returns from coffee have not been good and the strategy has serious costs, which can escalate as families remove land from food production to put it into coffee or another cash crop.

Related to these economic issues is the problem of massive rural unemployment. Job opportunities are few in the area, apart from self-employment, which requires capital. Many are able to get only casual work within the farming community. Approximately 70 percent of households surveyed indicated that one person within the household was seeking employment; 25 percent indicated that two or more members of the household were unemployed and seeking work. Lack of employment for people within the sublocations, as well as the difficulties in obtaining it outside the sublocations, results in a lack of cash for a variety of purposes, including more effective and efficient use of the land.

Much irony exists in a situation where employment opportunities are inadequate for the numbers seeking employment and labor is inadequate for increasing food crop production. Given the gender-based division of labor, the

designation of food crops for household consumption as a female responsibility, and the lack of cash for purchasing labor inputs, there is a shortage of labor
at critical times in food crop production. Males generally do not tend crops for
domestic consumption. They work outside the household only for pay. And
most households lack sufficient income to be able to place a priority on em-
ploying outside labor for food crops.

In this context, rural stratification continues apace with marked increases
in land sales and purchases in the 1980s. Figure 5.3 shows the increase in acquisition of land by purchase, rather than inheritance, in Mbusyani and Kyevaluki
in recent decades. Household interviews indicate that the main reason people
sell land is for school fees. With few other sources of income, land sales become a last resort to obtain the education for children, which people believe to
be vitally important for obtaining a salaried position. Most people are just becoming aware that their hopes may be misplaced.

Perhaps this growing awareness contributes to the perceptible discouragement felt in Mbusyani and Kyevaluki. Parents are worried about their children's
future, and young adults are worried about their own future. Though frustration
and anger accompany this sense of malaise, it is alleviated by some encouraging steps.

Attitudinal Changes

One of the promising trends in Mbusyani and Kyevaluki relates to attitudinal
changes. First, there are "generational" and "gender" assumptions and expectations concerning adjustments to new realities. For example, a handful of older
women in both areas, who were not widowed, had their own coffee shares.
They were members of the coffee society, dealt with the necessary arrangements for getting inputs and selling the coffee, and controlled the proceeds
from their sales.

Young women, particularly those with some secondary school education,
are questioning the traditional roles assigned to them. The prospect of early
marriage, early pregnancies, and a life of hard physical work cultivating their
fields, carrying water, and gathering firewood is one they wish, at the very
least, to delay for a few years. They search for other options, have new and
different hopes and dreams, and in some instances pursue them with vigor and
imagination.

Second, in both sublocations but particularly in Mbusyani, there is a growing awareness of the problems and issues that the communities face and an
interest in finding ways to deal with them. The people of Mbusyani demonstrated initiative and perseverance in arranging to attend workshops in a neighboring sublocation, Katheka, and organizing a PRA for themselves.

Finally, one can see emerging capacities to work together. The thirteen
mwethya groups in Mbusyani have organized the management and operation of
a maize grinding mill to service one portion of the community. The Mwangano

---

Figure 5.3   Households Acquiring Land by Purchase of Parcels

---

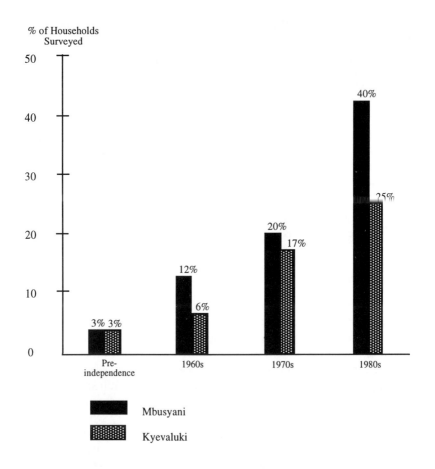

% of Households
Surveyed

Note: N = 200 (100 each sublocation).

Women's Group, the umbrella women's organization, oversees erosion control efforts on the part of the subsidiary groups. The Mbusyani Dam is a major effort on the part of the community to implement water conservation.

The parents of schoolchildren in Kyevaluki organized to implement the first steps of the Village Resource Management Plan by gathering materials for the school water tanks and contributing labor to the development of the roof catchment systems at four schools. These may be small steps, but they represent emerging capabilities on the part of the rural residents of Mbusyani and Kyevaluki.

LEARNING FROM MBUSYANI AND KYEVALUKI

The residents of Mbusyani and Kyevaluki face changing sets of norms and expectations. Gendered responsibilities are becoming somewhat more fluid as men migrate for jobs and as women join the ranks of the educated. In these communities, there are many fragmented families as husbands, sons, and daughters, though particularly men, seek employment elsewhere. Many note a gnawing concern about the numbers of children growing up within communities for whom there will be no land and for whom they fear there will be no jobs. Yet people are aware of new opportunities and challenges. Their attitudes reflect, among other things, changes in both generational and gender perspectives on rights, obligations, and accepted behavior patterns.

Evidence from Mbusyani and Kyevaluki indicates that men's and women's responsibilities are changing in the direction of greater flexibility. Yet there is a growing disjuncture between changing responsibilities and work load for women and their legal status. Cultural, social, and economic practices are being adapted to the reality of male out-migration and the exigencies that many households face. The legal system, land tenure, and other regulations have not been modified accordingly. A women's livelihood, and that of her family, depends on the land, yet insecure land tenure and lack of rights and control of land characterize a woman's legal relationship to the land.

Privatization of land has led to the transfer of virtually all common lands to private ownership and a widening rich–poor gap within these communities, with enormous implications for the work load, responsibilities, and levels of deprivation of women and their families, especially in the poorest households. These households have particularly relied on access to common forests and fields for food, fuel, and fodder.

Water is widely perceived in both communities as the critical resource issue. In the dry season, women may spend as much as three to four hours daily walking and queuing for water. In addition, access to fuelwood is a rapidly escalating problem. For both these resources, awareness of shortages and problems by community members is acute; household and community action of a preventative sort has begun in Mbusyani and, so far, is minimal in Kyevaluki.

The people of Mbusyani and Kyevaluki face complex challenges, for which they can draw on their personal resources of energy, determination, self-reliance, and a capacity for dealing with tough problems. They do, however, need accountable leadership, a supportive political environment, and access to some technical and financial resources, all of which will make a different future possible. Assisting them in their endeavor to build this different future requires knowledge, flexibility, and commitment on the part of the government, NGOs, and international agencies. As this analysis of rural change in Mbusyani and Kyevaluki demonstrates, it also involves an understanding of how gender-based responsibilities shape and are shaped by rural livelihood systems.

NOTES

1. Tiffen, "Productivity and Environmental Conservation"; Tiffen (ed.), *Environmental Change and Dryland Management;* Tiffen and Mortimore, "Environment, Population Growth and Productivity."

2. Tiffen et al., *More People, Less Erosion,* p. 13.

3. Tiffen and Mortimore, "Environment, Population Growth and Productivity," p. 361.

4. Tiffen, "Productivity and Environmental Conservation," p. 207.

5. Tiffen and Mortimore, "Environment, Population Growth and Productivity."

6. Tiffen, "Productivity and Environmental Conservation," p. 221.

7. O'Keefe and Wisner (eds.), *Land Use and Development.*

8. Mung'ala and Openshaw, "Estimation of Present and Future Demand for Woodfuel."

9. Mbithi and Barnes, *The Spontaneous Settlement Problem in Kenya*; Mbithi and Wisner, "Drought in Eastern Kenya."

10. Ondiege, "Local Coping Strategies"; Thomas-Slayter and Ford, "Water, Soils, Food, and Rural Development"; Thomas-Slayter, "Politics, Class and Gender in African Resource Management."

11. Rocheleau et al., "Environment, Development, Crisis and Crusade."

12. Rocheleau et al., "Single Perspectives on Separate Realities."

13. Ibid., p. 61.

14. Ondiege, "Local Coping Strategies," p. 129.

15. Ibid., p. 133.

16. Rocheleau et al., "Single Perspectives on Separate Realities," p. 63.

17. Ibid., p. 64.

18. Sen, "Gender and Cooperative Conflicts."

19. Bahemuka and Tiffen, "Akamba Institutions and Development, 1930–90"; Ondiege, "Local Coping Strategies"; Rocheleau, "Gender, Resource Management and the Rural Landscape"; Thomas-Slayter, "Politics, Class and Gender in African Resource Management."

20. Ondiege, "Local Coping Strategies," p. 130.

21. As mentioned in Chapter 3, the Akamba are alternatively called Kamba by some scholars.

22. Thomas-Slayter and Ford, "Water, Soils, Food, and Rural Development," p. 258.

23. Ondiege, "Local Coping Strategies."

24. Jaetzold and Schmidt, *Farm Management Handbook of Kenya,* p. 158.

25. Downing et al., *Coping with Drought in Kenya,* p. 17.

26. Munro, *Colonial Rule and the Kamba.*

27. Silberfein, "Differential Development in Machakos District."

28. Government of Kenya National Environment Secretariat et al., *Participatory Rural Appraisal Handbook.*

29. Bryson, "Women and Agriculture in Sub-Saharan Africa"; Davison (ed.), *Agriculture, Women, and Land*; Guyer, "Women in the Rural Economy"; Hunt, *The Impending Crisis in Kenya.*

30. Nzioki, "Effects of Land Tenure Reform"; Pala Okeyo, "Daughters of the Lakes and Rivers"; Rocheleau, "Gender, Resource Management and the Rural Landscape."

31. Staudt, "Uncaptured or Unmotivated?" p. 50.

32. Nzioki, "Effects of Land Tenure Reform," p. 63.

33. Moser, "Gender Planning in the Third World," p. 1.

34. Thomas-Slayter and Ford, "Water, Soils, Food, and Rural Development."

35. PRA survey data, 1989.

6

People, Property, Poverty, and Parks: A Story of Men, Women, Water, and Trees at Pwani

Dianne Rocheleau, Karen Schofield-Leca, Njoki Mbuthi

Pwani is a recently established resettlement village in Njoro Division, Nakuru District, Kenya. The resource and social stresses in this semiarid region also occur throughout Kenya and Africa as a whole. The study documents the gendered responses of the newly settled residents to their surroundings and the development of social and environmental conflicts between the community and the adjacent park. We analyze the ways individuals, households, and the community at large are influenced by and affect their local environments and the way their decisions are shaped by structures beyond their borders.

The story of Pwani represents the experience of recent settlers—people making a home in what was once another group's homeland and habitat. Pwani is located in Kenya's Rift Valley Province, on the edge of Lake Nakuru Park (see Map 6.1), on a swath of savanna that was once home to the Maasai people and their herds. It was settled by a colonial rancher-farmer in the first half of this century and, later, in the first decade after independence (1963), by share-holders in a land-buying company; this form of land acquisition contributed substantially to migration and the dramatic population growth rate in Nakuru District (6 percent between 1969 and 1979).[1] Although Pwani itself has not been directly involved, since 1992 the region has experienced violent clashes over land between ethnic and political groups.

Most of the current five thousand residents of Pwani purchased their land in 1969.[2] However, not until two recent waves of settlement, in 1976 and 1989, did they clear scattered trees and forest, establish farms, and move into the area. This experience is typical of many such settlements in that the shareholders bought into a legally constituted land acquisition group. They purchased lands made available by the newly independent government to hundreds of thousands of landless and near-landless people whose families had been displaced from or crowded out of their traditional highland homelands by colonial settlers and commercial interests.[3]

Map 6.1   Nakuru District

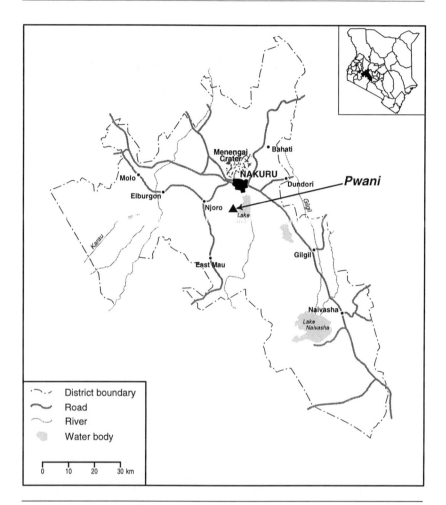

Source: Adapted with permission from Jaetzhold and Schmidt.

Given Pwani's origin and location, it shares many of the problems faced by subdivided settlements and also represents a condition typical of park periphery communities around the world. Pwani is unusual in that the population consists almost entirely of government forest service employees and their families, most of whom have spent their childhood in intensive farming areas of the highlands and several years in laboring for wages, farming, herding, and gathering in upland forests. In spite of these connections and their indirect influence on the formation of Pwani, the proximity of the park and people's employment in the forestry sector have not played a formal role in settlement, land use, and resource management planning in the community. Land was allocated and settled in Pwani as if it had been surrounded on all sides by other farming communities and as if its residents had never worked as foresters and forest farmers. Yet both of these features have affected resource management, with differing implications for men and women.

Pwani is also representative of settlement communities that have experienced dramatic changes in land cover, land use, resource management, and gender division of labor, within a single generation.[4] People at Pwani have moved from upland farms, to forest workplace and subsistence farms, to family farms at Pwani, and now to split urban–rural households with the rural root in Pwani and a branch in the city, plantation, or distant forest workplace. It further typifies settlement communities undergoing a rapid transition in the gender division of labor, knowledge, rights, and responsibilities—on farm, in the city, and between rural and urban domains.

Several methodologies were used to carry out this research. First, the researchers took part in a Participatory Rural Appraisal (PRA) in June 1990 (see the Appendix). The linkage of this case to a regular PRA provided an opportunity to learn about gender within the context of the community's history, its future aspirations, and its resource management and development problems. Government extension workers, representatives of NGOs, and university professors utilized a variety of techniques for gathering spatial, historical, institutional, and social data.[5] During the course of the PRA, residents provided the researchers and development officers with a sense of their community's character, its current situation, and its possible futures. The people of Pwani also had a chance to reflect on their own history, their somewhat precarious present, and their prospects for sustainable livelihoods, individually and as a community. The initial household and group interviews outlined the history, geography, and community organizations of Pwani, the various kinds of households, and the shape of people's daily lives. The second phase of the PRA focused on problems and opportunities related to resource management at household and community levels and the development of a Village Resource Management Plan (VRMP).

As both PRA participants and observers, the authors were able to interact with community leaders and residents to assess their resource management priorities and to learn more about the ways gender shapes the natural resource management choices of Pwani residents. Two researchers returned to Pwani in September 1990 to pursue gender-focused research on three aspects of resource management:

- What is happening to the resource base in the community?
- How are these changes affecting men's and women's use of, access to, and control of resources at household and community levels?
- How are people coping with and adapting to these changes?

Residents contacted during the first visit updated the researchers as to how local activities had progressed in the interim. A series of discussions with women, men, and youth about the daily activities in their households identified the pressures they face in making day-to-day and long-term decisions regarding scarce resources. In sharing their thoughts and experiences, they provided detailed knowledge of the linkages among resource issues, as well as the creativity and initiative needed to improve their life conditions.

We formulated a short, focused survey to gain a sense of the variety and concurrence of opinions and conditions among the residents. Local youth administered the survey to a random sample of 160 adults throughout the community, representing approximately 32 percent of the households. Their participation in the survey prompted the young enumerators to form a youth group, to more effectively influence the future of Pwani, and to share the trials and triumphs in their own lives.

COMMUNITY PROFILE

The Land

A distinctive feature of Pwani is its boundary with a national park covering just over 200 square kilometers, which is legally impenetrable but practically permeable.[6] The Nakuru National Park represents a popular site for international tourists (over one hundred thousand per year) because of its easy access from Nairobi (a two- to three-hour drive on paved highways), the dramatic backdrop of volcanic features in the landscape, and the scenic quality of the lake's world-famous population of pink flamingos.[7] International wildlife interests value the park and the lake as a refuge for endangered species, including a population of five rhinoceros under armed guard at the park rangers' station.[8]

Like many of the Rift Valley lakes, Nakuru is under increasing pressure from a combination of natural and human causes. The lake level is falling, alkalinity is increasing, and, as a result, both the aquatic and lakeshore plant and animal communities are changing. The flamingo population is declining because of the scarcity of food (specific types of plankton) in the lake, and some of the mammal populations have been plagued by fodder shortages and specific nutritional deficiencies due to their confinement in such a limited area.[9] At the same time, the surrounding town, industrial sites, and commercial farms have diverted clean water and have dumped polluted water into the lake, with unknown consequences.[10] Poachers have also degraded the plant and animal communities within the forest and grassland of the surrounding park.[11]

This combination of pressures has led national and international wildlife activists to consider the park as an important and vulnerable place under threat. They have identified local people at Pwani and other park boundary communities as threats to the ecological and commercial viability of the park. Encroachment by squatters into the park has already claimed over 1,800 hectares of its land.[12] The impact of these pressures, however, is not one way. The animals from the park (baboons, monkeys, impala, waterbuck, gazelles, warthogs, and eland) take a toll on the adjacent farmlands. Farmers complain of raids by marauding animals that eat, trample, and uproot their crops. Though this is not representative of the region, it is a concern common to park boundary communities the world over, from Yellowstone Park in the United States to the Maasai Mara Reserve in southern Kenya.

Pwani is situated in agroecological zone 4, a semiarid region designated as marginal for agricultural use. The dark brown and grayish clay soils are dry, best suited for cattle ranching and grazing small stock.[13] After the unreliable long (March–April) or short (November–December) rains—760 millimeters total in good years—crops bring shades of green to the landscape. During the dry seasons and the region's frequent droughts, only dispersed *Acacia* and *Euphorbia* trees punctuate the gently sloping land with green. Most of the dry forest (primarily the Acacia–Themeda association),[14] gallery forest, derived savanna, and bushland has been cleared for agricultural activities.

Pwani's 600 hectares are divided into smallholdings, on average 1 hectare each.[15] The farms consist of small grazing areas, a home compound, and one cropped plot. Most households in Pwani also have a few goats or one to two draft animals, and some households keep milk cows.

The village is adjacent to the western fence of the park. The nearest tarmac road lies some 20 kilometers away; Nakuru is an additional 10 kilometers beyond. Few public vehicles attempt the trip over the deeply rutted tracks leading into the village; the rare *matatu* (public bus or taxi) cost Ksh 20 in 1991 (a day's wage for local casual laborers—Ksh 20 converted to less than $1 at 30:1 in 1991). Women with produce for market or with children needing medical care must hope for a private vehicle to happen along.

Approaching Pwani from the south, from the chief's offices in Naishi 10 kilometers away, one first encounters the community dam—a poorly maintained facility used for doing laundry, watering livestock, bathing children, and fetching water for domestic use. The barbed-wire fence surrounding the dam is broken in several places, permitting goats and cattle to wander in at will. There are several trees on its eastern banks, however, which provide a sheltered spot where young men often gather.

The center of Pwani—at the jog of the main road transecting the village—is marked by some two dozen small wooden structures: retail shops; *hotelis* (small tea shops); a few repair shops; and several stalls set up for women who bring their beans or vegetables from the *shamba* (farm) to the marketplace. Behind the shops is an open area, shaded by several trees, where the chief's *barazas* (public meetings) are held.

In the opposite direction from the market center lies the Keriko Primary School, the only educational institution in the village. Farther along are Pwani's churches: Presbyterian, Church of the Province of Kenya (CPK), Full Gospel,

Apostolic Faith, and Free Mission. The Catholic church is the site of the weekly mobile clinic. At the crest of the hill, at the geographic center of Pwani, is the community cattle dip. Beyond this lie *shambas*, then the road continues for 25 kilometers to Nakuru.

History of Pwani

The area that is now Pwani was once Maasai grazing land. The first European settler, Captain Harris, arrived in 1911. He used a vast tract of land south of Nakuru to graze his herds of cattle and sheep. Only the Kenyans working on the ranch were permitted to live on the land, and their access to its resources was severely restricted.

After Kenya gained its independence in 1963, Harris's land was divided and sold to several settlers, who eventually sold it to the Mutukanio Land Buying Company in 1969.[16] Individuals throughout Kenya purchased shares in this company, responding to increasing land use pressure in high-potential zones. According to the usual procedure for such land purchases,[17] the entire tract was divided into plots of equal size, which were then allocated to shareholders by lottery. Whether a given household acquired 1 hectare of fertile valley land or a rocky windswept ridge was left to the luck of the draw. Some shareholders traded plots among themselves to gain property near their family or friends. Land demarcation in the area began in 1971 as part of the government's land adjudication program.

As in many of the shareholder settlements in the Rift Valley, the majority of the shareholders were Kikuyu people from the highlands who had lived in well-watered areas and were familiar with fairly intensive cropping and live-stock management systems. In this respect Pwani's condition is typical of a larger process in which near-landless people from well-watered highlands have moved to drier lowland areas formerly used by themselves or others for graz-ing.[18] Pwani is distinct in that most of the shareholders are part of a larger group of government forest service employees who lived and farmed in highland for-ests near their assigned posts. The government has periodically mandated an end to farming in the forest areas and evicted forest residents during the twenty-five years since independence. This threat of eviction led many forest employ-ees to purchase tracts in Pwani and similar sites. However, their status as forest service employees and an experimental program combining crop cultivation with reforestation efforts[19] spared many of the families from eviction and re-settlement until recently.

As in many settlement schemes, the men undertook the work of clearing the land and building houses, sometimes long before the arrival of their fami-lies. As forest employees, they knew about trees, but as both highland dwellers and foresters they saw dryland savanna trees as weeds on potentially produc-tive cropland. They also saw the savanna trees as capital—not as a form of investment but rather as assets that could be readily liquidated to finance house construction, other infrastructure (e.g., fences, cattle pens), and purchase of livestock and agricultural implements. As foresters they were also well connected to arrange for the sale of timber, poles, and charcoal from the trees on their land.

Although the women valued dry forest trees, shrubs, and herbs for fuelwood, food, fodder, medicine, fiber, oils, and dyes, most of them were not present during the period when their husbands made decisions about forest clearing and land preparation. Moreover, many forest employee households cleared and "improved" their plots as investment properties and back-up options that they hoped they would never need to settle. So women's knowledge, women's interests, and subsistence needs were divorced from the development of plots as investment property. In this commercial context the felled trees were a transitory bonus to be cashed in, whereas live trees had no intrinsic investment value and carried a negative value in terms of opportunity cost to agriculture.

The largest surge of settlers came in 1989, when many current Pwani residents were expelled from the forest reserves. The reluctance of shareholders to move onto their holdings, even to the present day, is an indication of the poor quality of the environment in Pwani. Families arrive in Pwani as they are forced, either by authorities or intolerable circumstances, to relocate.

Not all residents who come to Pwani stay, however. Like many rural communities throughout the world, Pwani is characterized by a high proportion of women-headed households or women-managed households with absentee wage laborer men. The exodus of men to the city in search of cash income has characterized most rural communities in Kenya since the middle of the century. This trend has been particularly pronounced among the Kikuyu, who were displaced from their homes in highland farming areas and were among the most heavily represented in the wage labor force at the time of independence.[20] The migration of male wage laborers has resulted in a new spatial division of labor by gender. Women remain in rural areas to manage small farms (often too small for subsistence under existing technology and economy), and men move to urban areas or plantations to earn cash. Remittances may flow both ways as women contribute food to men and men send cash, tin roofing, purchased inputs, or consumer goods home. The trend is shifting, however. Young men and women, too, seek jobs in the cities and towns, but their opportunities are limited, and many are employed for short periods of time, only to return to their parents' homes.

Pwani has grown considerably since 1971, when there were only six homesteads, those of cattle workers from Harris's day. From forty-five people in 1974, Pwani's population now stands at five thousand.[21] An average family has eight children, which creates intense land pressure for the rising generation. Social services (such as health facilities and schools), agricultural systems, and the surrounding ecosystem are straining to keep pace with prevailing rates and patterns of growth and movement.

Links to the Outside World

Though relatively isolated, Pwani is nonetheless enmeshed in the economic, social, and political realities that exist beyond its borders. Its very existence as a resettlement village is part of the larger government land utilization and allocation scheme. Government decisions about land use have restricted the residents' access to the forests and game reserves from which they relocated. The Lake Nakuru National Park is both a temptation and a nuisance; it holds many of the plants that the residents were accustomed to exploiting but now cannot, and the protected animals devastate the *shambas* along the fence while foraging for additional food. Knowledge of and exposure to new technologies and social services is limited within Pwani. Although residents are included in government extension services, the relative isolation of the community makes it a low-priority site for extension agents. Most innovations and new ideas from beyond Pwani are introduced by church agencies, most notably the CPK and the Catholic diocese.

GENDER, HOUSEHOLD, AND LIVELIHOOD IN PWANI

Who Lives in Pwani?

In Pwani, economic and resource management activities occur within both the household and the broader community. Most day-to-day decisions are made within the household, and it is at this level that choices and actions most immediately affect family members. Pressured by limited access to a degraded resource pool, families are confronted by frequent changes in the availability and quality of both natural resources and human energies. There is a great need to be flexible and to adapt individual responsibilities to meet the requirements of the entire family unit. Both the economy and the structure of the household set the parameters within which daily resource management decisions are made and implemented.

Household economy and wealth.   Households within the community are relatively homogeneous economically. Distinctions among classes of households are difficult to make as an outside observer; residents, even when specifically asked, don't divide themselves along strictly financial lines. However, during the survey, they noted several key indicators of household wealth: size of landholding, the presence of a water tank, the existence of cash income, and the educational attainment of children.

The most significant characteristic to differentiate households is that of land ownership, which brings secure access to other resources, such as fuel, fodder, and water. Access to the property of others and to public spaces is neither secure nor adequate to meet the needs of most households. Approximately 5 percent of the households in Pwani are landless. Among those owning land, the likelihood of greater affluence increases with the size of the holding, ranging from 0.1 to 4 hectares.

A second indicator of relative wealth is a household water tank. As water is a crucial and scarce resource in Pwani, those who have easier, more reliable access to water are better equipped to make the most of their other productive resources—materials as well as time. Because there are substantial labor and material costs involved in building a water tank, the poorest households rarely have one, whereas the better off sometimes do.

An external source of income—money other than that earned from the sale of basic subsistence crops, such as maize and beans—is a third distinguishing factor. Employment opportunities in Pwani itself are few, and there is strong competition for jobs in urban centers. However, some households in Pwani supplement their farming income with remittances from relatives employed elsewhere in local trading or marketing, and in casual labor both in and out of Pwani. This extra income is used for a variety of purposes: improved living quarters, hired labor, chemical fertilizers, and school fees.

The last criteria, educational attainment of children, is the least precise of the four. A child's educational progress is certainly contingent upon innate intelligence and application, but it is also directly affected by the opportunity to attend school at all. In Pwani, this depends on a parent's ability to pay school fees—in the form of contributions to building funds—and to replace children's labor in other activities, such as gathering fuel or water.

Given these four criteria, we identified four economic classes, representing the range of circumstances within the community:

1. *Landless.* Some households rent land; however, the rent in 1990/91 was about Ksh 1,750 (U.S. $55) per hectare per year, which is a great deal of money for an average individual. This group, although a small portion of the population (approximately 5 percent), can be further differentiated by the predominant economic activity. Even with rented land, landless households are generally unable to earn sufficient income from the sale of crops to cover the expenses of rent, and so they are employed, most frequently as local shopkeepers or mechanics. Those with jobs are better off than the unemployed, who are dependent on extension of credit from local shopkeepers, donations from neighbors, and support from external agencies for their livelihood.

2. *Near-Landless Smallholders.* Households in this group (approximately 15 percent) generally own between 0.1 and 0.8 hectare of land and a small, one-room wattle-and-daub house. They usually do not have a water tank, and they must purchase fuel or use maize residues. Most households in this group have no large livestock, though they may own a few chickens. They rarely have any cash income, and as a result their children get less than a Standard 8 education.

3. *Middle-Income Farmers.* Approximately 65 percent of the community falls into this group. These households have access to 1–2 hectares of land and live in small cement or timber homes with a few outbuildings. They might have

a water tank and generally can gather fuel on their own land or borrow from neighbors. They also have small livestock (sheep and/or goats). Because they occasionally earn cash income, their children generally complete Standard 8.

4. *Wealthiest Farmers.* The remaining 15 percent of the community is affluent by local standards. These households own 2–4 hectares. Their homes are large and built of cement, and they have many buildings in the compound. They have a water tank and fuelwood resources on their own land, as well as cattle and small livestock. There is a regular source of cash income within these households, so children will attend secondary school if they are capable, and most are able to use hired labor for a portion of the *shamba* work.

Household composition.   Although economic characteristics provide a partial description of households, family structure also distinguishes household interests and capacities in resource management. The household may consist of two or more (not necessarily consecutive) generations of extended family members. A notable fact of life in Pwani is the frequent absence of male heads of household because of either death, desertion, or, more commonly, employment in an urban center. The daily and long-term management of the household and its interaction with the larger community are dictated primarily by the age, gender, wealth, and status of household members. Therefore, we characterized households as headed by women, managed by women, or based on the presence of two adults (spouses) in the household.

1A. *Women-Headed.* Many households in Pwani are legally headed by women; some are widows, some have been deserted, and some are single by choice. Most women running households alone reported high levels of frustration due to the burden of providing sustenance and direction for the household without additional adult assistance.

1B. *Women-Managed.* Although these households have the support, albeit often little or sporadic in nature, of men who work in urban areas and who visit with varying degrees of regularity, the women are largely self-sufficient both economically and socially in daily life. They are responsible for the day-to-day management of the household, though long-term decisions are usually made by or with the male "head of household." Opinions vary about the realities of managing a household without a male partner to help on a regular basis. One woman commented that "women are better at managing their farms because they know kitchen necessities, and know what to plant." Another remarked that "most women don't have husbands at home; they sometimes don't have money, and there's no one to give them money."

The occurrence of women as legal landowners is uncommon in most communities throughout Kenya, yet a small but significant number of women (not all single heads of household) own their *shambas* in Pwani. Married women who own land are legally entitled to the privileges accruing from holding title to property, but they are generally unaware of such rights, uninformed as to how to access these benefits, or hesitant to use their land as collateral for loans. This may reflect the persistent perception of women's land ownership as socially inappropriate. One woman commented, "It looks like it's [the woman] who's having power [in the household]; if they do [own land], it's a family secret."

2. *Both Spouses Present.* Households where both spouses are actively involved in daily and long-term management decisions benefit from the added utility of two minds and two pairs of hands. The manner in which work is divided varies a great deal, however. Responsibilities and decisionmaking powers are sometimes equally shared, but, more commonly, women have a great deal of daily responsibility for providing sustenance, particularly performing the most time-consuming and repetitive tasks, while men reserve the right to make decisions regarding long-term household management.

Livelihood in Pwani

Most of Pwani's residents are farmers. The main crops are maize, beans, and a variety of vegetables, grown primarily for subsistence use. When the season is good, farmers are able to sell some surplus maize and beans for a small profit. Crop yields in Pwani are low in relation to national figures but not unusually so for smallholder farms in the drier parts of Nakuru.[22] No major cash crop is grown because the landholdings are small, and no one has yet identified a profitable crop that will do well here. Despite these and other problems, agriculture is generally the only local source of income. A few farmers grow small quantities of vegetables for the market.

A few of the landless, especially those with small businesses, can afford to rent a piece of land. Working in the *shambas* of those well-off enough to hire laborers provides another source of income for the poorest residents in Pwani. This is common among the very young and very old people who do not have any outside source of income; they generally earn Ksh 25 (less than U.S. $1) per day.

Small landholdings and a growing population have made paid employment a necessity for most families. Inputs to improve land productivity; school fees; health care; and food purchases all require money. However, roads and external communications are poor, and the economy of the village is subsistence based, providing few opportunities for earning a cash income. There is no industry in Pwani; those not employed in agriculture have small service businesses—*hotelis*, butcheries, repair shops—that meet the community's needs. Yet a retail establishment requires capital, which few individuals have. Some youth, especially young men with bicycles, earn some seasonal income in petty trading—buying beans from local farmers and selling them in Nakuru.

An alternative way of bringing cash into the household is through group activities. One group of women formed the Kuga no Gwika Bee Keepers to earn income from honey sales, and they have since begun keeping chickens. Another group, Amani, is buying cows for members and plans to earn income from the milk sales. In such cases success depends more on women's management of the enterprise and less on the size of their landholdings.

Although some men in Pwani are solely farmers, most have some sort of paid employment, either casual or regular, and contribute to household expenses and school fees. Employed men, when they are in residence, may also help in developing their homes. An example is Mr. W., who works for the Ministry of Lands and Settlement and comes home every weekend. He has built a good stone house and has extended the water tank built by his wife's self-help group. When he is at home he helps to look after cows, to build and repair fences, and to perform *shamba* work. He notes that his wife makes most of the decisions because she knows more about the farm than he does. If he had a choice, he would prefer to stay at home and manage the farm.

Because many adult men are absent, women are required to meet the subsistence needs of their families. Women find that they are often alone in facing the challenges of the changing times. They do not consider themselves lucky to be doing jobs that men used to do, such as looking after livestock, paying school fees, and building tanks. These women find their daily work load increasing as management pressures mount. Despite the small size of their holdings, they are generally not able to do all the required work alone. The net result is an ironic coexistence of unemployment and underemployment for youth and men and overburdening of women's productive capabilities. Though many survey respondents agree that tasks such as building a water tank traditionally would have been a man's responsibility, changing circumstances have required women not only to make the decisions but also to physically construct the tanks.

As in many rural communities with limited land, Pwani is home to a rising generation of unemployed youth with little hope of making a living as farmers. Not only is farming not a desirable future from their point of view, it is not viable considering the size and quality of the landholdings, which are too small to be efficiently shared among many children. Unlike some communities, Pwani has little to offer in the way of "marginal" or peripheral lands for new young families. Young adults are therefore unlikely to have access to land for their own use. Even with rapid and dramatic intensification of agriculture, Pwani's location would be disadvantageous relative to areas immediately surrounding the largest urban markets.

The primary school, forced to contend with too many pupils, too few teachers, and nearly nonexistent resources, cannot provide skills training beyond basic literacy. There is neither a secondary school nor a polytechnic in the village, that might improve a young adult's chances of competing in the overcrowded job market. The few existing educational and employment opportunities are available almost exclusively to young men. This is a national problem, but it is especially severe in Pwani because traditional social networks are weak and disrupted in such recent settlements. The next generation of youth brings rising expectations to a very limited, finite area whose natural capital (trees and soil fertility) has been heavily mined by their parents and outside interests. They are typical of rural youth in much of Kenya whose future depends on a reconciliation of urban values and rural realities and of commercial gain with subsistence security.

Although most commercial poachers now come from outside the area and local poachers confine themselves to medicinal herbs, fruits, and small game for food, poaching may become a compelling alternative to deepening poverty for Pwani's youth. They face the future from a finite tract of land already occupied by their parents, the park, or adjacent communities. Their horizon is short and will require creative vision to extend their future options beyond the present stalemate.

GENDER, LIVELIHOOD, AND COMMUNITYWIDE RESOURCE MANAGEMENT

Household-level resource management decisions are not made in a vacuum; they are limited by and contribute to the conditions in the community at large. It is necessary to examine these broader circumstances to gain an accurate view of what conditions are affecting the household and what responses are possible for both the household and the entire village. Some resources exist only on a larger-than-farm scale—for example, water points, cattle dips, and schools. When dealing with these larger, scarcer, or more expensive resources, the entire community context comes into play. Gender relations matter in terms of the process by which interactions occur and decisions are made and in terms of the impact that decisions have on various community members.

During PRA field interviews, communitywide meetings, and follow-up group meetings, Pwani residents identified water and fuelwood supply, lack of family planning services, low crop yields, livestock disease, and transgressions of the park boundary as the major resource management issues in their village. They all agree—regardless of class, gender, and age—that water scarcity is the single most important problem they face as individuals, as members of local households, and as a community.

There is less consensus on the relative importance of the other issues, although everyone recognizes each of the items as a valid concern. The six resource-related problems are shared by the whole community. However, they are experienced differently and ranked in different order by women and men. Class and age differences also affect the ranking of priority problems and the proposed solutions. People also note the lack of health care facilities, the poor condition of the road, the resulting isolation from marketing centers, lack of employment opportunities, and lack of a secondary school.

Water Scarcity, Water Quality, and Location of Water Points

Although water is undisputedly the most pressing problem, several points of difference arose during the various group meetings and follow-up surveys on gender and resources. Everyone is affected in some way by lack of water: the women are responsible for providing water to the household, both men and women are responsible for livestock watering (depending on household circumstances), and men, women, and children suffer from health problems caused by contaminated water. Some households already have roof-catchment water tanks for domestic water supply. These who do not may "borrow" or purchase water from neighbors, or they may draw their drinking water from the village dam, which is contaminated by runoff from the roads, the market, and cattle and other livestock that drink there.

For those with no tanks, domestic water supply is still at issue, whereas those with large tanks are now concerned only with the supply for their livestock. In group interviews, residents commented that only 10 percent of the population already have water tanks, and most women in the remaining households place a high premium on building a tank of their own. Many of the poorer households with no tanks have no livestock and therefore no long-term interest in the dam, once they manage to build a tank. In the short term, they are most concerned about the quality of the water from the dam and the need to keep livestock away from direct contact with the main body of water.

Among those who have no tanks, many women are members of self-help groups that provide rotating credit and labor pools to their members. Several of the groups in the vicinity channel their funds and labor into construction of water tanks for each of their members, in turns. One group, the Witeithie Wone Mai Women's Group, has already built fourteen tanks, and the women plan to construct one for each of the forty members. While the discussions reaffirmed the community's concern about water supply, some of the women's groups already have a plan and the will to carry it out.

The preferred solutions to the water problem vary among different groups. For example, community discussions about action on the water problem involved more men than women and a disproportionate number of wealthier members of the community. Many of those most active in the community meetings already have water tanks at home. Some of them financed the tanks themselves, whereas others had been at the top of their respective group's lists for tank construction.

Among these households—particularly among men with large numbers of livestock—the priorities for water concern restoration of the dam as a livestock watering point. Moreover, the discussion of community-level actions by officials and residents, both men and women, placed the emphasis on public, shared facilities rather than on group contributions to household-level infrastructure. The resulting village resource management plan gave top priority to dam rehabilitation, which implies a diversion of self-help group resources away from home water tanks and toward the dam as community infrastructure. This will benefit those who already have tanks and those with little hope of securing them in the near future who must use the dam for domestic water supply.

Both the discussion process and the substance of the proposed solutions affected men's and women's interests differently with respect to water resources. Women as a group have a more direct interest in domestic water supply because they are responsible for the daily provision of water to their households. Men, in general, are the legal owners of cattle and are responsible for the provision of livestock watering points, even if they delegate the daily management of cattle to their wives. The choice to give first priority to the community dam was forged from the convergence of three groups: (1) men in general, as cattle owners; (2) wealthy or influential women who already have water tanks; and (3) very poor women with little or no chance of building a home water tank through group efforts. All three groups shared a common interest in repairing the dam to expand the storage capacity, to stabilize the shoreline, and to protect the water quality. The group that would have placed home tanks as first priority includes those women who do not yet have household tanks but hope to build them with group assistance in the near future.

The distinct interest in various water development options, in spite of a consensus on the problem, demonstrates the importance of proportional representation of different groups, by gender and class, in the overall community meetings. Alternatively, it may be more effective to determine priorities of distinct interest groups in separate sessions and to use communitywide forums to negotiate the terms of joint or complementary efforts from these separate viewpoints. In either case it is critical to determine the nature of the interest groups (a mix of gender and class for water issues in Pwani), the relative numbers of people in each group, and the nature of the interests at stake.

Fuelwood

Throughout the survey process women raised the issue of fuelwood scarcity, both singly and in groups, but men were inclined to accord it a lower priority. The fuelwood issue came up at some household and group interviews but did not cause any controversy in those instances. All women report a scarcity of fuelwood, though there are several responses to their concerns. A few of the wealthier women can afford to buy good-quality fuelwood or charcoal. Most women either buy sawdust and wood chips from the nearby sawmill or use maize stalks, maize cobs, dung, and small stickwood from weedy fallows and fencerows.

The relationship between fuelwood and gender issues was clearly demonstrated in a discussion organized for the PRA exercise. The context for discussion of fuelwood scarcity was conditioned by the presence of officials and outsiders, the formality of the venue (a church), the combined presence of men and women, the high proportion of wealthy and influential community members, and the mixing of distinct groups in a public forum prior to reaching consensus separately, by group. All of this brought about a struggle over the meaning of women's work, women's resources, and women's voices in public affairs related to resource management. This was a clear demonstration of the effect of gender on problem definition, problem ranking, group process, and proposed solutions.[23] It also provided an object lesson in the proper place of outsiders in community affairs. The following summary captures the main points of the fuelwood debate during the problem-ranking exercise.

Though it was possible to reach an easy consensus on the primary importance of water scarcity through informal verbal assent, the fuelwood issue proved to be a somewhat more complex matter. One woman's suggestion that fuelwood be the second priority on the list drew an overall murmuring and nodding of approval from all the women present, whereas the men talked of roads and markets. The facilitator, a trainee, commented on the fuelwood point: "No, we mean a real problem." Some of the PRA team encouraged the women to raise their point again and to place fuelwood just below water as a major problem. However, there was a stalemate on the fuelwood issue, and by the end of the meeting fuelwood needs had been disregarded. A secondary school and roads were on the list, as was a hospital and, finally, more intensive, sustainable agriculture.[24]

The dynamic set in motion by the presence of outsiders and the unusual nature of this forum had firmly divided the room by gender, and it became clear that the matter being discussed was not merely fuelwood but rather women's place—in the household, in the landscape, and in community meetings. The issue of women's groups and the lack of men's groups arose, with strong statements on both sides. Women cited their heavy share of the labor on community work and men reminded them of their cash contributions. Several women strongly reasserted their claims on public attention and authority by stating that the women provided the organizational impetus, the ideas, and the labor, even when men contributed the cash for women's self-help group activities. So a simple discussion of resource management and development problems became an arena for struggles over meaning between men and women and between people with power and those they affect.

The resolution came the next morning, when the community leaders and residents present asked the PRA team and officials to leave them to a community meeting with no outsiders, to sort out the confusion of the previous day. They met for two hours, then announced that roads and hospitals were beyond the scope of the PRA follow-up and the community's own resources. The group left the secondary school in second place on the list.[25] They further noted that there is more to trees than firewood, such as timber, fodder, food, medicine, soil fertility, and soil conservation value. Thus was born the "tree planting and tree protection" priority rather than the fuelwood problem with a fuelwood solution. Men and women had renamed the contentious issue and had broadened it in the bargain. They also suggested that sustainable agriculture ought to include the practice of agroforestry and community tree planting, and they suggested moving that entire topic up to third place, right behind water and the secondary school.

Sustainable, Intensive Agriculture

As with the case of water, there is broad consensus on the importance of the problem of crop yields and several distinct approaches to solving it, based on household resources and composition. In group meetings and follow-up visits, several women showed a strong interest in group- and community-level seed banks for indigenous vegetable crops and herbs as well as improved crop varieties (maize, beans, vegetables) from elsewhere. This was dismissed by technical advisers and officials in the community meeting as a high-technology practice beyond the scope of rural communities and women's groups. Yet in follow-up visits, women showed substantial skill and interest in seed selection of their own traditional crops and in introducing drought-resistant vegetables, such as *Amaranthus* species from other regions.

Some individual women have their own small seed banks with indigenous plants, new species, and improved varieties purchased in Nakuru. However, their plots are not large enough for broad use, and access is limited to family, friends, and group members. Some of those interviewed noted the importance of local control over seed supply and quality. Under the current situation most women depend on traveling vendors and have little choice but to purchase whatever type of maize seed and other crop seed they may happen to bring to Pwani. There is often a shortage of all seed varieties at planting time. This concern was voiced almost exclusively by women throughout the PRA and follow-up and was not addressed by the first phase of the VRMP. It is, however, already part of the agenda for two church-based NGOs operating in Pwani.

Soil fertility and soil moisture problems were noted by both men and women. Many households now face declining crop yields after a few seasons of cropping. Because most residents are accustomed to wetter highland areas with fertile soils or to shifting cultivation in recently cleared forest, they have little experience with soil fertility management under dryland conditions. There is general interest in addressing this problem but little experience or experimentation thus far. No specific activities were planned to address this during the first phase of the management plan.

Overall, people agree that they need to restore and rehabilitate trees in the landscape and to bring multipurpose trees into croplands and home compounds. Only a few households still have gallery forest or patches of open woodland on their holdings, and these are under heavy pressure from neighbors. There is broad support for community and group tree nurseries, with farm-level planting by individual households.[26] Species choices include specific indigenous trees already known and liked, as well as exotic trees that might meet specific needs such as fuel, fodder, timber, and medicine. The Egerton University Forestry

Faculty has arranged to assist Pwani residents with tree seed, seedlings, training, and information.

Livestock Health

The issue of livestock health was raised by many of the men who had been
active in constructing and managing the cattle dip at Pwani. Tick-borne diseases are plaguing livestock keepers throughout Kenya, yet the village dip is no
longer functional. Several men complained that the government no longer provides the chemicals and veterinary services free of charge, and some residents
suggested that the pesticidal solution was diluted at those dips still functioning
on a fee-for-service basis. The content and process of this discussion identified
cattle keeping and veterinary medicine as a men's domain, heavily dependent
on government extension services.

A different impression emerged during follow-up visits to individual homes,
based on discussions of wild foods and medicinal plants with women. While
herding and veterinary medicine had traditionally been domains of men's work
and knowledge, many women in Pwani have been taught by their fathers to
care for cattle, to diagnose health problems, and to prepare herbal remedies for
common livestock diseases. Their fathers had noted the shift in the gender division of labor and the increasing migration of men in search of wage labor. Some
of the men with specialized herbal medicine skills also taught their daughters to
diagnose and treat people and to find and prepare the wild plants for specific
remedies. Women have, in fact, largely taken over traditional medicine, veterinary and human, as well as livestock management. Men are solely responsible
for the dip, and in wealthier families they usually purchase and apply chemical
sprays at home. Thus the gender division of labor and knowledge has shifted
from livestock versus agriculture to traditional versus "modern" commercial
technologies for disease control and treatment.[27] Many women are quite knowl-
edgeable about the current symptoms and conditions associated with livestock
disease and also know the water and fodder requirements of the animals because they either herd them or supervise children's livestock herding activities.

Nakuru Park and the People of Pwani: The Fence Has Two Sides

The conflict between the park and the people of Pwani is a double-edged problem. Though the park boundary is legally impenetrable, it is practically quite
permeable and is regularly crossed by people and wildlife. The poaching works
both ways: people poach on the plant and animal resources, and wildlife poaches
on the cropland of farmers closest to the park boundary. Each threatens the
living space and resource base of the other to some degree.

The poaching by people on park turf is closely related to the scarcity of
woodlands in the farming area and the demand for specific wild foods, condiments, medicinal herbs, and veterinary herbs in the community. Contrary to the
professional poachers from outside the area, Pwani residents do not threaten

the large mammals or primates in the park. For the most part, they enter the park in search of small quantities of renewable resources such as fruits, leaves, bark, roots, and small game species that are abundant in the woodlands around the lake. It seems that this widespread but low level of hunting and gathering has a relatively minor effect on the park as a whole.

The poaching on cropland by animals has a very pronounced effect on the narrow band of farms along or very near the park boundary but has very little impact on the community as a whole. Farmers whose lands are frequented by wildlife complain of serious damage to their grain harvests, fruit trees, legumes, and vegetables. Several of the farmers have changed their cropping strategy in response to frequent raids on their food and cash crops by baboons, warthogs, wild pigs, gazelles, and other wildlife. Some farmers keep vigil in their fields at night to guard their crops just before harvest time.

This issue was not raised explicitly in the context of the PRA but was raised by the farmers most affected by wildlife damage to crops. It was also raised by wildlife and natural resource management officers participating in the PRA and indirectly by women discussing their dwindling sources of wild foods, condiments, and medicinal herbs. Women's needs might well be met through special forest boundary nurseries and establishment of special forest stands for extraction of renewable forest products. Men's interest in small game might also be met through substitution of domesticated animals—which would create more work for women—or through stocking of small game in special stands outside the park. Both men and women share an interest in the park boundary issue, though their expertise and priorities are different with respect to specific resources within the park. Overall, there seems to be scope for negotiation of a more practical approach to the fence, which does indeed have two sides.

COMMUNITY RESPONSES

Progress to Date

Historical context.   Pwani's brief history is characterized by movement of population: waves of men, and then whole families, moving to the area and establishing homes and men going away again, seeking employment in urban centers. This continual state of flux shapes the local institutions within Pwani and dictates the nature and degree of interaction with the larger economic, social, and political context.

Pwani has not been characterized by community identification or unity until recently. These settlers have come from many places and, in resettling, have strained the traditional ties of family and community that have sustained people in times of need and provided a focal point of social interaction. Aside from close relatives and prior associations as forest employees, most households have little or no preestablished bond with other families in the community. Many have chosen to work independently and to strive for advancement based on their own individual efforts. However, this pattern of isolation has begun to change for several reasons.

Pwani is isolated, as a community, from larger administrative and economic units. Because of the community's remote location, no government extension personnel are specifically assigned the responsibility of tending to Pwani, and rarely do the "experts" visit, either to determine what is going on there or to give advice. Residents are prohibited from using the natural resources just on the other side of the park fence. Schools have been flooded with the children of recently arrived settlers, yet no new facilities or instructors have been provided. The natural resource base and local infrastructure, under demands from a booming population, have deteriorated, as indicated by the contamination and siltation of the dam, the scarcity of fuel sources, widespread livestock disease, and decreasing agricultural yields. These changes have created a strong need to pool resources to survive, which has been achieved in part by joining with other households similarly stressed.

Local institutions.   The first women's group, Umoja ("Unity"), was formed in 1980. Women's institutions were slow to assume major responsibilities within the community; individuals were hesitant to join, unconvinced of the potential benefits of such activity. Since 1987, however, self-help groups, often based on church membership, have proliferated rapidly. Comprising predominantly women members, these groups have formed most frequently around natural resource and financial problems—water, school fees, or household items—and have developed strategies to address these needs. In the process of tackling immediate needs, these clusters of women and men have begun to envision and plan for the future as a collective body rather than as isolated households.

External agents.   Pwani is not entirely ignored by larger regional and national institutions. Although there is little extension activity in Pwani at the present, a newly appointed assistant chief is attempting to redress this neglect. Some needs that cannot be appropriately met by individual households or small groups are being addressed by nongovernmental agencies. Egerton University has provided training in the construction of water tanks and has sponsored the Participatory Rural Appraisal exercise and follow-up activities on which this case study is based. A weekly mobile clinic, offering the only accessible health care for the community, is provided by the Catholic diocese, which has also encouraged the reintroduction of organic farming methods. World Vision and International Christian Aid provide school books and uniforms for impoverished students on an occasional basis.

The most striking external intervention in Pwani comes from the Church of the Province of Kenya (CPK). Following a communitywide self-survey and needs assessment in 1987, CPK began to provide both training and resources to match areas of interest and need identified by the residents. Training programs in leadership skills, group management, interactive process, health education, techniques for building water tanks, livestock management, organic farming, and small income-generating projects have provided a catalyst for the community's own initiatives and efforts.

Activities pertaining to resources.   Women's groups in particular have adopted activities to better manage or provide scarce resources. Nearly a dozen groups have been formed to build water tanks. Having come together around this common need, they have begun to help each other in different ways, sometimes working communally on large endeavors, like plowing, or providing aid to individuals in times of distress. Groups that have completed water tanks for all their members have gone on to other activities—most notably, constructing sheds for stall-fed livestock, purchasing crossbred cattle, or keeping chickens for sale.

Increasing capacities.   Largely as a result of past successes and assistance from the CPK, local institutions have expanded both their activities and their horizons. Groups have begun to look beyond Pwani's borders and are initiating cooperative efforts with similar groups in neighboring communities, creating what one individual called "development borders." Though originating from different regions and belonging to different religious denominations and occasionally different ethnic groups, many residents have broken down divisive barriers, and they work together in a spirit of neighborhood and community, as noted by the local CPK social worker.

Diversity also characterizes their activities. Rather than view each difficulty alone, groups now examine the linkages among problems and formulate strategies that can address several needs simultaneously. Beyond building water tanks, groups have taken on projects ranging from beekeeping to tree nurseries to building latrines. They have also decided to provide for themselves what the government has not; they have rehabilitated the cattle dip and are raising money to build a local secondary school.

This practice of cooperation and self-sufficiency has not prompted residents to discount government's role, however. Group members, bolstered by success in their endeavors, have come forward to demand accountability from their locally elected leaders and to remind government of its responsibilities to the community. A long-standing conflict over responsibility for planning and funding water projects was recently resolved when residents persuaded the new assistant chief to take up the matter with district-level officials.

FUTURE PROSPECTS

The convergence of gender, livelihood, and resource management issues in Pwani can inform future policy at local, national, and international levels. The argument to integrate policy across seemingly separate areas of concern rests on three premises, all demonstrated by the Pwani case. First, rural environmental quality and the quality of life of rural people are largely determined by settlement and land tenure policies, agricultural development policy (technologies and services), and the terms of local participation in land use and economic planning. Second, in park boundary communities, the ecological condition of the park and the surrounding areas may be damaged by the legal exclusion of local residents from any access to renewable resources within the boundary. Third, given the current gender division of rights and responsibilities in many rural communities, women tend to have use rights for, and therefore vested interests in, renewable resources on a regular, continuous basis. In contrast, men, who generally own the land and related resources, may tend to value resources as assets, to be accumulated over time or liquidated through sale or consumptive use. These points can be addressed by an integrated treatment of policy in four critical areas: (1) land tenure reform and settlement; (2) the provision of services and infrastructure to rural communities; (3) the practical management of park boundaries; and (4) participatory approaches to rural development and research.

Settlement and Land Tenure Policy

The Pwani case raises several points concerning the role of land tenure and settlement policies in shaping the landscape and the daily lives of the men and women who live there. The first question is whether the settlement of Pwani by former forest residents actually reduced deforestation in the long run. The eviction of forest employee families from national forest lands undoubtedly prevented additional deforestation in the moist upland commercial forests where they previously lived and worked. However, the forest employees who were forced to relocate then purchased land in dry settlement tracts. The result was almost complete deforestation and conversion to cropland over large areas of savanna.

The cost of providing water to households in Pwani, along with the long-term costs of deforestation in the savannas near Nakuru Park, may far outweigh the environmental costs of scattered smallholder settlements in the forest. Although the forests are government land and the settlement is private, the environmental costs in both cases will be shared by government as well as individual residents and will be unevenly divided between men and women. This indicates the need to treat forest evictions and shareholder land-buying schemes as part of one process of land use change and to evaluate the net result of resettlement in terms of environmental damage and livelihood at both sites. Both men's and women's work and their knowledge of resource use and management should inform such analyses. However, the more integrated treatment of forestry employee resettlement would not solve the problem if some other group were still to settle and deforest the savanna areas. To resolve the highlands/drylands resettlement question would require a more widespread analysis of net impact of land use and settlement change at district and national levels.

Pwani provides one specific example of the need for more holistic analysis and management of resettlement.

The second question is whether men's purchase of land as a private investment property and their initial occupation and clearing of farms might have influenced the treatment of trees and water resources in the local landscape. Had both men and women participated in the choice of settlement site, the location of specific plots, and land use plans for the whole area, they might well have left trees on ridges, streambanks, and rocky soils and in scattered stands in grazing land and croplands. Given the chance, they might also have developed domestic water supply and stock watering ponds at strategic sites, based on water harvesting at convenient points in the landscape.

However, with the prior subdivision of the land into blocks of equal size, settlers had no control over any land use decisions beyond their own property lines. There was little land left in the public domain, and none was officially allocated to shared use of fodder, wood, and other resources. At the farm level, men's concerns for buildings, fences, and cropland development took precedence over fuel, water, and fodder resources. The sequential settlement first by men and later by their families seemed to favor rapid conversion to cropland and a strong bias toward built infrastructure (other than water supply).

Policy options might include communitywide planning meetings, with men and women from all settler (or intended resident) households to decide on the number, type, and location of water sources; fuelwood production and gathering sites; community seed bank sites, fodder production, and grazing sites; and gathering areas for other products such as herbs, thatch, and fiber products. All these resources can be maintained on private plots, but it is unlikely that most smallholders could afford to establish or maintain them separately. Moreover, not all sites are equally well suited ecologically to all these functions. The administrative procedures that govern the establishment of new settlements might well incorporate such provisions, whether they be implemented by the national government, international development agencies, NGOs, or private land companies.

The third question has to do with the new spatial division of labor between men and women and the separation of male wage laborers from their families and their land. The ownership and control of land and water resources often rests with absentee men, whereas the responsibility for management falls to women who manage the farms on behalf of the household. Although the laws and procedures governing land purchase and ownership do not preclude women from owning or co-owning land, the usual practice vests exclusive legal ownership in male heads of household. Possible alternatives or supplements to this situation include cosigned title deeds by both spouses, if married; the allocation of common lands for shared use by women residents for such purposes as gathering fodder and producing fuelwood; the clarification and enforcement of women's use rights in both public and household lands; the establishment of local land use and resource management committees with equal representation of men and women; and administrative mechanisms to provide credit to women for farm improvements such as water tanks.

Agriculture, Health, and Related Extension Services

Pwani is typical of many dryland farming communities in its need for more frequent and more flexible extension services in health, agriculture, and veterinary care. One obvious response is to call for more extension officers in a number of specific fields, including women officers to work more effectively with women residents. However, the costs of extension services are quite high, especially over the long term, and expansion of these services is rarely a viable option for national government. This is especially true in Kenya, where various extension services are already quite heavily staffed relative to those in other countries in the region.

A more complex but perhaps more practical and cost-effective alternative is suggested by Woods (1903). Rather than train and maintain a large cadre of specialized extension officers spread thinly across the rural landscape, it may be preferable to focus on provision of good advice and information to local leaders and resident service personnel in rural communities. The latter can include appointed officials, teachers, NGO and church workers, women's group leaders, midwives, herbalists, and community-based health workers.

Besides the cost savings, other advantages include regular, widespread access to information at the community level among both men and women. In this case the information and advisory services are concentrated more at national and district levels, whereas local services are more widely available and accessible. This approach is also consistent with Kenya's District Development Focus. Although it does not guarantee equitable services for men and women, the flexible structure provides an excellent opportunity to reach both men and women with the information, advice, and products they require to maintain the health, livelihoods, and natural resources of their families and communities.

Practical Management of Park Boundaries

Each park has its own unique matrix of ecological and social conditions. However, Pwani exemplifies some circumstances that might well inform policy in other park boundary communities as well. Three options that might help to relieve the current problems at the interface of Pwani and Lake Nakuru include (1) experiments with carefully regulated "permeable" boundaries (i.e., controlled access to park by residents); (2) extension or relocation of selected park resources (or substitutes) outward into the surrounding communities; and (3) development of separate restrictions for renewable and consumptive resource use in or near the park. These seem relatively simple at face value but might well entail a major revision of park and wildlife policy currently based on the total exclusion of residents from nearby communities.

In practical terms, the revised policies on park access could lead to improved conditions in both the park and the nearby communities. For example, in some park boundary areas in other countries, farmers in boundary zones grow grain crops that are sold to the park service for supplemental animal feed. While this might not be reasonable in the case of Lake Nakuru, there are several possibilities for productive exchanges at the boundary. In return for vigilance against poachers and as compensation for damage to boundary zone crops, the park could help to provide herbs, condiments, wild foods and medicines, deadwood, tree nursery and extension services, and livestock dips for the community. Small enterprises based on these products might also employ local men and women from the farms most affected by crop damage. Women in particular spoke of herbs and condiments available only in the park. These are easily managed as renewable resources and could be produced in specific stands within the park or near the boundary. Alternatively, special-access permits might be issued to a few people to gather and sell specific products. Over the long term, the park could also provide water supply, nursery, seed bank, and extension facilities for Pwani and other communities.

Participatory Approaches to Development and Research Programs

Full and equitable participation by all land user groups in the community is essential to effectively address all the issues mentioned here. There is no single way to achieve broad-based participation, nor is there a single formula for how to involve local people in both research and development activities on resource management. Depending on the context and the players, it may be more appropriate to work with individuals, households, groups, or the whole community. Men and women may prefer to work separately or together, or their preference may vary depending on the particular issue or task. The key ingredient for appropriate structures and process is flexibility of format and method to suit the people, the place, and the task.

The choice of participating organizations and the selection of group representatives is critical, whether the topic is settlement, tenure, extension services, or park boundary issues. The recent experience in development and research circles suggests that rural people can bring unique skills and judgment to many tasks, from settlement planning and resource management to reforestation efforts and water development activities. The policy changes required to facilitate this approach are often procedural rather than legal, so change can often be initiated at district and local levels. At national and international levels, the policy changes often involve alternative approaches to the training of program and project planners as well as field personnel and may include retraining of existing personnel with regular assistance from experienced community facilitators.

In each of these areas, the Pwani case provides information and insights that could contribute to substantial revisions as well as specific refinements of existing policy at international, national, and district levels. Whether the policy changes are major or minor, the integration of gender, ecology, and community organization issues can help to restore the balance between men's and women's rights and responsibilities in the rural landscape and to close the artificial gap between economic and environmental policy.

CONCLUSIONS

Water, crops, trees, and wildlife at Pwani are embedded in a web of human social relations where gender matters. Throughout the PRA and follow-up discussions, the people of Pwani taught us much about the changing spatial and functional division of labor, knowledge, rights, and responsibilities. Part of what they demonstrated through their dealings with us and with each other is that nothing is written in stone. The meaning of gender divisions and the terms of gender conflict, cooperation, and complementarity in resource management are always subject to renegotiation.

From veterinary medicine to human health, and from livestock management to water tank construction, the gender lines are shifting, but they are not disappearing. In many cases, where women are taking on roles that were formerly those of men, it is not a negation of gendered work but a new rationale for the way men and women divide and share work and resources. Resource management programs with rural women who manage farms on behalf of absentee wage laborer husbands will still require an understanding of who controls the resource and the terms of shared access and authority. The knowledge, perspective, and legal rights of urban men may be critical to planning decisions taken by women in rural landscapes. Likewise, rural women's newly acquired veterinary skills and responsibilities may be crucial to early diagnosis and treatment of livestock epidemics.

Men's cash, women's labor, and women's social organizations have built the water tanks in Pwani. A similar joint effort will likely build the sustainable future that people in Pwani imagine for themselves. Resource management and development professionals cannot afford to ignore the relations of gender conflict, cooperation, and complementarity that shape the Pwani landscape as home, habitat, and workplace.

NOTES

1. Government of Kenya/National Environment and Human Settlements Secretariat et al., *Nakuru*, p. 30.

2. Estimates of Pwani's current population vary significantly between 3,500, the 1990 estimate of Pwani's school headmaster, and 5,000, the 1988 estimate by Church of the Province of Kenya survey.

3. Okoth-Ogendo, *Tenants of the Crown*; Hunt, *The Impending Crisis in Kenya*; Settlement Study Centre, "Planning Project"; Leo, *Land and Class in Kenya*, pp. 185–186; Leys, *Underdevelopment in Kenya*, pp. 90–91.

4. See Hunt, *The Impending Crisis in Kenya*, for a discussion of this phenomenon on a national scale.

5. See PRA chart in Government of Kenya/National Environment Secretariat et al., *Participatory Rural Appraisal Handbook*; Thomas-Slayter and Rocheleau, "Essential Connections."

6. Government of Kenya/National Environment and Human Settlements Secretariat et al., *Nakuru*, p. 22.

7. Ibid.

8. The park is one of the few in Kenya that is entirely fenced with a double wire (one electrified) perimeter about 25 feet between each fence.

9. Government of Kenya/National Environment and Human Settlements Secretariat et al., *Nakuru*.

10. Koeman et al., "A Preliminary Survey of the Possible Contamination of Lake Nakuru"; Curry-Lindahl, "Conservation Problems and Progress in Equatorial African Countries," p. 119; Greichus et al., "Insecticides, Polychlorinated Biphenyls and Metals"; Lincer et al., "Organochlorine Residues in Kenya's Rift Valley Lakes."

11. Government of Kenya/National Environment and Human Settlements Secretariat et al., *Nakuru*; Kariuki, "Integrating Conservation and Development."

12. Government of Kenya/National Environment and Human Settlements Secretariat et al., *Nakuru*.

13. Government of Kenya, Ministry of Economic Planning and Development, *Nakuru District Development Plan: 1979–1983* and *Nakuru District Development Plan: 1984–1988*; Jaetzold and Schmidt, *Farm Management Handbook of Kenya*.

14. Government of Kenya/National Environment and Human Settlements Secretariat et al., *Nakuru*.

15. The average land per person ratio for Nakuru District was estimated in 1989 at .34 hectare per person (see Downing et al., *Coping with Drought in Kenya*; Settlement Study Centre, "Planning Project"). Based on the PRA and the gender survey, most households have six to eight members and subsist on one parcel of 2.5 acres (1 hectare). This suggests that the land per person ratio in Pwani is less than the district average.

16. Land buying companies were formed after independence to enable indigenous Kenyans, who did not have the necessary financial resources, to buy back from the settlers the land they had fought to reclaim in the Mau Mau movement.

17. Okoth-Ogendo, *Tenants of the Crown*; Leo, *Land and Class in Kenya*; Government of Kenya/National Environment and Human Settlements Secretariat et al., *Nakuru*.

18. Mbithi and Barnes, *The Spontaneous Settlement Problem in Kenya*; Government of Kenya/National Environment and Human Settlements Secretariat et al., *Nakuru*; Soja, *The Geography of Modernization in Kenya*.

19. Oduol, "The Shamba System."

20. Soja, *The Geography of Modernization in Kenya*.

21. The 1988 estimate by Church of the Province of Kenya survey.

22. Downing et al., *Coping with Drought in Kenya*; Government of Kenya/National Environment and Human Settlements Secretariat et al., *Nakuru*, p. 62.

23. Thomas-Slayter and Rocheleau, "Essential Connections."

24. The idea for a hospital was actually derived from women's complaints about the lack of family planning services. "Family planning" was renamed by the men "hospital," which acquired a life of its own as an infrastructural need rather than an information and service need.

25. Although the school was not a resource management problem, it was related to teen pregnancy, family planning, and lack of direction among the youth. The PRA provided a forum to pressure local officials on a long-standing problem over school funding and land allocation.

26. As noted in the prior discussion of fuelwood, the PRA participants chose to include trees and the products under sustainable agriculture and to emphasize agroforestry approaches on-farm.

27. The same appears to be true in the realm of human medicine, although women must often raise the funds for treatment of themselves or their children in clinics.

7

A Pocket of Poverty: Linking Water, Health, and Gender-Based Responsibilities in South Kamwango

Elizabeth Oduor-Noah, Barbara Thomas-Slayter

South Kamwango is a puzzle. A small community in Migori District,[1] its climate, soils, water, and vegetation have the potential for abundant agricultural production and development. Yet, despite a strong resource base, the productivity of land and labor are low; water quality is poor; infant mortality is high; disease is rampant; and community institutions are fragmented. Over the years since independence, South Kamwango's problems seem to be growing more intractable; poor health and low productivity persist. Meanwhile, nearby communities are showing signs of development. To the north, in an adjacent location, people are emerging from conditions of deprivation, and to the southeast in the next district, they are thriving. South Kamwango appears to be a pocket of poverty, a phenomenon existing not only in Kenya but in other parts of Africa as well.

This chapter examines the struggles of the people of South Kamwango to manage the particularities of their local environment and production system and to come to terms with political and social constraints on that system. It considers socioeconomic conditions within South Kamwango and how the community is linked with economic and political systems beyond its borders. It examines gender roles within households and community, the gender-based division of labor, the competing demands on women's time and resources, and their domestic, cultural, and economic obligations, as well as their access to the resources necessary to meet them. It explores not only the particularities of the environment but also the interactive processes involving the environment, specific resources, family welfare, and broad economic and political systems within which local communities exist. All these issues provide insights relevant to understanding South Kamwango's severe environmental and health problems as they relate to questions of resource access, community institutions, and gender.

We argue that particular attention to gender—assuring sensitivity to both men's and women's roles, perspectives, and responsibilities—can suggest de-

Map 7.1   Migori District and South Kamwango Sublocation

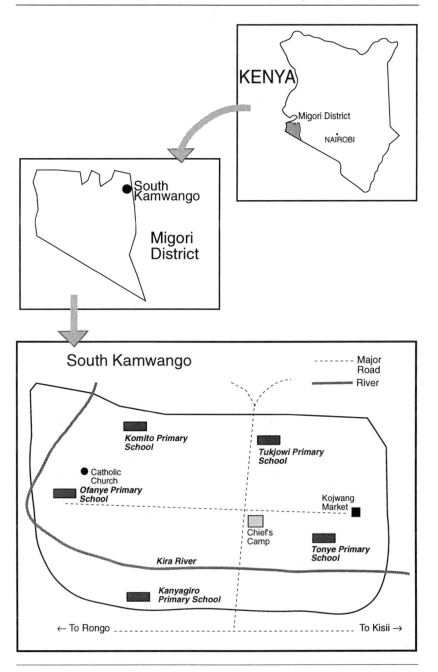

velopment approaches that will strengthen capacities of households and community institutions to address the problems they face. Further, we suggest that when government agencies and NGOs incorporate a gender perspective into their program and project analysis, the likelihood increases that communities will organize and act on issues of environmental degradation, resource management, and health.

THE APPROACH

In late 1990, the district officer of Rongo Division, Mr. Kiama Gachanja, invited a research team from Kenya's National Environment Secretariat and Clark University to explore the puzzle of South Kamwango, one of his area's lagging sublocations. Mr. Gachanja indicated that South Kamwango was a community with comparatively inactive organizations, where people were having difficulty sustaining their livelihoods and the institutional infrastructure was fragile. He was eager for insights and observations on ways to strengthen this community, its institutions, and the processes of development. Research in this sublocation provided an opportunity to consider the following:

- A community regarded as a pocket of poverty where, despite a strong natural resource base, poverty persists
- The underlying social, political, and economic factors that either encourage or hamper the capacities of community groups to respond to changing resources and ecological conditions
- The range of resource issues confronting South Kamwango and the ways households and community organizations are addressing them
- The interactions of gender-based responsibilities, health, and environmental problems within this community

The team addressed four questions that incorporate a focused interest in health, nutrition, water, and agriculture: (1) What is happening to the resource base in this community? (2) How are these changes affecting men's and women's use of resources, access, and tenure at household and community levels? (3) How are people coping with or adapting to these changes? (4) What policies would assist communities like South Kamwango to address the problems facing them, including those emanating from the larger political, ecological, and economic systems of which they are a part?

Methods for gathering data included household interviews with members of sixty randomly selected households, 30 percent of the two hundred in the sublocation. The team conducted the majority of interviews with the responsible adult woman of the household, although men were included as well. From these interviews, the team was able to gain a clear picture of the conditions and problems confronting the households in South Kamwango. Team members met with key informants, including officials at the division level, the assistant chief, extension officers, headmasters, the chairs of the women's groups, and others who might have insights on central issues, constraints, and opportunities for the sublocation. Another formal survey in the community was administered to one hundred adults from households that had not participated in the household interviews. The survey covered topics such as cash income for the household, labor requirements for the farm, group membership, and specific agricultural knowledge. Finally, through the assistant chief, the research team organized a public meeting of approximately fifty people to exchange views on topics such as health, water, schools, sources of income, family planning, food production, and trees.

THE CONTEXT

Migori District

Migori is one of the seven districts of Nyanza Province. Formerly it was part of South Nyanza District, which was Kenya's fourth most populous district. In 1993, South Nyanza was divided into two new districts: Migori and Homa-Bay. Situated in the southwest corner of Kenya, Migori comprises 3,116 square kilometers and is bordered by Tanzania to the south and Lake Victoria to the west. It has a population of approximately 602,000,[2] largely from the Luo (or Joluo) community, part of the more than 2,000,000 Luo residents of South Nyanza Province. Despite considerable labor migration to towns and plantations outside the area, the Luo homeland is one of the most densely populated rural areas of East Africa. In 1979, densities averaged about 181 people per square kilometer; by 1994, they had reached 315.[3] Migori suffers severe problems in health, nutrition, and water quality. Historically, as part of one of Kenya's poorest districts, it has had the nation's highest rates of early childhood (birth to two years) mortality.[4]

Migori offers an opportunity to explore men's and women's roles in securing a livelihood and sustaining the family within the context of severe problems in health and nutrition, which are reflected in statistics on child health and mortality. Some of these problems relate closely to the circumstances in which women of that district find themselves. They face constraints deriving from polygamy, early marriages, high birth rates, and their children's chronic disease, malnourishment, and ill health. Women are the primary care providers, responsible for the health of young children. Throughout much of this district, women face acute difficulties in securing the health and well-being of their families, particularly for children under five years of age.

In addition, many households face increasing pressures in their struggle to meet cash needs. Until recently, the vast majority of farmers grew sugarcane as their major cash crop, which was the primary commodity through which South Kamwango was linked to the cash economy. In 1989, production of sugarcane in South Kamwango was prohibited. While the factors underlying this decision are complex, the decision has resulted in hardship for many households, escalating the struggle of local residents to meet cash needs and having a significant impact on the allocation of labor for both men and women in the community.

South Kamwango and Its Resource Base

South Kamwango Sublocation comprises an area of 15 square kilometers, with two hundred households and a total population (in 1990) of 3,825 (1,798 male, 2,027 female). It is located in North Kamagambo Location 2 kilometers from a tarmac road and about 10 kilometers from the division headquarters at Rongo, just inside Migori District's border with Kisii District.

Land: quality, access, and ownership.   South Kamwango falls within Kenya's agroecological zone 3, characterized by fertile agricultural land and reliable rainfall. Endowed with a good climate and suitable environment for productive economic activities, especially for agricultural and livestock development, it has a medium to high potential for agricultural production. Its fertile, loamy soils offer good prospects for the cultivation of a wide variety of both cash and food crops, although the potential has not been fully utilized. Black cotton soils characterizing parts of the sublocation are prone to waterlogging. Overall, the area does not experience severe soil erosion.

For the Luo, as for many other Kenyan ethnic groups, land is the most important and treasured asset a man can bequeath to his sons. As the head of household, a man holds all the property in trust for the family. When he dies, his widow manages the property until her sons are mature enough to share it among themselves. Should the husband in a polygamous marriage die, the wives share the property and hold it in trust for their sons. Although recent national law provides daughters with rights to inherit land, customary inheritance laws bestow this right only on male progeny. It is assumed that daughters will marry and have usufruct rights within their new households.

During the first part of this century, "territorial confinement of ethnic groups under colonial authority, the advent of the ox-plow, and the falling death rate due to medicine and consequent rises in population growth all contributed to competition for land and to local imbalances in the ratio of population to land."[5] Since independence, processes of land consolidation, adjudication, and registration have taken place in Luoland, as elsewhere in Kenya. Shipton notes that many Luo continue to disapprove of land sales and that the process has diminished the legal land rights of women and other social groups.[6] Since women's rights to and control over land and other property are determined in large part by traditional laws rather than statutory laws, women do not usually inherit or own land. As polygamous households and a rapidly growing population begin to feel land pressures, questions of ownership and control, including that by women and young men, become increasingly acute. As Shipton states, "The descent-based Luo land system, once well suited to conditions of gradual lineage movement and territorial expansion, has proved unsatisfactory under conditions of territorial confinement and crowding."[7]

Water: issues of contamination and protection.   Water quality is the central resource issue in this sublocation. Groundwater is an important supply for domestic use, and most households either own or have convenient access to hand-dug wells and boreholes. There are no roof catchment systems. The Kira River, widely used within the sublocation, provides abundant quantity but poor quality. Most of the wells are not protected; the river is severely polluted, and groundwater is contaminated by domestic, agricultural, and/or municipal waste.

Forests and fuelwood: a growing problem.   The sublocation has no forest reserves. A few farmers have casually maintained woodlots, and most households grow *Eucalyptus* trees to provide income, primarily from the sale of poles for building purposes. There are scattered *Grevillea* trees. Although people identify fuelwood as a growing problem, particularly during the wet season, the sublocation has no significant tree planting activities. Bushes, shrubs, and maize stalks from the farms are the primary sources of fuelwood. One women's group had planted seedlings but had not separated and distributed them to members in time to avoid excessive crowding of the roots. In general, the afforestation effort seems sparse and scattered.

Agriculture: high potential, low returns.   Most of the farmers cultivate smallholdings of 4–6 hectares and practice mixed subsistence farming. Maize, sorghum, beans, millet, and sweet potatoes are widely grown as food crops. At the present time there are no major cash crops. The good climate supports two growing seasons a year, and there is opportunity for introducing new cash crops, such as robusta coffee, tea, and tobacco. The extension agent underscores the strong, untapped potential for market gardens. This potential is further enhanced by the low incidence of crop pests and crop diseases. Moreover, since the erodability of the soils is low, production costs per unit area are minimal.

Although there is great potential for high yields sufficient for family needs, many households report a food deficit of approximately two months per year. This appears to result from insufficient utilization of the land for food production and a shortage of labor at critical points in the agricultural cycle, given the gender-based responsibilities for agricultural production. Holdings are adequate, but it is difficult for a woman to cultivate more than 1 hectare of maize under current labor and technological inputs. Given large families, there is a disjuncture between the productivity of the woman's labor for subsistence production and the needs of the household.

According to the agricultural extension agent, the trends in agriculture show increased food self-sufficiency. Many farmers have some knowledge of extension and are practicing recommended agricultural methods, including the use of fertilizers, improved seeds, and cultivars. On the other hand, many women respondents believe the fertility of the soil is declining, and they express a need for more agricultural advice from the extension agents. A major problem affecting food production in the sublocation is the spread of the striga weed, which attacks maize and sorghum, the area's major cereal crops.

Livestock.   Livestock rearing is practiced at moderate levels. Many households have five or six head of the indigenous zebu cattle. Disease is the major problem faced by those rearing cattle, particularly east coast fever and trypanosomiasis. Grade cattle cannot survive without protection from these diseases, and people hand spray rather than dip the few grade cattle found in South Kamwango; there are no cattle dips in the whole of North Kamagambo Location.

One women's group in South Kamwango has been involved in an experiment managing a dairy cow. This group is the first in the community to keep stall-fed cattle, practicing zero grazing, in which the group grows the forage and brings it to the cattle pen. As dairy cows can thrive in this area, extension officers hope that this project will serve as an example to other farmers.

CULTURE AND CLASS

Polygamy and Patriarchy

In South Kamwango, as in other Luo communities, the family system is patrilineal, and the senior male has final authority over the home regarding all decisions. As Shipton puts it, "The Luo give a high public profile to males. Patriliny, bridewealth, and polygyny all reinforce each other."[8] Polygamous marriages are commonplace. Figures from 1989 for South Nyanza District indicate that 40 percent of currently married women have one co-wife or more and 25 percent of young men (15–24 years) are in polygamous unions.[9] Women are dependent upon their fathers until they marry, when their husbands gain control over them.

Our data suggest that virtually all households in South Kamwango are polygamous, having anywhere from two to five co-wives. Men accrue status and prestige with their capacity to support more than one wife. In turn, a man's wives cultivate his increasing landholdings, augmenting his prosperity. In related research among Luo in southwestern Kenya, Johnson observes a relationship between the levels of productive resources a person controls and the attainment of formal position by that individual.[10] Social standing reflects the size of landholding; the largest landowners are the most powerful men in the area. The control of productive resources as a precondition for the attainment of social position is clearly linked to the capacity to mobilize nonwage labor. The number of wives a man has to work in his fields directly affects his status.

The reproductive capacity of wives (i.e., the number of children they bear) similarly enhances a man's prestige. The value, for a man, in having more than one wife was clearly articulated in a meeting in South Kamwango Sublocation where one senior male participant stated, "He who has only one wife will not be heard in the public meetings! Such a person will not command authority and respect in South Kamwango."[11]

After the immediate household and homestead, according to Diamond, subclans remain the fundamental unit of social organization for the Luo.[12] The lineage system is segmentary, in addition to being patrilineal, and new subclans eventually break off from existing subclans when a particular branch becomes quite large. Subclan membership implies a set of rights and responsibilities to other members of the same subclan. A subclan is both a lineage and a spatial division with varying degrees of wealth and status among homesteads.[13]

In polygamous households, the decisionmaking power of the women is concentrated in the senior wife. She initiates the agricultural cycle, settles disputes between other women, and is always the first to be consulted on domestic issues. Households observe a strict division of labor, and women's tasks include all the preparation and cooking of meals, rearing children, and looking after immediate household needs like water and fuelwood. They are also involved in economic activities on a gender-specific basis.[14] In fact, according to Shipton, "gender charts the possibilities of a Luo's economic life."[15]

For the women in Migori, early marriage is common. The average marrying age is sixteen to eighteen years. District records (for Migori and Homa-Bay as South Nyanza) indicate that 25 percent of women who have ever married did so before their fifteenth birthday, and 66 percent married before their eighteenth birthday.[16] Current data from South Kamwango suggest that the cultural inclination toward early marriage continues. One headmaster lamented that a thirteen-year-old had just left school to marry. Some young women of seventeen or eighteen, who had been married for several years and had borne children, were among the junior wives in the households interviewed by the research team.

The birth rate in Migori is high, with a total fertility rate of 8.2; one out of every three women has given birth to six or more children.[17] Of the households interviewed, middle-aged women had, on average, six or seven living children and had lost two or three. However, there are large variations. One respondent had lost fifteen out of sixteen children she had borne, before they reached the age of five, and another had borne fifteen, of whom five had survived. Several young women had lost their first two babies either at birth or as infants and were expecting their third. Households in South Kamwango bear out Migori's position as one of the districts with the highest infant mortality rate in the country. In fact, most of the households the team members visited had lost two or three children to early childhood diseases, malaria, or complications from malnutrition.

In many ways, the women sharing a polygamous household in South Kamwango are supportive of one another. Yet interviews revealed keen competition among co-wives as they vie for cash income, educational opportunities for their children, and benefits brought by the husband to the household. This competition occurs under conditions of increasing scarcity. In general, each wife separately maintains her own fields, granary, trading activities, purse, hearth, and children.

These characteristics of South Kamwango—related to polygamy and patriarchy, early marriage, high birth rates, and high infant mortality—are critical sociocultural dimensions shaping women's responsibilities in this rural community. They also shape the capacities of women, as primary care providers, to respond to essential environmental and health issues.

Class Structure and Household Portraits in South Kamwango

Although there are no wealthy families in South Kamwango, economic stratification exists. Health problems, infant mortality, and low levels of productivity affect everyone, but some households are better off than others and some are extremely poor with few options for improving their material conditions. Households in South Kamwango are divided very broadly into the following categories:

- Relatively prosperous families, of which there are few
- Average households
- Very poor households

The more prosperous homes are characterized by a sturdy house in good repair with a metal roof, several cattle (perhaps even a grade cow), furniture, the capacity to hire laborers, and a nonagricultural source of cash income. Approximately 20 percent of the households have a family member with regular employment providing a monthly income; more than half of these family members are teachers.

In this community, families of average socioeconomic standing have adequate land to meet the needs of the household and keep a few cattle. For cash, they depend on limited returns from the sale of some crops, from casual labor, or from trading undertaken by the women. Usually, they are able to hire an ox and plow to prepare the land for cultivation. Often, they must buy food at the end of the season. There is no money available for expenditures such as secondary school fees for any of the children.

The poorest households support large families on 2 hectares or less without a major source of outside income. They are unable to keep cattle, cannot afford to hire oxen and plow, and therefore must dig the land with hoes. They may, in the South Kamwango context, be suffering particularly from the prohibition on sugarcane cultivation.

A prosperous household.   Cyprosa Okech is a widow who is about seventy years old. She married just before World War II and bore five children, of whom four are living. Two sons work outside the community, and their wives and children stay in the compound. One son died and his two widows with their children also live in the compound. Thirteen grandchildren are in residence;

two grandchildren died several years ago—one from malaria, the other from measles.

The main house has plastered walls, an iron sheet roof, and a pit latrine in back. Flowers provide evidence of care and attention to the compound. However, an open, shallow well on the land stands unprotected.

The family owns 11 acres. Every adult woman in the household has her own maize plot; each also grows groundnuts, beans, sorghum, and bananas. "The food is sufficient for the family," says Cyprosa, adding, "if we do not donate to the needy." They use fertilizer and hire an ox and plow to prepare the soil for planting. While she herself is "uneducated," Mrs. Okech proclaims vigorously, "Ignorance is why we are behind."

In the past, the family sold sugarcane to obtain some income. Since this is no longer an option, Cyprosa wants to learn how to increase food production to sell extra produce. With the income, she would hire workers, thereby further expanding agricultural production and refocusing the household on these new sources of income. Meanwhile, a son employed in Moyale provides financial support, which is used for school fees.

An average household.   Serafina Aoko and Salima Adhiambo, both about fifty years old, are co-wives, each managing her own household within a larger family compound. Currently residing with them in the household are their husband, five sons, four daughters-in-law, and twelve grandchildren. Three daughters are married and living elsewhere; two sons work outside the district. Of the eleven children Serafina has borne, six have died. Of the ten Salima has borne, five have died. All deaths occurred before the age of three and are attributed to either kwashiorkor, tetanus, malaria, measles, or witchcraft. It is evident that the grandchildren are suffering from malnutrition and respiratory infections.

Each co-wife cultivates her own plots with the help of her daughters-in-law. The sons do all the plowing together and help with building, tending cattle, and digging. The daughters-in-law weed, fetch water and firewood, wash clothes, sweep the compound, cook, and care for children. The whole family participates in planting, but Salima and Serafina do the harvesting. Their crops include maize, millet, groundnuts, beans, potatoes, and fruits (papayas, pineapples, mangoes, and bananas) primarily for home consumption. They used to grow sugarcane, but the land is now idle as they contemplate alternatives for cash crop production. The husband tends the household's seven cows (the local breed). Since the family must buy food at the end of the season, and since sugarcane cultivation is no longer an option, they have three avenues for acquiring cash. Serafina and Salima sell bananas, their husband does casual labor, and their sons occasionally send money.

A poor household.   Kazia Akienye was married in 1965 and moved to her present 4-acre farm twelve years ago from another *shamba* within the sublocation. There are three co-wives, each possessing a small home with mud walls and a thatch roof. All the houses are in need of repair. The household has only one small granary. There is no latrine, and the wives do not see the need for one, despite the small size of the *shamba* and the presence of twelve people—five adults and seven children. None of the adults has regular employment.

Kazia's husband makes decisions about what is grown and sold. All adults participate in the farm work and use only *jembes*, or hoes. They do not own or hire an ox and plow. Before the ban, they used to devote 1 acre of their land to sugarcane, from which they derived jaggery, the central ingredient for brewing *changa'a*, the local beer. They sorely miss the income from jaggery sales and still hope for the establishment of a sugarcane processing factory one day. Now they sell small amounts of maize and beans to earn a little income; however, this is no indication of a surplus of food. They have to buy food for one month of the year.

The family has an unprotected well on their land, and the drinking water is not boiled despite its muddy color. Several children of the three co-wives have died of various diseases, but the adults do not associate the illnesses with possible water contamination.

Their land yields insufficient fuelwood, and the women often burn maize stalks for cooking (in the past they used sugarcane stems). The women have planted a few tree seedlings given free of charge by the Ministry of Agriculture nursery at Rongo, but they do not perceive these trees as the answer to their increasingly serious firewood shortage. This scarcity of firewood is a deterrent to boiling water to purify it for drinking.

LIVELIHOOD SYSTEMS AND GENDER ROLES

Diversifying Livelihood Strategies

All households pursue multiple strategies for supporting the extended family. These include farming, small-scale trade of agricultural commodities, casual labor, and off-farm employment. Twenty percent of South Kamwango's households (forty households) have a family member who works outside the community. Of these, nearly half are teachers, usually employed in primary schools within the district. The remainder are divided between those holding positions within local government administration (including police and clerical workers) and those who work as factory laborers, usually in tea or sisal industries outside the district. Most residents are involved in agriculture and petty trading. The men seek casual labor on public works, if and when it becomes available. Some men and a few women engage in small business. (See Figure 7.1.)

The majority of households have 5–6 hectares of fertile land and plentiful water. However, labor and land have low levels of productivity. Yields and, hence, options for sale of produce are limited by hoe technology, inadequate resources for inputs, and insufficient labor for managing more intensive agriculture or the cultivation of more fields.

Currently, most households meet only their most urgent cash needs through small sales of groundnuts or maize and through women's clever trading in small-scale commodities such as fish and bananas. One relatively prosperous household had half an acre planted in groundnuts. In a good year that half-acre could yield sixty tins, or about one and a half bags of nuts, at prices per tin varying from Ksh 27 to Ksh 50 (1990 prices; Ksh 1 = U.S. $.04). The maximum income from the groundnuts for this household was Ksh 3,000. Several households had as much as 1.5–2 acres in groundnuts. Women indicated that groundnut cultivation is highly labor-intensive and that its profits come at considerable cost in the form of their work.

Because of the rising cost of living, entrepreneurship and trading activities are increasing. These activities involve both men and women. Women tend to trade in fish, bananas and other agricultural produce to earn extra income. Men, besides seeking casual labor, trade in different products, particularly cattle and lumber or poles.

Given the rapid increases in population and current inheritance patterns, the size of the agricultural holdings per household in South Kamwango is likely to diminish over the next generation. Off-farm activities will be extremely important for future sources of income and employment. At present, however, much can be done to improve both utilization and yields within the current cultivation patterns.

Figure 7.1   Primary Source of Household Income in South Kamwango

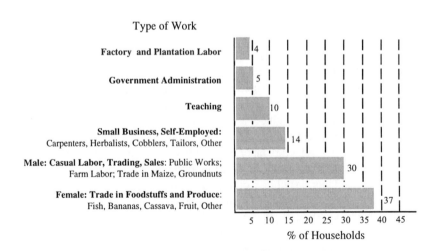

Type of Work

% of Households

Overall, most respondents expressed views varying from resignation to despair on the question of cash income. They specified that their biggest problem in relation to land and other resource use stems from government restrictions on growing sugarcane and their inability to find a suitable crop to replace it as a source of income.

Cash, Commodity Production, and the Changing Role of Sugarcane

As mentioned, until recently sugarcane was widely cultivated in South Kamwango as a cash crop. However, in 1989, the government prohibited its production in this sublocation for three reasons.[18] First, most of the farmers in South Kamwango were noncontract cane farmers. That is, they did not have contracts with a factory to produce cane for processing at that factory. The only processing plant in the district does not have sufficient capacity to accommodate noncontract farmers. To be a contract farmer, one needs to be within a specified radius of the factory, and South Kamwango did not fall within the limit. Because of the distance to the factory and the difficulties of ensuring that the cane would be purchased by the factory, most farmers in South Kamwango sold their cane locally for use in making jaggery for home-brewed beer.

Second, an increase in production and consumption of the local brew in South Kamwango had prompted the government to ban sugarcane cultivation. Brewing liquor is an illegal activity.

Third, it was widely believed that households in the community were growing sugarcane at the expense of food crops. Government extensionists wished to discourage sugarcane production and encourage cultivation of nutritional food crops. In fact, there was considerable evidence, not only in the sugar growing areas but in other cash crop areas as well, that malnutrition was increasing.[19]

The ban on sugarcane came as a surprise to the residents of South Kamwango. In the larger national context, the policy might seem ill advised, given recent below-average production and Kenya's heavy reliance on imported sugar.[20] Respondents to the household interviews registered keen dismay over the prohibition on sugarcane cultivation as it prevented access to a significant source of income. Most were complying, but they articulated a desperate need for an alternative cash crop and were discouraged about the prospects of finding a good one.

Evidence from South Kamwango does not support the view that there was a direct tradeoff for households between growing sugarcane and food crops. There are two dimensions of this issue: allocation of fields and allocation of labor. Sugarcane is a man's crop, and food crops are women's responsibility. Household interviews and surveys indicate that sugarcane and food crops were not competing with one another for labor time. This finding is corroborated by the Kennedy and Cogill study of the impact of sugarcane production on women's income, time allocation, and child care practices.[21]

On some of the smaller holdings, however, decisions may well have been made to remove land from food cultivation and place it in sugarcane production, using the proceeds to purchase food and other household needs. Kazia Akienye's household is an example of such a situation, in which 1 of 4 acres was under sugarcane cultivation before the ban. It is likely that this was a rational choice giving them some flexibility and purchasing power for foods or nonagricultural goods needed by the household.

It is clear that households that are no longer planting sugarcane are seeking alternatives. One option, not a popular one, is coffee. A few farmers grow coffee, though without much enthusiasm because the coffee factory is extremely late with returns from sales and the prices are low. There is some progress in expanding coffee production as an alternative cash crop, but this effort is marginal. Given the cooperative's pattern of late payments, few of those who have given up their sugarcane wish to take up coffee growing. In fact, one woman stated that she had pulled up her coffee trees since payment was such a problem, and she is now using the land for maize. Bananas and groundnuts are minor cash crops produced and managed by women and are widely grown in the sublocation. If the government mounts a major effort to introduce tea and coffee production, it will alleviate local concerns for ways to address cash needs. However, the important objective of increasing the nutritional status of families will not be met by substituting tea and coffee for sugarcane, particularly given erratic payment by local cooperatives.

It is ironic that the prohibition on sugarcane production has had some unanticipated impacts on women's responsibilities. The first concerns the production of maize and groundnuts. Because these crops are usually cultivated by women, their substitution for sugarcane (a man's crop) has inevitably increased women's agricultural responsibilities.

Second, cane sales were the major source of income for many households. The household interviews indicate that, now that this is no longer the case, many women find it necessary to increase both the time spent trading and the quantities of produce sold to help meet the households' cash needs. The intensification of this activity puts pressures on time and labor allocations for agriculture and child care. Thus, the ban on sugarcane cultivation appears to have had an immediate detrimental effect on family nutrition, child welfare, and women's work loads. Residents of South Kamwango hope that these pressures will be short-lived as the government activates agricultural extension services and other programs for the community.

Women's Productive Activities: Issues of Access and Control

In South Kamwango, women's primary economic activities are in agriculture and petty trading. Many women spend several days per week trading in the market to earn income for the family. Besides selling produce from their own farms, they buy commodities, such as fish, in the nearby town of Rongo and sell them in the smaller markets near their homes. Alternatively, they may purchase bananas from neighbors and take them to town to sell at a small profit.

Several respondents buy bananas from neighbors, divide them into small bunches, and go to Rongo twice a week to sell them. Profits for this activity are approximately Ksh 25 (U.S. $1 in 1990 values) per week.

One enterprising woman goes once or twice a week to Rongo to purchase *omena*, a fish similar to sardines, which she then sells in the local community on a daily basis. On a trip in October 1990 she bought 20 kilos of fish for Ksh 100, which she divided into small dishes and then sold for Ksh 2 or 3 per dish. A kilo of fish sold in this manner yields Ksh 20 per kilo, and thus her profits are Ksh 300. Normally she cannot sell more than 3 kilos per day. Whereas a woman working as an unskilled agricultural laborer might earn Ksh 5–15 per day for weeding, this woman earns at least Ksh 45 per day through petty trading. Her income is extremely important to the household, as it had previously relied heavily on income from sugarcane and jaggery production. The pressures on this woman are clear. With five young children showing strong evidence of nutritional deficiencies, she is keenly concerned about their health and the family's need for income.

In addition to trading and domestic duties, women in South Kamwango are also involved in the agricultural cycle, especially during planting, weeding, and harvesting periods. Female children and relatives in the home carry out tasks similar to those of the wife or co-wives. However, the husband makes the decisions on what crops are to be cultivated. In one typical situation, two co-wives reported that they do their agricultural work separately, each on her own plot. They grow the same things, primarily food for the family and a small amount of produce for sale. Each grows groundnuts, and they give the profits from that crop to their husband. They keep the returns on the bananas for themselves. Clearly, the choice of new commercial crops to replace sugarcane is key in regard to the gender division of benefits and costs.

Further, there are important differences in the kinds of property sales benefiting women versus men. Women's sales are small scale; men may sell cattle or land and may have access to cash income through employment or the sale of a commercial crop. Shipton notes that the access to new and large amounts of cash—with its qualities of transportability, concealability, and divisibility—has upset the balance of control over wealth between the sexes.[22]

Men's Productive Activities: Issues of Access and Control

Men have authority and economic control over the home. On the farm, male family members make the key decisions on crops and prepare the land, which may involve hiring oxen and plow or doing the actual plowing with hand tools. Traditionally, the men also herd the cattle and make decisions concerning cash transactions involving cattle. They often seek work outside the farm as casual laborers as well.

Until recently, as indicated, many men in South Kamwango have grown sugarcane. With half an acre of sugarcane a man could earn Ksh 5,000 after processing it into jaggery. This would represent less than twenty days of labor. Expenses would include those for hiring oxen for milling and for hiring a laborer to assist with making the jaggery. A *debe* of processed sugarcane makes five or six jaggery containers, which are sold for Ksh 4. Thus the farmer can earn Ksh 20–24 per *debe*. The cost of milling is Ksh 3 per *debe*, and a team of oxen can grind fifteen *debes* per day at a total cost of Ksh 45. A laborer to assist with the process of boiling the cane earns Ksh 10 per day. Returns therefore could be seventy-five to ninety jaggery containers, or Ksh 300–360 for a day's work. After expenses are deducted, the farmer may earn Ksh 255–315 for a day's jaggery making. These returns are substantially higher than those for casual labor or small-scale trading.

A comparison of results for alternative uses of both land and labor shows that sugarcane ranks high in terms of yield. Half an acre of groundnuts yields Ksh 2,875 whereas half an acre of sugarcane yields Ksh 5,000. Sugarcane requires approximately one and a half years to mature, so annual returns would be approximately Ksh 3,325. Many households cultivated 1 acre of sugarcane, earning Ksh 6,650 annually.

The prohibition on this crop, without the substitution of another cash crop, has had a strong impact not only on household cash income but also on both male and female economic activities. It has left men struggling to find alternative agricultural or nonfarm work. It has pushed women toward more active trading and selling of their agricultural products, some of which are needed by the family. Both men and women are discouraged over the prohibition on sugarcane production. Many are eager to explore alternative crops with some assistance from the government.[23]

COMMUNITY RESPONSES: FLEDGLING INSTITUTIONS AND CHANGING RESOURCE CONDITIONS

Responsibility for planning and implementing Kenya's rural development shifted to the districts in the mid-1980s to enable rural communities to make decisions on their priorities in regard to development projects. The District Focus for Rural Development policy assumes a complementary relationship among the ministries, with their different sectoral approaches to addressing local needs.[24] The objective is to broaden the base of rural development and encourage local initiatives to improve problem identification, resource mobilization, and project design and implementation.

A well-organized institutional structure at the grassroots level is required to facilitate any kind of project activity. At present, South Kamwango is heavily dependent on local government for development initiatives. Local institutional infrastructure is thin; people are inexperienced in working at the community level; and the urgency of household and family problems has prompted many to focus their attention at that level. They may even be unaware that the scope of some of their problems is not contained within the boundaries of their own household.

Local Institutions in South Kamwango

Pressures on a slim infrastructure: the government. The government is the most important institutional actor in South Kamwango, whether in terms of direct administration or various extension services. South Kamwango was created as a separate sublocation only in 1986. Thus, Assistant Chief Charles Omburo is relatively new in his position; in 1990 he had been in office for only three years. At that time, he was still in the process of consolidating his authority. Clearly committed to fostering development in the area and to raising the socioeconomic standards of the residents of South Kamwango, he faces the challenge of rallying support from all segments and factions of the community.

A sublocation development committee, chaired by the assistant chief, consists of members of the community, among them extension agents, elders, and teachers. This committee's mandate is to discuss matters of social and economic importance pertaining to the sublocation. However, its potential is yet to be realized—it is semidormant and rarely meets.

Leadership questions, issues of accountability, capacity to mobilize the public, and ways to build a development-conscious community are of paramount importance in South Kamwango. The role of the assistant chief is central to addressing these issues. His relationship to the chief of the location is an important element of local leadership because the needs of the sublocation must ultimately be incorporated into the overall planning efforts of the entire location of North Kamagambo. It is evident that leaders in the sublocation are still grappling with building a strong and effective base. The issues they face demand imagination, conscientious leadership, and vision.

Limited operations: NGOs, churches, and schools. Two NGOs perform limited activities in the community. The Catholic diocese of Kisii provides health services for mothers and children and family planning services through a mobile clinic, which comes twice a month to the sublocation. CARE-Kenya has funded a small agroforestry program through the Ofwanga Women's Group. The government's Lake Basin Development Authority (LBDA), a semiautonomous agency involved in the provision of rural water supply, has built a protected well in the sublocation at the site of the mobile clinic.

There are ten church congregations in the sublocation, although there are no church buildings. A Catholic church is under construction. Three congregations are Catholic, three are Seventh-Day Adventist, and the remaining four belong to smaller sects. All but the Catholic church confine their activities to religious concerns. Not only does the Catholic church support the clinic, it also helps support several schools. One Catholic parish sponsors a group of men and women who carry out some fund-raising activities for the church.

The sublocation has three primary schools with a total student population of slightly over one thousand pupils. There are no secondary schools and no nursery schools. The primary schools are semipermanent structures that are not well maintained and have inadequate water and sanitation facilities. All the schools are teaching some resource management awareness through tree planting activities despite the difficulties in procuring seeds.

Nascent organizations and scarce resources: women's groups.   Six formal women's groups in South Kamwango have from ten to forty-three members. All the groups have been started under the umbrella of Maendeleo ya Wanawake, the national women's organization, taken over by the national political party, KANU, in the early 1990s. The main objectives of the South Kamwango groups are to generate income and improve the welfare of the members' families, although many of the members are not clear how to go about accomplishing these goals. The women also view their groups as forums where they can exchange views freely and gain knowledge on various kinds of development issues.

The women's groups were started in 1987–1988, just after the sublocation's reorganization, as part of the government's efforts to encourage local development in that community. Of the six, in 1990 three were still in an early organizational stage. Activities include a zero grazing scheme for grade cattle, a tree nursery, and a beekeeping scheme that was just being launched. Two groups discontinued their tree nurseries because the women felt that they were not generating sufficient income to justify the effort. At the time of the survey, these groups had not decided on their next activity.

The Ofwanga Women's Group carried out the zero grazing and tree nursery projects. In regions where cattle diseases are widespread, this is the preferred management for grade cattle, which are excellent milk producers but highly susceptible to disease. A women's group qualifies for a grade cow if it is able to construct a shed for the cow and plant an acre of napier grass. The women in this group had done so and were caring for a grade cow. The group had received instruction on fodder growing and management and was benefiting from regular extension advice from the government and from CARE-Kenya. By late 1990, the Ofwanga Women's Group was in a position to raise funds through milk sales and to demonstrate zero grazing techniques for a community with the potential for engaging in improved dairy farming. At that time political and administrative leaders in Rongo Division widely encouraged zero grazing projects, although little effort had been made specifically in South Kamwango. The Member of Parliament for the area supported the zero grazing scheme of the Ofwanga Women's Group.

The Tonye Women's Group, with thirty-five women and eight men, maintained a nursery through which members sell a variety of seedlings, drawing on advice from the government and from CARE. They planned to undertake a zero grazing project, had rented land under a four-year agreement, planted the napier grass, and were building the cow shed. This group rotates labor, working collectively for its members on each of their farms. Occasionally the group works for nonmembers for a fee. It maintains a bank account and has plans for future investment in a building in Rongo. The chairperson and inspiration behind this group was a woman teaching in a primary school in South Kamwango.

Aside from the members of the Ofwanga and the Tonye women's groups, most of the women of South Kamwango are not enthusiastic about participation in women's groups. They are constrained from participating in activities outside the home by time commitments and work loads. In addition, they are not persuaded that there are benefits from belonging to such groups. These conditions, combined with difficulties the groups face in procuring capital for initiating projects, have led to a lack of motivation for group activities among the women. With few exceptions, the women have not benefited from systematic training that could enable them to make good project choices for generating income. (In 1994 investigation in South Kamwango revealed that the women's groups were faltering. The cow that the Ofwanga Women's Group was caring for in 1990 had died. No other group had undertaken zero grazing activities. The challenges for institution building remained substantially as they were in 1990.)

Most of the women of South Kamwango have very little or no formal education. A leader in one of the women's groups summarized this situation: "The level of education is so low in South Kamwango that it is the biggest drawback in raising awareness and knowledge levels of the women." Most of the women who are active leaders in the South Kamwango groups are resident in the sublocation by virtue of marriage or having been assigned to the sublocation through the educational service. Thus, they have broader experience and higher educational levels than natives of the sublocation, and they can imagine conditions different from those existing within South Kamwango.

TRENDS IN SOUTH KAMWANGO

Demographic Trends

South Kamwango is beginning to experience pressures on resources related to rapid population growth. It is common to find households with two or three wives each with four or five living children. Some people recognize and can articulate the impact of these statistics on their own families. They recognize the troubles their children will have in obtaining sufficient land for cultivation; they lament their inability to provide secondary education for their own children. One man asserted, "If I had money, I would rather educate one and leave five home to starve."[25] Although he may have overstated the case, he was acutely aware of the desperate need to provide a new avenue out of poverty.

Migori's population is young. Those aged fifteen years and younger constitute about 50 percent of the entire population. As a result, the dependency ratio is high. Although there is considerable awareness of family planning, and

85 percent of the adult population is familiar with the concept, the acceptance rate is only 5 percent.[26] The increase in population and the continuing inclination for large, polygamous families are leading to a reduction in the available, cultivable land per household. For most households in South Kamwango, this is not yet a critical issue. Many respondents, however, face daily pressures on other natural resources, particularly fuelwood. Few are systematically responding to the impact of fuelwood shortages and increased time involved in gathering firewood, but they are aware of the toll on their time and energies.

The overall effects of population increase on resources are well understood, yet this understanding, under present circumstances, does not necessarily shape household decisions on family size. At the public meeting, several women and older men spoke in favor of family planning and limiting family size. Several younger men opposed it. "How," one asked, "can we have family planning when so many of our children die?" It is clear that questions of population growth can be examined only in the context of South Kamwango's health situation and its extraordinarily high infant mortality rates. (Figure 7.2 indicates the extent of child mortality in South Kamwango.)

Trends in Health and Sanitation

The continuing presence of severe, environmentally related health problems is one of the most significant issues for South Kamwango. The widespread and commonplace assortment of diseases can be attributed to several factors. The water is sufficient but the quality is poor. Rare is the family that has a protected well or boils its drinking water. The Kira River, which runs through the sublocation and which many households use for drinking water, is seriously polluted. Furthermore, sanitation is poor. Fewer than half the households have a latrine; groundwater levels are high, and the opportunities for the spread of disease are evident. Obeng, a leading expert on African freshwater ecosystems, states, "The incidence of diarrhoeal and other diseases is greatly increased by the use of contaminated water for drinking and bathing, together with insufficient education on environmental sanitation and hygiene."[27] South Kamwango households provide supporting evidence.

The poor health status of the community, especially children, is caused largely by factors that are preventable (in addition to environmental sanitation). Most children die from preventable diseases like measles, even though a health outreach facility is available twice a month. One respondent asserted, "These days children are dying from measles because of the mother's ignorance. Women do not follow through on immunization. They do not understand the preventative aspects of inoculations. Even the Women's Guild of the Catholic Church has met to discuss this issue."

The South Kamwango survey suggests that more than half the deaths of children under five are related to measles and its complications (usually, secondary pneumonia in children younger than two years old, as well as postinfection encephalitis). Measles is a severe disease among malnourished children.[28] Figure 7.3 indicates respondents' perceptions of the causes of deaths of children under five within their own families. On average, each mother has lost 2.2 children; the range in the survey varied from zero to six.

Malnutrition in the form of marasmus, kwashiorkor, and various vitamin deficiencies has reached epidemic levels, but most mothers do not associate conditions caused by malnutrition with poor diet. With the emphasis on cultivated foods, they have lost access to and knowledge of several important wild green vegetables that are traditional sources of vitamin A. Similarly, they do not relate the increasing numbers of stomach ailments and skin infections to the quality of water. Nor do people link these problems to the general health status and levels of sanitation. Measures that would improve family health, such as boiling drinking water, are not undertaken, primarily for three reasons: the women have no basis for understanding a cause–effect relationship between water quality and health, firewood may be in short supply, and there are time constraints. In one typical household, the respondent said, "Our water is not good. It has worms. We use a sieve, but we do not boil it. We dug a latrine, but

Figure 7.2   Births and Child Survival in South Kamwango

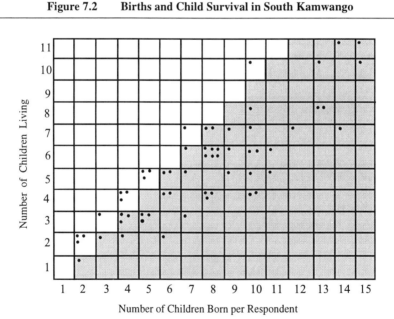

Number of Children Born per Respondent

Notes: • = 1 household; N = 60. Only those households in unshaded squares have not had children die before the age of five (20% of total). All households in shaded squares have lost one or more children before the age of five.

we do not like to use it. A lot of mosquitoes collect in the hole. We have serious problems with malaria, but we do not know what brings it. . . . My son died from stomach problems."

Child care is the exclusive domain of the woman. The status of children in the sublocation reflects the nature of women's knowledge regarding nutrition and disease. The household interviews revealed that most mothers have some knowledge of the nature of diseases but do not conceptualize the cause–effect relationship of environmental conditions and their children's health problems. There is very low awareness of the constellation of hygiene, nutrition, and sanitation factors and their relationship to environmental quality, settlement, and land use. Repetto reminds us of the importance of women's knowledge on these and other issues. He states: "Where rapid gains in reducing mortality have been achieved, improvement in the educational and social status of women has been a key. The mother is the basic health worker in all societies."[29]

Apart from problems caused by specific environmental conditions, there are notable changes in life-styles, especially dietary patterns, which are having a detrimental impact on health. Many respondents made two observations: diets have become less varied and nutritious in recent decades, and health, particularly that of children, has deteriorated noticeably in recent years. Indigenous foods that at one time provided essential nutrients have been discarded in

Figure 7.3   South Kamwango Perceptions of Causes of Mortality of Own Children Who Have Died Before the Age of Five

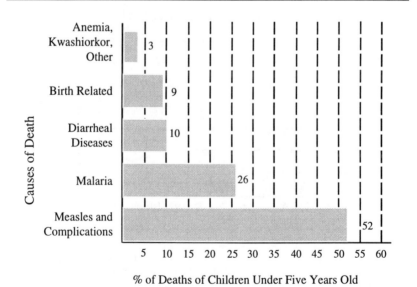

favor of less nutritious foods. Specifically, maize is now the staple food, serving as the central element in children's diets from an early age, and it does not provide them with the nutrients they need. Few residents of South Kamwango are using indigenous vegetables. They do not like them, claiming that they are too bitter. In addition, people previously cooked with milk, but they no longer do so since they keep few cattle.

Malnutrition contributes to the high levels of infant mortality in South Kamwango. As noted earlier, infant mortality rates in Migori and Homa-Bay Districts (formerly South Nyanza District) are the highest in the country (130–160/1,000). Most deaths of children from birth to 3 years are caused by immunizable childhood diseases, by dehydration from diarrhea, and by complications from severe malnutrition. Despite the availability of health services, most people are openly ambivalent about using them. One woman stated emphatically, "A hospital injection means that children die easily; when they are treated with traditional medicine, they usually survive."[30] Many prefer to adhere to traditional beliefs and practices in dealing with their health problems.

Thus, there is an urgent need to increase women's understanding of the nature and origins of many illnesses and thereby to improve both their willingness and capacity to address the root causes of these problems. Knowledge about matters of health, sanitation, and nutrition should be central to the lives of women in South Kamwango. At present, trends in these areas are negative. If people-centered development is to take place in South Kamwango, reversing these trends in health, nutrition, and sanitation is essential.

Trends in Conceptualizing the Community

Thinking about the community and long-term change.   The pace of development in a community is affected by the ways communitywide issues are understood. It was quite evident that many individuals do not have a clear sense of communitywide problems or possible solutions. They identified household concerns and personal problems but simply did not recognize options for dealing with their concerns at the community level. They had difficulty with or were unwilling to think about the potential of community-managed development over time and the impact such changes might have on their community and their own households.

In some instances, this perspective seemed to derive from the respondent's relative inexperience in dealing with affairs beyond the immediate household. In others, it related to direct observation of project achievements within the community. For example, provision of the mobile clinic has not done much to decrease the community's chronic morbidity; as another illustration, the work of the agricultural extension service is not linked to awareness of improved incomes and nutritional status of South Kamwango residents and is regarded as a relatively isolated government activity.

Respondent reluctance or inability to consider possibilities for and benefits of long-term community-managed changes may arise from personal inexperience or from the jaded cynicism of involvement with fruitless community-level activities. Whatever their origin, these attitudes are unlikely to change without vision and leadership at the community level. Only with such human resources are people likely to look beyond the concerns of the moment to explore long-term solutions to problems.

The role of education and new opportunities.   Education and training of various sorts can offer new opportunities to those who take advantage of them. In South Kamwango some households have responded positively to efforts of the agricultural extension officer to encourage the use of organic manure and hybrid seeds. Some have received extension advice on management of the striga weed. Introduction of the zero grazing project through the Ofwanga Women's Group generated interest on the part of some individual farmers in owning a grade cow. Women's groups have been the beneficiaries of a cockerel exchange program organized by the agricultural extension service. Thus, there are important areas in which local residents respond to new ideas and practices. Agricultural practices are among them.

Sometimes, however, there is resistance to new ideas. For example, many people in South Kamwango believe that a child will grow up to be strong only if he or she contracts measles. Given that 20 percent of the children do not see their fifth birthday and that it is possible to prevent measles through an inoculation obtainable at a nearby clinic, this belief seems surprisingly persistent and counterproductive.

Whereas people respond to innovations in agriculture, the areas of health and environmental management seem to be more intractable. This may be in part because complex behavioral changes are required if the transmission cycles of water-related diseases are to be broken.[31] Even if the household has clean drinking water—and most in South Kamwango do not—the fecal–oral pathogens that cause many waterborne diseases may still be ingested if hands and dishes are not clean. In the case of South Kamwango, the issues are not scarcity, distance, and expense but the acquisition of pure drinking water and the use of water for improved hygiene and sanitation. These depend on information, health education, and motivation.

Receptivity to learning new ways relates, in some measure, to levels of education, to attitudes of inquiry obtained through education, and to the usefulness of the knowledge to be acquired. It also relates to cultural attitudes, which change slowly. Levels of education are indeed low. Few middle-aged women have completed more than Standard 3; most have no education. Many younger women have completed up to Standard 6 or 7. For older men, typically the standard reached is 4 or 5, and for younger men, 6 or 7. The schools of South Kamwango are hard-pressed; dropout rates are high.

Increasingly, people perceive education as a way out of poverty, yet the difficulties of providing education seem nearly insurmountable. Meanwhile, the lack of knowledge on current conditions of nutrition, sanitation, and disease is apparent. Also apparent are wide-ranging problems that focus people on such a difficult present that it is nearly impossible for them to design a different future.

LEARNING FROM SOUTH KAMWANGO

Why, in this community of strong potential, have productivity and well-being been so elusive? Why is South Kamwango considered a pocket of poverty? What can we learn from the opportunity to become acquainted with this community? And of what relevance is gender to the process of encouraging people-centered development? These questions can be addressed by considering the following five factors.

First, respondents in almost every household interview identified health as their critical household problem. Measles, malaria, tetanus, polio, nutritional conditions such as marasmus and kwashiorkor, skin diseases, acute respiratory infections, diarrheal diseases, and intestinal worms are among the illnesses mentioned or for which there was evidence. Survey data confirmed that infant mortality is high, averaging 25–33 percent per mother; occasionally it is as high as 66 percent or even 90 percent. Poor health conditions were evident in virtually every household, particularly in the one-to-five age group. Most of the common diseases derive from a lack of potable and safe water, inadequate environmental sanitation, insufficient protection through inoculations, and malnutrition. All of these causes fall within the purview of women's responsibilities. The nexus of gender roles, water, nutrition, and health—particularly child health—is evident.

Second, women's roles involve not only domestic duties and agricultural responsibilities but also high levels of skill and entrepreneurship at small-scale trading, primarily of foodstuffs and produce. In this latter area women from South Kamwango are savvy and well informed. However, they have inadequate knowledge on a variety of important health and nutrition-related topics. Most women can effectively describe the symptoms of the diseases that affect their children. However, few seem to link causes, such as unclean water, and consequences in the form of disease. As the headmaster of one school emphasized, "Most parents are very ignorant on health matters." Most are also uninformed on matters of nutrition and water quality under current conditions of land use, food supply, and water management. This is particularly the case for younger age groups. Older women seemed to have relevant traditional knowledge on balanced diets and basic herbal remedies. Evidence points to the importance of both preserving indigenous knowledge on long-term practices and educating women in regard to water pollution and related risk factors in areas of increasing population density and encroaching modernization.

Third, many households continue to struggle to meet cash needs. Until 1989, when the government banned sugarcane growing in South Kamwango, it was the primary commodity through which the sublocation was linked to the cash economy. Although a few households still produce sugarcane, most have complied with the policy by burning the cane and are searching for alternative crops to provide them with a source of cash. This pressure on finding new income opportunities is felt in many communities across Kenya; it is unusually acute here given the ban on a crop long grown in the area and given the inability of the community, local entrepreneurs, and the government to arrange appropriate marketing facilities to accommodate it.[32] Nor has the government put substantial effort into helping local residents find alternatives to sugarcane.

Fourth, community institutions in this locality are fragile. NGOs, churches, and women's groups have shallow roots. Unlike Gikarangu (Chapter 4) and Mbusyani (Chapter 5), there is no track record of community organizations with strong social agendas. Certainly, organizations with environmental agendas are nonexistent, despite the urgency of addressing some environmental issues. Overall, South Kamwango is characterized by an absence of community efforts for addressing common problems. Furthermore, there appears to be a general reluctance among respondents to consider issues at the community level. A common voice might enable South Kamwango residents to begin to address some of the health and environmental issues they face, both individually and collectively, and might give strength to dealing with some of the economic and social issues confronting them.

The final issue relates to leadership approaches and vision within the community. Discussions reveal that notions of political accountability, community mobilization, and public awareness are just beginning to emerge in South Kamwango. The district officer for Rongo Division is encouraging leaders throughout his division to adopt a development-oriented style. This includes a more participatory approach to development, involving efforts to engage all members of the community—men and women—in addressing community problems and in seeking both the vision and the accountability of those who lead them.

South Kamwango Sublocation is a community with enormous potential as well as enormous problems. Although its people are acutely aware of many of them, they are only beginning to identify alternatives and solutions. Findings of this study point to the critical, yet often overlooked, roles of women in establishing the conditions under which family welfare and improved livelihoods can emerge in South Kamwango and in other communities like it, not only in Kenya but in other parts of Africa as well. The findings also underscore the importance of nurturing community organizations that can become focal points for community action in addressing environmental, resource, and health problems. Women, as well as men, are central to this venture.

South Kamwango is neither isolated nor remote, yet the benefits of development seem to have passed it by. As one respondent said, "We have not yet seen the fruits of independence." This community's problems are aggravated by the following:

- Insufficient attention to the knowledge, resources, awareness, time constraints, and motivation of women as the primary family caretakers in the areas of health, sanitation, and nutrition
- The pressures of poverty, intensified by the larger political and economic systems, in which South Kamwango finds unfavorable terms of exchange and costly requirements for entry and access as reflected in recent agricultural policies
- Conditions shaped by impure water and poor sanitation leading to high child mortality, as well as other harmful demographic and health trends
- Fragile institutions, which are just beginning to address communitywide issues

The men and women of South Kamwango face extraordinary challenges. They need resources for addressing them. They also need information, organization, and a catalyst for action. The task ahead involves dislodging the intertwined roots of poverty and poor health.

NOTES

1. This study was undertaken in 1990 when Migori was part of South Nyanza District. In 1993, South Nyanza District was divided into Homa-Bay District and Migori District. District-level data derived from information gathered before 1993 is based on statistics for South Nyanza District.

2. Government of Kenya, Ministry of Economic Planning and Development, *Migori District Development Plan, 1994–1996*, p. 9.

3. Ibid, p. 13.

4. Youri, *South Nyanza District Health Situation*, p. 56.

5. Shipton, *Bitter Money*, p. 30.

6. Ibid.

7. Shipton, "Lineage and Locality as Antithetical Principles," p. 126.

8. Shipton, *Bitter Money*, p. 19.

9. Youri, *South Nyanza District Health Situation,* p. 58.

10. Johnson, "Social Investment in a Developing Economy," p. 342.

11. Participant, village meeting, October 26, 1990.

12. Diamond, "Trees for the Poorest?" p. 13.

13. Ibid., p. 27.

14. Pala Okeyo, "Daughters of the Lakes and Rivers"; Hay and Stichter (eds.), *African Women South of the Sahara.*

15. Shipton, *Bitter Money*, p. 19.

16. Youri, *South Nyanza District Health Situation*, pp. 7–9.

17. Ibid., p. 58.

18. In several meetings in October 1990, Mr. Gachanja, district officer for Rongo Division, discussed the reasons for the ban on sugarcane production.

19. Personal communication, Isabella Asamba, June 11, 1994.

20. Government of Kenya, Central Bureau of Statistics, *Economic Survey, 1994.*

21. Kennedy and Cogill, "The Case of Sugarcane in Kenya."

22. Shipton, *Bitter Money*, pp. 51–52.

23. In 1994, discussions with NGO professional staff working in Rongo Division revealed that the ban on sugarcane continues and that the absence of efforts on the part of the government to introduce other cash crops is glaring. More lands are under food crops, and people are somewhat better off nutritionally. However, it needs to be determined whether the reason is the increase in fields planted to maize or the discovery of gold nearby. A number of South Kamwango men are now working in newly opened gold mines. Though they are not getting rich, they are increasing levels of household income for basic purchases. Most of those who are reaping the greatest benefit from the discovery of gold are traders from outside the community.

24. Government of Kenya, Ministry of Planning and National Development, *National Development Plan, 1989–1993*.

25. Participant, group meeting, October 26, 1990.

26. Youri, *South Nyanza District Health Situation*.

27. Obeng, *Population and Environment*, p. 5.

28. Gordon, *Control of Communicable Diseases in Man*, p. 146.

29. Repetto (ed.), *The Global Possible*, p. 149.

30. Respondent, South Kamwango, 1990.

31. Cox and Annis, "Community Participation in Rural Water Supply," p. 68.

32. This seems quite surprising given the rising demand for sugar and the need to import large quantities—for example 65,200 tons in 1993 (see Government of Kenya, Central Bureau of Statistics, *Economic Survey, 1994*).

Part 3

Considering Policy

8

Policy Implications and Opportunities for Action

Barbara Thomas-Slayter, Dianne Rocheleau, Charity Kabutha

Understanding rural livelihood systems is central to policy formulation and program and project design for sustainable resource management. The five case studies in Part 2 of this book examine six rural communities in a variety of agroecological zones in Kenya to explore the following: (1) the relationship between gender and environment in rural livelihood systems, particularly the ways gender-based roles and responsibilities affect the sustainable management of natural resources at household and community levels; (2) the responses of local communities to changing resource conditions, with emphasis on understanding community-based institutions and leadership; (3) the impact of these responses on resource management, employment opportunities, and, broadly, the prospects for sustainable development; and (4) the relevance of the findings to policymaking for rural communities, sustainable management of resources, and livelihood security for both women and men.

Attention given by policymakers to gender-based responsibilities, community organization, and the effective management of natural resources can help improve conditions for these rural communities and their households. Analysis of the changes that have come—and continue to come—to these communities can illuminate the ways national and international governments and development agencies might contribute to this process. In fact, the convergence of gender, livelihood, and resource management issues, as demonstrated in the communities investigated, can inform policy at local, national, and international levels.

Increasingly, the boundaries among community, national, and global systems are blurred and shifting. Although the cases in Part 2 focus, in each instance, on the microlevel, the processes shaping them and the implications of the findings relate to local, national, and international arenas. The cases provide information and insights that can contribute to substantial revisions as well as specific refinements of existing policy. Whether the policy changes are ma-

jor or minor, the integration of gender, ecology, and issues of community organization into policy can help to strengthen the balance between men's and
women's rights and responsibilities in rural communities; can integrate important elements of economic, environmental, and social policy; and can address
economic and political barriers to environmental sustainability.

All nations—North and South—need to overcome deep-rooted economic
and political causes of poverty and ecological crisis. Governments, NGOs, and
international agencies, for example, must make the link between the human
consequences of the economic crisis and the massive debt burden of many developing countries, including Kenya. Governments that are heavily indebted
and struggling with structural adjustment have cut domestic social services,
often to the detriment of the nation's children. The UNDP's *Human Development Report* for 1994, assessing human development since World War II, em-
phasizes that an arresting picture emerges of unprecedented human progress
yet unspeakable human misery, of rich and poor nations alike afflicted by growing
human distress.[1] The report asserts that understanding a new conceptualization
of human security—of which health would be a key element—is an important
step toward securing sustainable livelihoods. In the struggle for livelihood that
we have observed in six communities in rural Kenya, women are the key actors
in the domains of health, food security, and management of natural resources.

WHY GENDER MATTERS

Gender matters in the context of sustainable resource management and development policy primarily for four reasons. First, the responsibilities for managing resources are designated according to gender. In rural Kenya, women have
major responsibilities for managing soils, water, trees, and agricultural productivity. Second, women often must undertake new responsibilities without adequate knowledge, technology, resources, and time. Third, women are the majority of the rural constituency and therefore are most affected by environment
and development programs and policy. Fourth, the responses to the environmental crisis are largely initiated collectively by women who see the basis of
their livelihood system eroding.

Gender shapes the opportunities and constraints women and men face in
securing viable livelihoods and strong communities across cultural, political,
economic, and ecological settings. Moreover, as Sen states succinctly, "The
systematically inferior position of women inside and outside the household in
many societies points to the necessity of treating gender as a force of its own in
development analysis."[2] Although the relative deprivation of women vis-à-vis
men varies around the world according to specific context, this fact does not
diminish the importance of gender as an analytical tool. If policy is to reach the
grassroots with effective prescriptions and action for sustainable management

Figure 8.1   Gender, Environment, and Development

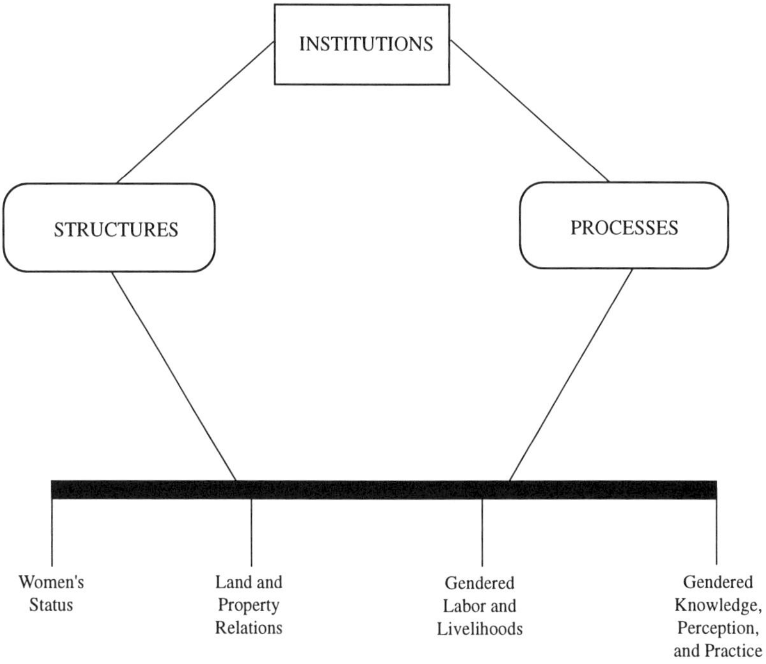

of resources, it will have to address the concerns of men *and* women and the ways both genders, individually and collectively, relate to the state, the economy, and the land.

As we stated in Chapter 1, resource and gender issues are central to debates about the nature of Kenyan society, the claims women and men can make on this society, and the realities of distributional justice. Our discussion is predicated on the assertion that gender is a variable that must be used to inform development planning, policies, programs, and projects. Gender is central to positioning both men and women vis-à-vis the institutions that determine access not only to land and other immediate resources but also to the wider economy and policy.[3] Thus, we begin with the institutions considered in the five case studies, emphasizing key points about both structure and process as they bear on policy considerations. We draw on illustrations from the communities presented in Part 2 and relate the findings from the cases to four analytical categories: women's status in its political, social, and legal dimensions; gendered land and property relations; gendered labor and livelihoods; and gendered knowledge (see Figure 8.1). For each category we identify several key policy options that address the vital roles women play in managing resources as they strive to build more secure livelihoods.

INSTITUTIONS

Structural Focus

We focus briefly on the state at the national level and on the community, recognizing that in the case of Kenya there is a gap, a "hollow middle," between community-based and national institutions and practices with respect to resource management.[4] In spite of the policy emphasis on district-level development, the infrastructure, procedure, personnel, and policies are not yet in place in most districts to allow for an integrated treatment of resource management and environmental protection.

The community is the world in which we all live, work, create meanings, and structure realities from a myriad of experiences. Macrostructures shape the political and economic environments of local communities. National and international policies establish the context in which local networks, associations, and organizations exist; in effect, they set the terms of reference, but the action is played out in the local community and can in turn affect the broader context.

Attention to rural communities and local institutions is critical for addressing ecological decline and restoring the productivity and sustainability of rural Africa. As noted in Chapter 1, many also find local organizations and grassroots movements central to effective social change and the empowerment of women. Both formal and informal structures are relevant to these processes, actively linking the state, public policy, development plans, external agents, and the rural household. Understanding how such structures function and what their impact is on the women and men who participate in them is central to determining appropriate development interventions for achieving sustainability. NGOs as well as governments can contribute to the processes of strengthening local institutions.

Local communities.   Local organizations constitute an important part of the rural landscape. In most instances, membership, participation, and activities in these organizations are determined by gender. This gendering has implications not only for the access of individuals and households to resources but also for stratification patterns within communities.

Evidence from the five case studies indicates that rapidly changing economic opportunities and constraints are affecting relationships within and between households. New patterns of cooperation, reciprocity, and exchange are emerging, particularly among both formal and informal women's groups, to ensure household security, improve livelihoods, and promote individual and collective welfare. Local women's organizations exist in all the sublocations investigated. In Kathama, Mbusyani, Gikarangu, and Pwani they have great potential and are currently underrepresented as centers for decisionmaking and action on resource management and community welfare issues. Women in Kathama have organized themselves around routine agricultural work and mutual assistance with births, deaths, and illnesses in the family. They have extended their organizations to deal with subsistence, famine relief, and access to resources, as well as rotating credit, marketing of baskets and rope, house construction, terrace construction, and tree nurseries. In Mbusyani, a women's organization owns and operates a maize grinding mill. Women in Gikarangu have identified steps for educating young women and are addressing the problems of teenage girls. In Pwani, women have taken on the task of providing domestic water supplies to group members.

Significant portions of the populations in the six sublocations under investigation have been experiencing the pressures of increasing commercialization of agriculture and displacement of food crops (Gikarangu); ecological decline due to watershed degradation (Mbusyani); resource scarcity in crowded resettlement areas such as Pwani; declining agricultural productivity and deteriorating human health, as in South Kamwango; and poverty, land scarcity, and out-migration in Kathama. Through informal networks and formal associations and organizations men and women in these communities seek access to resources, to public and private goods and services, and to centers of power and decisionmaking. They also create mechanisms to channel their own individual efforts into community-based action.

Gender and the state. Women do not experience the state in the same way as do men, whether one is considering its ideological, legal, political, administrative, or developmental dimensions. Evidence from the case studies demonstrates that the view of the state from the bottom (i.e., at the local level) differs for men and women. Direct evidence of these differences permeates all five case studies. Women have limited access to the state and few occupy official positions. Laws, norms, and ideology shape different political meanings for men and women. The intended and unintended consequences of state action also affect men and women differently.[5]

In South Kamwango, for example, the ban on sugarcane, intended to increase food production and improve nutrition, actually put increased pressure on women to allocate more time for trading activities away from home. The laws against uprooting coffee or intercropping coffee with other crops in Gikarangu, during a time of low coffee prices, resulted in negligible returns, either in produce or in cash, from the best land of many households, placing a major burden on women for feeding their families. In just about any community in Kenya, one can observe the inconsistencies and contradictions of policies that are intended to promote economic well-being at the national level but that diminish livelihood security for many households.

Many national-level policies, when observed from the community level, appear to be biased in favor of men. Gender is central in terms of access to the state and in terms of state resource allocation. In fact, as we observed in Chapter 1, states are characterized by distinctive gender ideologies that guide resource allocation decisions and shape the material realities with which people live.[6] For many women in the six communities we explored, as well as in others across Kenya, the state is experienced as insensitive to gender issues; policies reflect and are shaped by either the "invisibility" of women and their interests or an active gender bias.

Moreover, evidence from these sublocations suggests that a patriarchal ideology and the presence of women's organizations have sometimes provided officials with the opportunity to control women's collective labor for public purposes. Increasingly, women are seeking ways to redefine expectations at the intersection of gender-based responsibilities and the requirements of the state.

Process Focus

How institutions carry out their work is central to addressing the issues under consideration, whether they are governmental institutions functioning at the local, district, or national level; NGOs; or international donor agencies. We propose three critical process elements: consider the user, create an enabling participatory setting, and acknowledge women's responsibilities in community resource management.

Consider the user.   In focusing on the resource user, one makes no assumptions about who is performing the various tasks—farming, managing the coffee, trading, plowing, providing animal care, running the shop, and so on. This focus directs extension services, credit, technology, information, and resources to those who need and will use them, irrespective of gender. It strips away notions of what men are supposed to do and what women are supposed to do— increasingly, as evidence from four of the six communities demonstrates, old assumptions about gender roles no longer apply. Throughout rural Kenya, changes are occurring that require a focus on resource users—these changes include the introduction of new crops, the pull of the cash economy, newly divided households, women taking up animal care and long-distance trading, and men taking up long-term migration and French bean growing. Increasingly, all public and private agencies working on resource and development issues must ask "Who is doing what, now?" and "What are the trends for the future?" because livelihood structures are under stress and in flux.

Despite its obvious practicality and common sense, such an approach must take into account that access to and use of resources are often contested terrain and therefore involve the exercise of power and resistance to it. Indeed, in many parts of the world, management of resources and environmental activism involve struggles against expropriation by outsiders as well as resistance to exploitation by local elites. That resistance might involve active confrontation, or it might be waged with the "weapons of the weak."[7] Stakeholders in the local environment, acutely aware of the issues, have strong incentives for managing resources sustainably. Disenfranchised stakeholders may, in turn, express resistance to any resource management initiatives pending recovery of lost lands and resources. A user focus will more effectively bring government policymakers into accord with stakeholder concerns. A nuanced understanding of women's and men's daily lives must shape the agendas of organizations, and these agendas must reflect needs and opportunities across environment, development, and gender lines as they are currently positioned in NGOs and government bodies.

Create an enabling participatory setting.   Agencies should strive to create an enabling environment for local development activities. Without a supportive national milieu, favorably disposed to local initiatives, such initiatives are not likely to emerge. This means that in the policy arena, governments (aided by NGOs and international donors) should encourage discussion of approaches that enable local communities to assess and address their needs for managing resources effectively and for gaining access to more secure livelihoods. Additionally, rural communities need clear channels to communicate demands on the state for action that is beyond the scope of local groups.

Community empowerment, as well as the elements of programs and projects, will be strengthened significantly by involving local people in data collection as well as decisionmaking and implementation processes. Such involvement can encourage community awareness, understanding, and commitment; facilitate decisionmaking, consensus building, and conflict resolution; and build collaboration among outside researchers or development workers and the community. This cooperation can assist processes of empowerment and sustainable development. Using participatory methods, local community members can readily identify and begin to address their most critical problems, such as inadequate sources of income, poor health, polluted water, limited institutional capacity, low food productivity, insufficient fuelwood, and a lack of knowledge in specific areas.

At the district and local levels, participatory approaches to problem definition and local activity within rural communities can be encouraged. NGOs can provide both political and monetary support for participatory research and action methodologies. NGOs with highly specific mandates, such as the Kenya Water and Health Organization (KWAHO), and others with more generalized approaches (e.g., CARE) can readily find a niche in many communities where their efforts would be valuable, productive, and appreciated. Often, opportunities are coordinated with the ongoing work of local groups (as in Kathama) or the long-term initiatives of church-based organizations, such as the Church of the Province of Kenya (CPK) in Pwani and the Presbyterian Church of East Africa (PCEA) in Gikarangu.

The capacities of local communities and institutions can be strengthened by approaches that mobilize local resources, build consensus, identify and resolve conflicts, engage diverse social groups in decisionmaking and participation, and identify patterns that eliminate poverty and lead to empowerment. At least four of the six sublocations are in a position to benefit from NGOs that pursue strategies connecting a local project via community participation and institution building with broader problem-solving initiatives and programming for sustainable development. For example, group gardens in Mbusyani would benefit from a multipronged NGO approach to engage in increasing agricultural productivity, to provide water, and to develop market linkages. Kathama groups built on prior experience with public infrastructure, spring water distribution, soil conservation, and agroforestry to take on a major water project with the UNDP's Africa 2000 Network.

Currently, many participatory methodologies—such as Participatory Rural Appraisal (PRA) and Participatory and Learning Methods (PALM)—do not specifically address issues of social relations, the exclusion of particular social groups, or the gender variable. Pursuing a formal integration of social analysis and participatory methodologies—in which issues for both the researcher/agent and the community are identified and tools are formulated, operationalized, and tested in rural settings—is a key step in long-term capacity building and empowerment for development agencies and the rural communities they intend to serve. Participation should not become the prerogative of a privileged few who become partners in a widening, but still quite small, circle of decisionmakers. Likewise, the privileged few should not be allowed to capture the labor of the poor majority through "community-based" projects that in fact selectively serve the most powerful.

At a policy level, it is necessary to devise productive ways for communities, NGOs, and the public sector to address common problems. One agenda for NGOs in the 1990s involves "creating a policy environment favorable to participatory development."[8] Many are recognizing the importance of engaging both NGOs and local communities in broad social and political debates about resources and development.[9] Long-term "enabling action" is needed, as well as partnerships with local groups that can connect community participation to a broader participatory democracy.[10] Many Africans, specifically many Kenyans, seek to address such challenges of governance and the democratic process.

Acknowledge women's responsibilities in community resource management.   Women are key resource managers involved in community work across rural Kenya. It is therefore essential to consider the relationship between gender-based participation and community structures that can strengthen opportunities for sustainable resource management and development. Acknowledging the significant responsibilities of rural women in community activities, particularly resource management, the government and NGOs can recommend ways women should be included in decisionmaking and implementation of development projects. They can also take steps to direct financial and technical resources to women's groups and other self-help groups carrying out such activities.

Full and equitable participation by all residents in a community, including women, is essential for effectively addressing the issues that confront them. Government and NGOs can encourage formal inclusion of women in these processes. There is no formula for involving both genders in development activities; the most suitable approach will vary according to the context and the people involved. As Rocheleau, Schofield-Leca, and Mbuthi observe, "Men and women may prefer to work separately or together; their preference may vary depending on the particular issue or task. The key ingredient for appropriate structures and process is flexibility of format and method to suit the people, the place and the task."[11]

The theme of the government of Kenya's *National Development Plan, 1994– 1996* is "Resource Mobilization for Sustainable Development." It indicates the plan's central purpose: to mobilize the creative energies of all Kenyans to generate sustainable development that satisfies the needs of the present generation without jeopardizing and compromising the needs of future generations. The plan recognizes that past development has tended to marginalize women and specifies that a gender orientation will be strengthened during this plan period.[12] In particular, it recognizes women's concerns in the areas of energy, water, sanitation, land rights, and community decisionmaking. Hence, it is timely to bring a discussion of gender, resources, and development into the debate.

Such acknowledgment can encourage NGO support for women's activities. The women's groups in places like Mbusyani, Pwani, Kathama, and Gikarangu are well organized for making optimal use of financial and technical support and other services that organizations might provide. Given that women are particularly involved in managing natural resources at the community level, it is natural to begin building this infrastructure within their associations. Women's groups should not, of course, bear sole responsibility for the task of resource management in the public interest. They can be the point of departure for discussion of the issues and development of strategies for broader community-based efforts.

WOMEN'S STATUS: POLITICAL, SOCIAL, AND LEGAL

Questions concerning the status and position of women in society underlie many of the concerns about gendered access to and control of resources and gendered differentials in the development process. Historically, in a traditional setting, both men's and women's rights were carefully defined and mediated within broad social structures of subclan, clan, or ethnic community, albeit often within uneven relations of power. Regarding changes that have occurred in the last century—including privatization of land and social, political, and economic links to a world beyond Kenya—men have been given more sharply defined preferences in the balance of rights and responsibilities. Urban and, increasingly, rural women are well aware of this shift.

Many factors shape women's position in society. Many analysts agree, however, and the *National Development Plan, 1994–1996* reflects, that education is the single major factor that can "narrow the gender imbalances in all sectors of development."[13] Females are disadvantaged at all levels of education in terms of access, participation, completion, and performance. Gradually, professionals are giving their attention to this issue. Both men and women are making greater efforts to address educational opportunities for girls, the position of girls and women within Kenyan society, and the relevance of the curriculum and academic experience to building competence, confidence, and self-respect in young women. A broad issue, relevant at a level of macropolicy, it affects how women throughout Kenyan society perceive themselves and respond to their responsibilities and opportunities.

In Gikarangu and Mbusyani, recent economic trends have caused a decline in the enrollment of girls in school, as family finances have been constrained and girls have had to either seek employment or help out at home. In Kathama, men and women alike are concerned about the number of teenage single mothers leaving school as well as the unemployment of those who do complete primary and secondary school. In South Kamwango, few girls have gone beyond primary school, and often their experience at that level is limited. Kenyans at all levels recognize that the quality of education for girls and young women is a critical item for a policy agenda.

Education also relates to perceptions about entitlements, particularly insofar as access to natural resources is concerned. In exploring these cases, it has been evident that women's entitlements are embedded within family and kinship relationships. In some cases these entitlements are normative. In others they are labor based, shaping the conditions under which both men and women can seek labor or participate in labor sharing groups. Sometimes they are based on capital—determining access to land, credit, or other capital goods. Some entitlements are being broken down through processes such as migration, the increased number of female-headed households, and sheer population pressure on high-potential agricultural land.

As Kenyans come to grips with issues of gender and livelihood security, they will need policies that recognize that gender relations are as significant as those of class, race, and ethnicity in influencing property matters and in generating other entitlement inequities. The concept of entitlements must be expanded to take account of gender as a dimension central to the process of alleviating poverty and achieving livelihood security.[14]

Usually the residents of poor rural communities understand very well the connections among gender, entitlements, economic and environmental concerns, sustainable development, and community organizations. There is likely to be an acute awareness that if local residents do not undertake certain kinds of tasks, they will remain undone. As a resident in one sublocation in Machakos stated, "There isn't anyone who can help us. The Government never comes here. We have to do it ourselves."[15] This community has received precious little help from public authorities. It is at the end of the line, isolated and often forgotten. Virtually the only resource it has is the labor of those who reside within it, and that labor is largely female. If they want certain basic improvements in their environment and their services, for the most part they will have to do it themselves. This is a source of dismay, but it is a reality that most recognize and reluctantly accept. Thus, residents of this community have organized themselves into local groups for community action. Until outsiders (government bodies, NGOs, and international donors) recognize that these communities, often made up overwhelmingly of poor women, old (and poor) men, and young children, face barriers within the larger political system because of gender-based disadvantages, progress toward effective and equitable management of resources will be slow.

GENDERED LAND AND PROPERTY RELATIONS[16]

Gendered division of property—land as well as other resource use, access, and control—emerges as a key to resource management and livelihood strategies in each of the case studies. The complex and ambiguous mix of land ownership with land, plant, animal, and water use rights has strong implications for women's and men's interests in any given production and resource management system; it also has implications for their interests in the integration of new rules and technologies into these systems at farm and community levels. This is equally true both in the densely populated and well-watered highland sites such as Gikarangu and in the semiarid but still densely settled areas of Pwani, Mbusyani, and Kathama. Women of all ages in Kathama, Mbusyani, and Kyevaluki note a reduction in the quality and supply of water, fuelwood, and fodder resources relative to what was available to previous generations. In Mbusyani and Kyevaluki young women in particular point out the difficulty in accessing fuelwood and water supplies and lament the time and labor they must divert away from other productive pursuits to deal with this situation.

Those who are in control of the factors of production (land, water, labor, capital, information) will determine in part the distribution of costs and benefits from new technologies and land use systems in communities across Kenya. Because control is often determined by gender and class, proposed changes in farm-level production systems, improvements in community-level infrastructure, and the introduction of new technology at both levels should take into account the variability in amount and type of resources available to different groups.[17]

Examples from the case studies illustrate the ways gender and class division of resource tenure interacts with technology and management interventions to create distinct effects on different groups within and between households. In Gikarangu, men have control over land and the choice of crops to plant, although women are the primary food producers. The promotion of coffee as a monocrop favors the commercial interests of men and displaces women as producers and their subsistence crop production from limited landholdings. Intercropped systems, rotation of French beans with food crops, or alternative cash crops that grow well with local staples could accommodate the interests of both men and women on the same plot. In sites where women and men have full control over different plots, this might not be an issue. Likewise, in places with more land or where women control the decision over choice of crop to plant, the maintenance of a cash monocrop might not affect women and the household food supply in the same way as in Gikarangu.

In Pwani, the class and gender differences in rights, responsibilities, and resource endowments affected the distribution of costs and benefits of alternative water supply infrastructure at the community level. One group (consisting of mostly men and a few women from wealthy households that already had water tanks and women from very poor households with little prospect of ever getting a water tank) chose to repair the community-level dam for domestic water supply and livestock watering. The majority of women placed a higher priority on the construction of individual tanks for domestic water supply.

How can such communities and their collaborators resolve conflicts over allocation of scarce community financial and labor resources in the face of such differences in private resource endowments and in terms of control over shared resources? One approach would be to include distinct options scaled to different levels of resource access; a second approach would be to integrate complementary resources creatively at a larger-than-farm scale. For example, in a situation like the one in Pwani, a combined approach might involve allocating some community funds to women's groups for building tanks; the groups would provide labor to the effort at the dam. Alternatively, the women's groups active in tank construction might be exempt from labor at the dam, and wage-earning men might arrange to pay young men to work at the dam site or send a man or older boy from their household to work at the dam site.

How can policy at the international, national, and district levels promote land use and tenure practices that foster complementarity or resolve conflicts in the gender division of control over resources, production processes, and products? Perhaps the most feasible and practical action would be to encourage planners and fieldworkers to adopt a flexible, user-focused approach, as detailed earlier and in other discussions of a land user perspective.[18]

National- and district-level research and extension agencies can also place greater emphasis on multiple use of land, water, plants, and animals; renewable versus consumptive use of each; and access and use rights. This contrasts with the current policies that tend to favor—even if only by default—simple ownership, exclusive-use rights, single-purpose production systems, and consumptive use. Such a shift in administrative and training priorities in agricultural, forestry, and resource management agencies could create scope for experimentation and creative precedents in gendered resource tenure by interested planners and fieldworkers in specific sites or programs. Employment of both women and men as planners, researchers, extensionists, and paraprofessional field staff could also help to promote more equitable participation of men and women in production and/or conservation programs as well as in daily practice.

However, these measures would not suffice without broader changes in the legal and administrative framework governing the gender division of rights and responsibilities in rural land use and production systems. Ecologically sound and equitable development will require fundamental conceptual and procedural changes in the ways national and district agencies deal with the gender division of resources, knowledge, work, and benefits of traditional and experimental systems of land use. Policy interventions on five key points could foster more equitable sharing and division of control over both the means and the fruits of rural production.

First, national agencies and legislative bodies could promote legislation and procedural regulations that define people's access to land, water, livestock, and plants to accommodate multiple uses and users. This would include women's use and access rights that are nested within property controlled by male relatives, community groups, or local officials. In the case of Kathama this might have resulted in the definition of common gathering areas on hillslopes and riversides, creating a community reserve outside the private plots marked by the land survey in 1972.

Second, government agencies and NGOs could foster the legal and administrative recognition of gathering as a valid use of land, particularly in fragile or special environments. Carefully controlled rights of access at such sites could serve gatherers (often women), the community at large, and national interests in environmental conservation. This would apply particularly in the case of Pwani and other communities bordering parks and resources.

Third, extension and marketing agencies could promote men's and women's complementary involvement in and control of the processing and marketing of specific products of land use systems. Conversely, they could foster development of new land use systems that include a mix of separate products and processing or marketing activities already controlled by either men or women. The need for this approach is best exemplified by the experience of women at Gikarangu, where French beans have become largely a male domain and even the selling of bananas may become a male domain as it becomes a more lucrative venture.

Fourth, the national legislature and the courts could consider the revision and formal recognition of customary law with respect to men's and women's rights of use and access to land, plants, and products to restore the balance between rights and responsibilities under changing conditions of land use and family structure. In 1990, the government of Kenya issued an administrative directive to the effect that women may inherit and construct on land from their parents. Though most communities are not yet grappling with issues pertaining to women's access to land, a few are. In Kathama, for example, the elders have already begun to change the rules of inheritance to reflect the changing structures of young families and the needs of single women and their children.

Finally, outside agencies—whether global, national, or local—could involve women's organizations and popular or religious organizations with strong representation of women in the formulation and enforcement of codes or project contracts that protect both men's and women's rights to land, water, animals, plants, and their products.

An alternative approach, linked to the issue of women's legal, social, and political status, would be to focus on property ownership and to promote women's rights to cosign title deeds. However, this would still not address the issues of multiple and overlapping use of land and other resources by a number of users, many of whom are not even from the same household as the landowner. The fact remains that at present most rural women in Kenya are dependent on residual adherence to former customary law governing their rights of use and access to land and resources controlled by men for specific purposes related to women's responsibilities.[19] Resource management and land use changes both affect this system of gendered tenure and are affected by it, because most new production and conservation practices will either strengthen or displace men's and women's respective current uses of particular plants and places. New plants and places allocated to women may also be displaced later unless their rights of use and access within men's property are recognized and upheld by projects or local authorities.

GENDERED LABOR AND LIVELIHOODS

Two key attributes of labor and livelihoods in the sublocations investigated concern spatial distribution and gendered utilization. A phenomenon encountered widely in four of the six sublocations is that of the divided household, most often with men seeking employment outside the community. In Gikarangu, Pwani, Kathama, and Mbusyani such a household structure was commonplace. Land remains under the ownership and control of the men, but the women carry out the daily management of farm and household. Women get drafted into male enterprises to provide labor but may not share in the benefit. The current system does not compensate them for work done, and they are not co-owners of most farms or businesses. Mbusyani women were regularly managing the coffee farms while their husbands were employed (perhaps in salaried positions or as casual laborers) in Nairobi, Mombasa, or elsewhere. In Pwani, many women were managing new smallholdings while their husbands worked outside the community. They had all the drawbacks of cultivating semiarid lands with limited technology yet without opportunities for seeking credit and other resources accompanying land ownership. An important next step for many women is to find ways to recognize or identify their contributions to family maintenance and productivity and to enable themselves to share in the ownership of assets.

The second point concerns labor utilization. In some communities food self-sufficiency at the household level would be enhanced by an improved utilization of labor. Communities in agroecological zone 3 with population densities similar to South Kamwango need not suffer from food shortages. A substantial effort is needed to bring more inputs of labor (as well as land and technical knowledge) into food production. The focus should be on women farmers and on modifying the traditional gender-based division of labor, which prevents men and boys, even if they have time available, from joining in many tasks related to food production. Similarly, in the other sublocations under investigation, severe pressures on women's time are accompanied by underutilization of male labor for livelihood security. Indeed, the assistant chief in Mbusyani lamented that when the coffee prices were so low that cultivation was not worthwhile, the men were idle and the burden for family well-being fell on the women.[20]

A broad initiative to involve men more fully in the household economy and community activities could combine complementary strategies to reintegrate men into farm-level agricultural production and community-level work, in both cases on terms not simultaneously disadvantageous to women's authority, autonomy, and entitlements. Developments in Kathama suggest possible strategies for coordinating community work in the broader, national context. The self-help groups during the 1980s consisted almost exclusively of women, and men's groups began to appear in the early 1990s. In some cases they were clan or family based, and in others they were organized by neighbors. In one case in Mbiuni Location, in which Kathama is located, unemployed men returning from city and plantation workplaces formed a group to improve their farms and to secure local employment in farm and conservation activities. Such activities included road repair; land rehabilitation; commercial tree crop plantations on members' farms; tree nurseries and sale of seedlings; reciprocal farm labor on terraces and fencing; and wage labor (gang labor) on wealthier farmers' land. The men's groups, however, often included women and called upon wives and women relatives of members to contribute labor to group activities, leaving the women to work without the voice they would enjoy as members of women's groups.

The men's groups in Mbiuni did not appear to be conducting public work on a regular basis. The most consistent, continuing group work by young men seems to be in the form of mutual aid in house construction, terrace construction, and agricultural work among groups of three or four neighbors or among more senior men in the form of extended family- and clan-based activities, ranging from tree nurseries to crop storage and petty trade.

More recently, women's groups approached the chief to suggest that he call on labor from every household rather than place the mandate for public works on women's groups. This represents a demand that men in general, and all households within this sublocation, be brought back into public works to maintain and manage community resources. It is a message that reflects gender, class, and age differences in group participation, and it represents a demand from the most overburdened group for accountability from public officials and the public at large, including the youth and men. The chief succeeded in mobilizing the required work parties from the general population, as requested. This recent experience in Kathama suggests that there is ample scope for the reintegration of men into the labor and management tasks required to maintain and improve community infrastructure and shared resources in other areas.

There is an equally clear case for policies that make farm-level agricultural production for food security and sales more attractive to men—enough to secure their full- or part-time involvement. Options include making pricing policies more favorable to the farmer. For example, in Gikarangu men participate in cultivating French beans, which for most is a commercial crop, not a subsistence crop. The situation illustrates that relatively favorable prices for horticultural crops have encouraged male involvement in agriculture with possibilities for strengthening household food security. Presumably, men would respond positively to cultivating other crops with strong commercial, as well as subsistence, value if such options were made available. International, national, and local organizations as well as appointed officials might well provide leadership on this point by organizing community resource management and farm-level production activities specifically geared toward the involvement of young men or the joint and equitable involvement of all the youth, both men and women. Of course, before such activities are structured, one would need to evaluate carefully these new groups and their effects on women's rights, responsibilities, and authority.

GENDERED KNOWLEDGE, PERCEPTION, AND PRACTICE

The gendered basis of local knowledge and practice emerged in the course of researching each of the communities studied. Gendered knowledge and perceptions were reflected in the South Kamwango case, for example, in terms of health problems and remedies; in Kathama in respect to responses to famine; in Pwani in relation to resettlement processes and management of water and fuelwood supplies; in Gikarangu in terms of shifting control over commercial crops; and in Mbusyani and Kyevaluki in relation to group soil conservation practices. The changing boundaries of gendered knowledge were particularly important to resource management and the well-being of women in Kathama, South Kamwango, and Pwani.

In each case, men's and women's distinct roles in daily work and in the broader gender division of labor are reflected in their knowledge about various elements—the physical environment, use and management of resources, production systems, nutrition, and health care. Women and men each possess the knowledge needed to carry out their respective tasks. The gender division of knowledge, like the gender division of labor, is not fixed and permanent but is constantly subject to change, governed overall by a principle of flexible complementarity.[21]

For example, women's detailed knowledge of shrub and tree species and of their intended uses allows them to choose the best available fuelwood for specific purposes. Gendered knowledge is also at play in women's selection of seeds for the next year's crops,[22] although the exercise of that knowledge is sometimes pre-empted by crop failure, food shortage, and seed shortages, as noted by women's group members at Pwani. In Kathama, Gikarangu, and Pwani, the changing responsibilities for livestock management have resulted in women acquiring knowledge that was formerly part of men's repertoire of local production and health sciences. It allows them to choose the most appropriate fodder for their livestock, whether in times of plenty or in the midst of a drought (as in Kathama), and to find medicinal plants to treat minor ailments of domestic animals (as in Pwani). Women in Pwani have taken over the traditional treatment of livestock disease, once a man's domain, and men have specialized in the administration of injections and purchased modern remedies.

Likewise, both women and men have substantial knowledge about wild foods and can teach children to locate and identify nutritious wild fruit and nut snacks to supplement regular meals. Women, however, usually have more specialized knowledge of wild vegetables to supplement cultivated staple foods in cooked meals or to stave off hunger in times of famine, which proved so crucial to many of the poor in Kathama in 1984 and 1985. Men generally know more about roots and grasses on the rangelands because of the gender division of labor that prevailed when they were taught by their fathers to herd livestock and to survive on long treks across open range. These men's skills are disappearing rapidly because they are no longer commonly called into play; many men now work in wage labor rather than herding, as noted by residents in Kathama.

Gendered sciences of production are by no means limited to traditional knowledge of plants and animals; they are also a key consideration in the design and management of experimental programs in agriculture, livestock production, and forestry, as demonstrated by the history of the Kathama Agroforestry Project. Women and men will bring different bits of knowledge as well as distinct perspectives about the desired outcomes of experimental programs; they might also learn and experiment in different ways and in distinct social contexts.

In terms of livelihood security, NGOs, government bodies, and international agencies can support research institutions investigating trees and plants for food, fodder, fuel, and building material for household or small-scale commercial uses. Research and technical assistance programs would be particularly useful to women in poor households if they focus on indigenous vegetation known to the local men and women or on other plants that can thrive in the particular environment, have multiple uses suited to local needs and plant product preferences, and are compatible with food crops and other plants already known and used by people in the area.

For example, action research by government agencies and NGOs could build a high level of expertise for identifying and/or developing cultivars suited to particular landscapes. For semiarid lands, it would be invaluable to conduct research on new crops suitable for these regions or on adaptations of familiar crops for cultivation and use in this environment as well as for commercial sales.

The dynamic nature of gendered knowledge, resource management, and household needs is also evident in the area of health education. Women bear primary responsibility for the health of the family. As was abundantly clear in the South Kamwango case, traditional medical knowledge does not deal with many new health problems related to environmental sanitation, increased population densities, and new diseases.

The capacity to improve overall health conditions is central to issues of livelihood security and sustainable development in many rural communities. The 1994 UNDP *Human Development Report* indicates that Kenyans' access to medical facilities, including doctors and nurses, is well below average for poor developing countries. Further, the typical Kenyan's average daily calorie intake is 86 percent of daily needs.[23] While absolute expenditures for health care have been increasing, the proportion of development expenditure devoted to health care has been decreasing.[24] Infant mortality figures have improved significantly over the last several decades, yet malaria, diarrheal diseases, anemia, and AIDS continue to impair the health and threaten the lives of children and adults alike.[25] These health concerns have an obvious impact on family welfare, productivity, and livelihood security, issues brought out in the case of South Kamwango, a pocket of poverty. Yet women in the region are not prepared either by their formal schooling or by the traditional teachings of women elders to confront these new problems.

An answer to the needs in South Kamwango lies somewhere in the domain of broad public education, directed at both men and women, addressing the links among agricultural production, nutrition, resource management, water supply, and sanitation infrastructure, all of which cross gendered domains of knowledge, labor, authority, and responsibility. The government and NGOs can introduce health education (including knowledge of nutrition, sanitation, and environmentally caused diseases) at the earliest stages in primary schools in ways that combine both women's and men's traditional knowledge and practice with national and international sources of information and understanding. Many communities would benefit from programs of public education on child health that relate the causes of childhood diseases and morbidity to the appropriate preventative measures in environmental management, household nutrition, and health care. International agencies can support intensified efforts to provide information and resources to improve child health and nutrition and environmental hygiene, therefore helping to raise child survival rates.

FROM NAIROBI TO RIO TO BEIJING AND BEYOND

Across the boundaries of nation and culture there is a new awareness with respect to the interrelationships of women, the environment, and development. This new perspective recognizes not only the complex interactions between human beings and the environment but the central roles of women as actors in that dynamic. This perspective incorporates the two elements of a conceptual framework that we identified in Chapter 1 as central to our analysis of gender and livelihood struggles in Kenya: first, a focus on human interests, values, and activities as they relate to the ecosystem; and second, the relevance of local organizations and grassroots movements for effective social change and management of resources. Women are at the center of this worldview not only because the responsibilities of most involve daily management of the resource base in pursuit of a livelihood but also because their knowledge and concern for the community in which they live and work necessitate that their voices be heard.

The 1985 Nairobi Conference commemorated the end of the UN Decade for Women. The conference concluded that, after ten years of worldwide focus on their needs, women around the world continued to be victims of environmental devastation, suffering from the consequences of long-term, large-scale, ill-conceived development programs and an array of forces external to their communities that are harming the resource base and increasing the material poverty of their households. The Nairobi Conference confirmed women's restricted access to productive resources, their limited ability to influence decisionmakers through formal channels, and the various impediments they face—economic, political, cultural, legal—to building secure livelihoods.

In June 1992 the UN Conference on Environment and Development (UNCED), known as the Earth Summit, and the parallel nongovernmental conference, the Global Forum, were held in Rio de Janeiro. *Agenda 21*, the major document to come out of the Earth Summit, outlines in forty chapters actions recommended to move the planet toward sustainable and equitable development. Women are mentioned throughout the document. Chapter 24 is entitled "Global Action for Women towards Sustainable and Equitable Development" and contains a mandate that the UN agencies involved in the implementation of *Agenda 21* "ensure that gender considerations are fully integrated into all policies, programs and activities."[26] The intent of *Agenda 21* is to alter both the international agenda and the public debate by focusing on improving the access of the poor to resources and by addressing the reverse flow of resources from developing countries, connecting this issue to sustainable development.[27]

At the Global Forum were more than twenty thousand participants representing nine thousand organizations from 171 countries. The treaties drafted there contained a vision of global interdependence challenging existing models and practices of development in both North and South. Among the issues the forum emphasized were inappropriate development and inequitable distribution, wasteful overconsumption of resources, the burden of debt, and the exclusion of many people, especially women, from participation in decisions that affect their livelihoods and even their survival. The Global Forum, along with the Global Assembly, emphasized the ways individuals can make a difference and the ways people—especially women—are stakeholders in their environment and can be its most effective stewards if they are well informed, organized, and secure in equitable access to land and other resources.[28]

Now planners are shaping the agenda for Beijing. No doubt they are asking what progress has been made since the Nairobi Conference. Has such a forum made a difference to the lives of women in rural communities around the world—communities like Gikarangu, where women are struggling to retain control over the banana trade; South Kamwango, where difficult health conditions drain the energies of the most resilient, and Kathama, where women's traditional organizing and sharing mechanisms are essential to supplement inadequate national and international famine relief policies?

Many African women have high expectations, hopes, and determination to use the political space created by a growing pluralism and new efforts at democratization in their countries to integrate gender into participatory processes. In Kenya women have had a marginal role in formal politics, and at the local level they have had a central role in community institutions. Throughout the nation women share a heightened concern about ecological and social problems. As Kenya faces the challenge to increase democratization and accountability to all her citizens, women raise their hopes for people-centered development built on effective and equitable management of resources and secure livelihood systems.

We know that individual women can make a difference in their local communities. We have seen the stamina of the founder of a girls' school in Gikarangu, the calm organizational skills of the chair of the Mwangano Women's Group in Mbusyani, the outspoken demand for accountability from a traditional leader in a chief's *baraza* in Kyevaluki. We now need to see the structural changes to support their actions. If the Beijing Conference can move all of us—individually and in our collectivities—to a new and renewed commitment to equitable development and environmental sustainability, and if it can strengthen support for the numerous roles of women in achieving these goals, it will have addressed an enormous challenge. It remains for all of us in our various capacities to take the first steps. The women of rural Kenya are already doing so.

NOTES

1. UN Development Program, *1994 Human Development Report,* p. 2.
2. Sen, "Gender and Cooperative Conflicts," p. 123.

3. Thomas-Slayter and Rocheleau, "Research Frontiers."

4. Roe and Fortmann, *Season and Strategy.*

5. Charlton et al., *Women, the State, and Development.*

6. Parpart and Staudt, *Women and the State in Africa*, p. 6.

7. See Scott, *Weapons of the Weak.*

8. Brodhead, "NGOs: In One Year, Out the Other?" p. 1.

9. Weatherly, "NGO Outreach Project," p. 7.

10. Nyoni, "Indigenous NGOs," p. 55.

11. See Chapter 6.

12. Government of Kenya, Ministry of Planning and National Development, *National Development Plan, 1994–1996*, p. 253.

13. Ibid., p. 255.

14. For a valuable discussion of the issues of poverty and entitlements, see Kabeer, "Gender Dimensions of Rural Poverty."

15. Thomas-Slayter, "Politics, Class and Gender in African Resource Management."

16. This section draws on fieldwork conducted by Rocheleau, Wamalwa, and Jama in 1991 and summarized by Rocheleau in Jama et al., *Farmer Participatory Research on Farming Systems*, and in works in progress by all the authors.

17. For further discussion of gender and technology in Africa, see Stamp, *Technology, Gender and Power in Africa.*

18. Jiggins and Feldstein (eds.), *Tools for the Field;* Kabutha et al., *Participatory Rural Appraisal Handbook*; Rocheleau, "The Gender Division of Work, Resources and Rewards"; and "A Land User Perspective for Agroforestry."

19. Pala Okeyo, "Daughters of the Lakes and Rivers"; Okoth-Ogendo, "Some Issues of Theory in the Study of Tenure Relations"; Rocheleau, "Gender, Conflict and Complementarity" and "Women, Trees, and Tenure."

20. Discussions with Chief Isaac Kaku, June 9, 1994.

21. Rocheleau, "Gender, Ecology, and the Science of Survival."

22. Ferguson, "Gendered Science."

23. UN Development Program, *1994 Human Development Report*, p. 153; Redfern, "Kenya Tops in Development," p. 12.

24. Government of Kenya, Central Bureau of Statistics, *Economic Survey, 1994*, p. 194.

25. Government of Kenya, Ministry of Planning and National Development, *National Development Plan, 1994–1996*, pp. 226–235.

26. UN Conference on Environment and Development, "Global Action for Women."

27. Fisher, *The Road from Rio.*

28. The Global Assembly of Women and Environment (Miami, November 1991), in preparation for the Rio Conference, addressed these issues from women's perspectives, drawing in particular on success stories of the ways women are managing the environment. These issues have also been analyzed by Development Alternatives with Women for a New Era (DAWN) and other participants in UNCED for their impact on women and for women's views on how to address them.

Glossary

baraza	A public meeting called by a village chief
changa'a	The locally brewed beer
cockerel	A high-quality cock used for breeding purposes
coppice	To cut certain tree species close to ground level to produce new shoots from the stump
debe	A container holding approximately 5 gallons
duka	A small general store
githaka	Clan land (Kikuyu)
grade cow	Imported, milk-yielding breed, such as a Holstein
Greenbelt Movement	A people's environmental movement organized in Kenya by a prominent Kenyan environmentalist, Wangari Mathai
groundnuts	Peanuts
harambee	Self-help
hoteli	A small store selling such items as eggs, salt, and soda
jaggery	A solid form of molasses that is the central ingredient for brewing *changa'a*
jembe	A short-handle hoe
jua kali	The informal sector or any informal, self-generated enterprise
kwashiorkor	Severe malnutrition in infants and children that is characterized by stunted growth, changes in the pigmentation of the skin and hair, edema, fatty degeneration of the liver, anemia, and apathy; caused by a diet excessively high in carbohydrate and extremely low in protein
mabati	Corrugated iron; name for the women's groups that do roofing
Maendeleo ya Wanawake	The national umbrella women's organization of Kenya
matatu	A public bus or taxi
mbari	Communal clan property
mwethya	Local work group

nongovernmental organization (NGO)	A term used to refer to development organizations, although it technically includes any nonprofit organization, such as educational institutions and arts organizations
omena	A small sardinelike fish
posho	Corn meal
shamba	A farm, usually referring to a smallholding; also used to refer to croplands and specific plots
striga	A weed common in western Kenya and exceedingly harmful to crops
umoja	Unity
zebu	The breed of cattle found in much of Kenya

Acronyms

ACTS   African Centre for Technology Studies
CARE   Cooperative for American Relief Everywhere
CPK   Church of the Province of Kenya
ECOGEN   Ecology, Community Organization and Gender project
EID   (Office of) Economic and Institutional Development (USAID)
ELCI   Environment Liaison Centre International
FAO   Food and Agriculture Organization
FORD   Forum for Restoration of Democracy
GDP   gross domestic product
GNP   gross national product
ICRAF   International Center for Research on Agro-Forestry
ILEIA   Institute for Low External Input Agriculture
KANU   Kenya Africa National Union
KENGO   Kenya Energy and Environment Non-Governmental Organization
KWAHO   Kenya Water and Health Organization
LBDA   Lake Basin Development Authority
NEAP   National Environmental Action Plan
NES   (Kenyan) National Environment Secretariat
NGO   nongovernmental organization
PALM   Participatory and Learning Method
PCEA   Presbyterian Church of East Africa
PRA   Participatory Rural Appraisal
SADCC   Southern Africa Development Coordinating Committee
SAP   Structural Adjustment Program
SAREC   Swedish Agency for Research and Economic Cooperation
SARSA   Systems Approach to Regional Income and Sustainable Resource
            Assistance
UNCED   UN Conference on Environment and Development
UNDP   UN Development Programme
UNEP   UN Environment Program
UNICEF   UN International Children's Emergency Fund
USAID   U.S. Agency for International Development
VRMP   Village Resource Management Plan

Appendix: Eight Steps to Participatory Rural Appraisal (PRA)

1. Site Selection: Choose a location to conduct the exercise.
2. Preliminary Visits: Meet with village leaders to clarify the nature of PRA.
3. Data Collection:
   A. Spatial Data:
      1. Village Sketch Map: Identify characteristic physical and economic details.
      2. Transect: Determine subzones and distinct microecologies.
      3. Farm Sketches: Identify the variety of farm management techniques utilized.
   B. Time-Related Data:
      1. Time Line: Record important events of the community's history.
      2. Trend Lines: Determine patterns of changes in resource issues.
      3. Seasonal Calendar: Track patterns in resource issues for 12–18 months.
   C. Social Data:
      1. Farm Interviews: Survey households to complement the farm sketches.
      2. Village Institutions: Construct diagrams of group relationships.
   D. Technical Data: Perform economic and technical feasibility studies.
4. Data Synthesis and Analysis: Organize data and list problems and opportunities for action.
5. Ranking of Problems: Prioritize issues to be addressed.
6. Ranking of Opportunities: Choose appropriate activities to address problems.
7. Adopting a Village Resource Management Plan (VRMP).
8. Implementation: Carry out the activities.

Bibliography

Agarwal, Bina. *Cold Hearths and Barren Slopes: The Woodfuel Crisis in the Third World.* New Delhi: Allied Publishers, 1986.

————. *Structures of Patriarchy: The State, the Community, and the Household.* London: Zed Books; New Delhi: Kali for Women, 1988a.

————. "Neither Sustenance Nor Sustainability: Agricultural Strategies, Ecological Degradation and Indian Women in Poverty." In Kali for Women (eds.), *Structures of Patriarchy.* New Delhi: Kali for Women, 1988b.

————. "Engendering the Environment Debate: Lessons from the Indian Subcontinent." CASID Distinguished Speaker Series, no. 8. East Lansing: Michigan State University, 1991.

————. "Gender Relations and Food Security: Coping with Seasonality, Drought, and Famine in South Asia." In *Unequal Burden, Economic Crises, Persistent Poverty, and Women's Work,* edited by Lourdes Beneria and Shelley Feldman. Boulder, CO: Westview Press, 1992.

Ahlberg, Beth Maina. *Women, Sexuality and the Changing Social Order.* Philadelphia: Gordon and Breach, 1991.

Ali, Taisier, and O'Brien, Jay. "Labor, Community, and Protest in Sudanese Agriculture." In *The Politics of Agriculture in Tropical Africa,* edited by Jonathan Barker. Beverly Hills, CA: Sage Publications, 1984.

Alila, Patrick O., Kinyanjui, Kabiru, and Wanjohi, Gatheru. "Rural Landlessness in Kenya: Dynamics, Problems and Policies." Occasional paper, no. 57. Nairobi: Institute for Development Studies, University of Nairobi, 1993.

Alsop, Ruth. "Whose Interests? Problems in Planning for Women's Practical Needs." *World Development* 21, no. 3 (1993): 367–377.

Antrobus, P. "A Journey in the Shaping: A Journey without Maps." Mimeograph. Cambridge, MA: The Bunting Institute, 1987.

Ayot, Theodora, and Okonji, Grace. "Economic Activities: Women's Groups in South Nyanza District." Report prepared for the government of Kenya, 1990.

Bahemuka, Judith Mbula, and Tiffen, Mary. "Akamba Institutions and Development, 1930–90." In *Environmental Change and Dryland Management in Machakos District, Kenya, 1930–1990: Institutional Profile,* edited by Mary Tiffen. ODI Working Paper, no. 62. London: Overseas Development Institute, 1992.

Barkan, Joel D., McNulty, Michael L., and Ayeni, M. A. O. "'Hometown' Voluntary Associations, Local Development, and the Emergence of Civil Society in Western Nigeria." *The Journal of Modern African Studies* 29, no. 3 (1991): 457–480.

Barker, Johnathan S. *Rural Communities Under Stress.* Cambridge: Cambridge University Press, 1989.

Bassett, Thomas. "The Political Ecology of Peasant-Herder Conflicts in the Northern Ivory Coast." *Annals of the Association of American Geographers* 78, no. 3 (1988): 453–472.

Bebbington, Tony. "Farmer Knowledge, Institutional Resources and Sustainable Agricultural Strategies: A Case Study from the Eastern Slopes of the Peruvian Andes." *Bulletin of Latin American Research* 9, no. 2 (1990): 203–228.

Bergdall, Terry D. *Methods for Active Participation, Experiences in Rural Development from East and Central Africa.* Nairobi: Oxford University Press, 1993.

Bernard, F. E., and Thom, D. J. "Population Pressure and Human Carrying Capacity in Selected Locations of Machakos and Ktui Districts." *Journal of Developing Areas* 15 (1981): 381–406.

Bernard, F. E., Campbell, D. J., and Thom, D. J. "Carrying Capacity of the Eastern Ecological Gradient of Kenya." *National Geographic Research* 5, no. 4 (1989): 399–421.

Berry, Sara. "Coping with Confusion: African Farmers' Responses to Economic Instability in the 1970s and 1980s." In *Hemmed In: Responses to Africa's Economic Decline,* edited by Thomas Callaghy and John Ravenhill. New York: Columbia University Press, 1993.

Berry, Sara, ed. *Access, Control and Use of Resources in African Agriculture.* Special issue of *Africa* 59, no. 1 (1989): 41–55.

Bhatt, Ela. "Toward Empowerment." *World Development* 17, no. 7 (1989): 1059–1065.

Blaikie, P. *The Political Economy of Soil Erosion in Developing Countries.* London: Longman, 1985.

Blaikie, P., and Brookfield, H. *Land Degradation and Society.* London and New York: Methuen Press, 1987.

Boserup, E. *Woman's Role in Economic Development.* New York: St. Martin's Press, 1970.

Bradley, P. *Women, Woodfuel, and Woodlots.* Vol 1, *The Foundation of a Woodfuel Development Strategy for East Africa.* London: Macmillan Education, 1991.

Bradshaw, York W. "Perpetuating Underdevelopment in Kenya: The Link between Agriculture, Class, and State." *African Studies Review* 33, no. 1 (April 1990): 1–28.

Braidotti, Rosi, Charkiewicz, Ewa, Hausler, Sabine, and Wieringa, Saskia. *Women, the Environment and Sustainable Development: Toward a Theoretical Synthesis.* London: Zed Books, 1994.

Bratton, Michael. "Farmer Organizations and Food Production in Zimbabwe." *World Development* 14, no. 3 (1986): 367–384.

———. *The Politics of Government–NGO Relations in Africa.* Working paper, no. 456. Nairobi: Institute for Development Studies, University of Nairobi, 1987.

———. "Beyond Autocracy: Civil Society in Africa." In *Beyond Autocracy in Africa.* Working papers from the inaugural seminar of the Governance in Africa Program. Atlanta, GA: The Carter Center of Emory University, February 17–18, 1989.

Bray, David Barton. "'Defiance' and the Search for Sustainable Small Farmer Organizations: A Paraguayan Case Study and a Research Agenda." *Human Organization* 50, no. 2 (1991): 125–135.

Brodhead, Tim. "NGOs: In One Year, Out the Other?" *World Development* 15, supplement (Autumn 1987): 1–6.

Bromley, D. "The Common Property Challenge." In *National Academy of Science Proceedings of the Conferences on Common Property Resource Management.* Washington, DC: National Academy Press, 1986.

Brown, L. David. *Bridging Organizations and Sustainable Development.* Working paper, no. 8. Boston: Institute for Development Research, Boston University, 1990.

Bryson, Judy. "Women and Agriculture in Sub-Saharan Africa: Implications for Development (an Exploratory Study)." In *African Women in the Development Process,* edited by N. Nici. London: Frank Cass, 1981.

Callaghy, Thomas M. "Debt and Structural Adjustment in Africa: Realities and Possibilities." *Issue* 16, no. 2 (1988): 11–18.

Callaghy, Thomas M., and Ravenhill, John, eds. *Hemmed In: Responses to Africa's Economic Decline.* New York: Columbia University Press, 1993.

Carney, Judith. "Struggles Over Land and Crops in an Irrigated Rice Scheme: The Gambia." In *Women and Land Tenure in Africa,* edited by Jean Davison. Boulder, CO: Westview Press, 1988.

———. "Peasant Women and Economic Transformation in the Gambia." *Development and Change* 23, no. 2 (April 1992): 67–90.

Carney, J., and Watts, M. "Manufacturing Dissent: Work, Gender, and the Politics of Meaning in a Peasant Society." *Africa* 60 (1990): 207–241.

Castro, Alfonso Peter. "Indigenous Kikuyu Agroforestry: A Case Study of Kirinyaga, Kenya." *Human Ecology* 19, no. 1 (1991): 1–18.

Cege, Alex. "Disasters: An Act of God or Follies of Our Own Making?" *Daily Nation* June 1, 1994, p. 3.

———. "The Key to Ensure National Food Security." *Daily Nation* June 1, 1994, p. 8.

Cernea, Michael M. "Farmer Organizations and Institution Building for Sustainable Development." *Regional Development Dialogue* 8, no. 2 (1987): 1–24.

———. "Nongovernmental Organizations and Local Development." World Bank Discussion Papers, no. 40. Washington, DC: World Bank, 1988.

Chambers, Robert. *Putting the Last First.* London: Longman, 1983.

———. "Shortcut Methods of Gathering Social Information for Rural Development Projects." In *Putting People First,* edited by M. Cernea. London: Longman, 1985.

———. "Shortcut and Participatory Methods for Gaining Social Information for Projects." Mimeograph. University of Sussex, 1990.

Chambers, R., Pacey, A., and Thrupp, L. A., eds. *Farmer First: Innovation and Agricultural Research.* London: Intermediate Technology Publications, 1989.

Charlton, Sue Ellen, Everett, Jana, and Staudt, Kathleen, eds. *Women, the State, and Development.* Albany: State University of New York Press, 1989.

Chavangi, N. A. "Cultural Aspects of Fuelwood Procurement in Kakamega District." KWDP Working Paper, no. 4. Nairobi: Kenya Wood Fuel Development Project, 1984.

———. "Household Based Tree Planting Activities for Fuelwood Supply in Rural Africa." In *Development from Within: Survival in Rural Africa,* edited by Fraser D. R. Taylor and Fiona Mackenzie. London: Routledge, 1992.

Chazan, Naomi. "Gender Perspectives on African States." In *Women and the State in Africa,* edited by Jane L. Parpart and Kathleen A. Staudt. Boulder, CO: Lynne Rienner Publishers, 1989.

Chazan, Naomi, and Rothchild, Donald. "The Political Repercussions of Economic Malaise." In *Hemmed In: Responses to Africa's Economic Decline,* edited by Thomas Callaghy and John Ravenhill. New York: Columbia University Press, 1993.

Chazan, Naomi, Mortimer, Robert, Ravenhill, John, and Rothchild, Donald. *Politics and Society in Contemporary Africa.* Boulder, CO: Lynne Rienner Publishers, 1988.

Clark, John. *Democratizing Development: The Role of Voluntary Organizations.* West Hartford, CT: Kumarian Press, 1990.

Clark, John, Khogali, Mustafa, and Kosinski, Lezek A., eds. *Population and Development Projects in Africa.* Cambridge: Cambridge University Press, 1985.

Cloud, Kathleen. "Women's Productivity in Agricultural Systems: Consideration for Project Design." In *Gender Roles in Development Projects,* edited by Catherine Overholt, Mary Anderson, Kathleen Cloud, and James Austin. West Hartford, CT: Kumarian Press, 1985.

Collier, Paul. "Contractual Constraints on Labour Exchange in Rural Kenya." *International Labour Review* 128, no. 6 (1989): 745–768.

Collins, Jane. "Women and the Environment: Social Reproduction and Sustainable Development." In *The Women and International Development Annual 2,* edited by Rita S. Gallin and Anne Ferguson. Boulder, CO: Westview Press, 1991.

Collinson, Michael. "Research Planning Study. Data Presentation: Parts of Lower, Drier Areas of Northern Division, Machakos." Nairobi: CIMMYT/Medical Research Centre, 1979.

Conway, Gordon R. "Agricultural Ecology and Farming Systems Research." In *Agricultural Systems Research for Developing Countries,* edited by J. V. Remenyi. Canberra: Australian Center for International Agricultural Research, 1985.

———. *Rapid Appraisal Techniques for Sustainable Development.* London: International Institute for Environment and Development, 1988.

Cornell University, Institute for African Development. "Development in the Arid and Semi-Arid Areas of Kenya." Report of workshop convened at Cornell University at the request of the government of Kenya, January 1988.

Cox, S., and Annis, S. "Community Participation in Rural Water Supply." In *Direct to the Poor: Grassroots Development in Latin America,* edited by Sheldon Annis and Peter Hakim. Boulder, CO: Lynne Rienner Publishers, 1988.

Crossette, B. "Study Sees Rise in Child Death Rates." *New York Times* May 9, 1992, p. 1.

Cubbins, Lisa A. "Women, Men, and the Division of Power: A Study of Gender Stratification in Kenya." *Social Forces* 69, no. 4 (1991): 1063–1083.

Daily Nation. "A Most Welcome Sober Approach." Editorial. May 26, 1994, p. 6.

Dankelman, I., and Davison, J. *Women and Environment in the Third World: Alliance for the Future.* London: Earthscan Publications, 1988.

Davison, Jean. *Voices from Mutira: Lives of Rural Gikuyu Women.* Boulder, CO: Lynne Rienner Publishers, 1989.

Davison, Jean, ed. *Agriculture, Women, and Land: The African Experience.* Boulder, CO: Westview Press, 1988.

De Janvry, Alain, Sadoulet, Elisabeth, and Thorbecke, Erik. "Introduction to State, Market, and Civil Organizations: New Theories, New Practices, and Their Implications for Rural Development." *World Development* 21, no. 4 (1993): 565–575.

Development Alternatives. "Strategies for Small Farmer Development: An Empirical Study of Rural Development Projects." Washington, DC: USAID, 1975.

Dewees, Peter A. "The Woodfuel Crisis Reconsidered: Observations on the Dynamics of Abundance and Scarcity." *World Development* 17, no. 8 (1989): 1159–1172.

———. "Trees, Farm Boundaries, and Land Tenure and Reform in Kenya." Mimeograph. Oxford: Oxford University, April 1992a.

———. "Tree Planting and Household Decision Making Processes Amongst Smallholders in Kenya." Mimeograph. Oxford: Food Studies Group, Oxford University, April 1992b.

Dey, Jennie. "Development Planning in the Gambia: The Gap Between Planners' and Farmers' Perceptions, Expectations and Objectives." *World Development* 10, no. 5 (1982): 377–396.

Diamond, Nancy K. "Trees for the Poorest? Equity and Agroforestry Extension in Southwestern Kenya." Ph.D. diss., University of California, Berkeley, 1990.

Domen, A. "A Rationale for African Low-Resource Agriculture in Terms of Economic Theory." In *Indigenous Knowledge Systems: Implications for Agriculture and International Development,* edited by Michael Warren et al. Studies in Technology and Social Change Series, no. 11. Ames: Iowa State University, 1989.

Doornbos, M. "The African State in Academic Debate: Retrospect and Prospect." *The Journal of Modern African Studies* 28, no. 2 (June 1990): 179–198.

Downing, T., Gitu, K., and Kamau, C., eds. *Coping with Drought in Kenya: National and Local Strategies.* London: Lynne Rienner Publishers, 1989.

Drabek, Anne. "Development Alternatives: The Challenge to NGOs—An Overview of the Issues." *World Development* 15, supplement (Autumn 1987): ix–xv.

Durning, Alan. "Poverty and Environmental Decline." *World Education Reports* 29 (1991): 5–7.

Ecosystems LTD. Machakos District—Report for M. I. D. P. 4 vols. Nairobi: Ecosystems Ltd., 1981.

Ekins, Paul. *A New World Order: Grassroots Movements for Global Change.* London: Routledge, 1992.

Escobar, Arturo, and Alvarez, Sonia, eds. *The Making of Social Movements in Latin America: Identity, Strategy, and Democracy.* Boulder, CO: Westview Press, 1992.

Etienne, M., and Leacock, E., eds. *Women and Colonization: Anthropological Perspectives.* New York: Praeger, 1980.

Everett, Jana. "Incorporation Versus Conflict: Lower Class Women, Collective Action and the State in India." In *Women, the State, and Development,* edited by Sue Ellen Charlton, Jana Everett, and Kathleen Staudt. Albany: State University of New York Press, 1989.

Fatton, Robert. "Gender, Class, and State in Africa." In *Women and the State in Africa,* edited by Jane L. Parpart and Kathleen A. Staudt. Boulder, CO: Lynne Rienner Publishers, 1989.

Feldstein, H. S., and Poats, S. V. *Working Together: Gender Analysis in Agriculture.* West Hartford, CT: Kumarian Press, 1989.

Feldstein, H. S., Flora, C. B., and Poats, S. V. *The Gender Variable in Agricultural Research.* Ottawa: IDRC, 1990.

Ferguson, Anne. "Gendered Science: A Critique of Agricultural Development." *American Anthropologist,* in press.

Fernandez, Maria. "Technological Domains of Women in Mixed Farming Systems of Andean Peasant Communities." In *Gender Issues in Farming Systems Research and Extension,* edited by S. Poats, M. Schmink, and A. Spring. Boulder, CO: Westview Press, 1988.

Fisher, J. M. *Reports on the Kikuyu.* Nairobi: Government of Kenya Archives, 1952.

Fisher, Jule. *The Road from Rio: Sustainable Development and the Nongovernmental Movement in the Third World.* Westport, CT: Praeger, 1993.

Fleuret, Anne. "Methods for Evaluation of the Role of Fruits and Wild Greens in Shambaa Diet: A Case Study." *Medical Anthropology* (Spring 1979).

Fleuret, Patrick. "Food, Farmers and Organizations in Africa: Anthropological Perspectives, with Implications for Development Assistance." Mimeograph. Washington, DC: USAID, 1985.

Fleuret, Patrick, and Fleuret, Anne. "Social Organization, Resource Management, and Child Nutrition in the Taita Hills, Kenya." *American Anthropologist* 3, no. 1 (March 1991): 91–114.

Fliervoet, Els. "An Inventory of Trees and Shrubs in the Northern Division of Machakos District, Kenya." Nairobi: International Center for Research on Agro-Forestry; Wageningen, The Netherlands: Wageningen Agricultural University, 1982.

Folbre, Nancy. "Women on Their Own: Global Patterns of Female Headship." In *The Women and International Development Annual 2,* edited by Rita S. Gallin and Anne Ferguson. Boulder, CO: Westview Press, 1991.

Food and Agriculture Organization. *Restoring the Balance.* Rome: FAO, 1988.

Ford, Richard, Lelo, Francis, and Kelly, Laura. "Pwani Village and Village Resource Management Plan." Worcester, MA: Clark University, 1991.

Ford, Richard B., and Brown, Janet Welsh. "Land, Resources, and People in Kenya." In *In the U.S. Interest: Resources, Growth, and Security in the Developing World,* edited by Janet Welsh Brown. Boulder, CO: Westview Press, 1990.

Fortmann, L. "The Tree Tenure Factor in Agroforestry with Particular Reference to Africa." *Agroforestry Systems* 2 (1985): 229–251.

Fortmann, Louise, and Rocheleau, D. "Women and Agroforestry: Four Myths and Three Case Studies." *Agroforestry Systems* 2 (1985): 253–272.

Fowler, A. "NGOs in Africa: Naming Them by What They Are." In *Non-Governmental Organizations' Contributions to Development,* edited by Kahiru Kinyanjui. Nairobi: Institute for Development Studies, University of Nairobi, 1985.

Fox, Jonathan. "How Do Regional Peasant Organizations Sustain Accountability and Autonomy? Lessons from Mexico." Rosslyn, VA: InterAmerican Foundation Report, 1988.

Freire, Paulo. *Pedagogy of the Oppressed.* New York: Herder and Herder, 1970.

Geertz, C. *Agricultural Involution: The Processes of Ecological Change in Indonesia.* Berkeley: University of California Press, 1963.

————. *Local Knowledge: Further Essays In Interpretive Anthropology.* New York: Basic Books, 1983.

Ghai, Dharam. "Participatory Development: Some Perspectives from Grass-Roots Experiences." *Journal of Development Planning* 19 (1989): 215–248.

Ghai, Dharam, and Vivian, Jessica M., eds. *Grassroots Environmental Action: People's Participation in Sustainable Development.* London: Routledge, 1992.

Gielen, Hans. "Report on an Agroforestry Survey in Three Villages of Northern Machakos." Nairobi: International Center for Research on Agro-Forestry; Wageningen, The Netherlands: Wageningen Agricultural University, 1982.

Ginneken, J. van. "Second Progress Report on Analyses of Demographic Data of Joint Project, Machakos, between 1974 and 1980." Nairobi: Medical Research Centre, 1981.

Ginneken, J. K. van, and Muller, A. S. *Maternal and Child Health in Rural Kenya: An Epidemiological Study.* Kent: Croom Helm, 1984.

Gladwin, Christina H., ed. *Structural Adjustment and African Women Farmers.* Gainesville: University of Florida Press, 1991.

Glavanis, K. "Aspects of Non-Capitalist Social Relations in Rural Egypt: The Small Peasant Household in an Egyptian Delta Village." In *Family and Work in Rural Societies,* edited by Norman Long. London: Tavistock, 1984.

Gordon, David F. "Debt, Conditionality, and Reform: The International Relations of Economic Policy Restructuring in Sub-Saharan Africa." In *Hemmed In: Responses to Africa's Economic Decline,* edited by Thomas Callaghy and John Ravenhill. New York: Columbia University Press, 1993.

Gordon, J. E. *Control of Communicable Diseases in Man.* New York: American Public Health Association, 1965.

Government of Kenya. *African Socialism and Its Application to Planning in Kenya.* Sessional paper, no. 10. Nairobi: Government Printers, 1965.

———. *National Atlas of Kenya.* Nairobi: Government Printers, 1970.

———. *Economic Management for Renewed Growth.* Sessional paper, no. 1. Nairobi: Government Printers, 1986.

———. Central Bureau of Statistics. *Economic Survey, 1994.* Nairobi: Government Printers, 1994a.

———. *1989 Census.* Nairobi: Government Printers, 1994b.

Government of Kenya, Ministry of Culture and Social Services. *The Government Achievements in the Development of Women (1963–1993).* Unpublished document, 1993.

Government of Kenya, Ministry of Economic Planning and Development. *Migori District Development Plan, 1994–1996.* Nairobi: Government Printers, 1994.

Government of Kenya, Ministry for Planning and National Development. *Nakuru District Development Plan: 1979–1983.* Nairobi: Government Printers, 1980.

———. *Nakuru District Development Plan: 1984–1988.* Nairobi: Government Printers, 1985.

———. *National Development Plan, 1979–1983.* Nairobi: Government Printer, 1979.

———. *National Development Plan, 1984–1988.* Nairobi: Government Printer, 1984.

———. *National Development Plan, 1989–1993.* Nairobi: Government Printers, 1990.

———. *National Development Plan, 1994–1996.* Nairobi: Government Printers, 1994.

Government of Kenya/National Environment Secretariat, World Resources Institute, Egerton University, and Clark University. *Participatory Rural Appraisal Handbook: Conducting PRAs in Kenya.* Washington, DC: World Resources Institute, 1990.

Government of Kenya/National Environment and Human Settlements Secretariat, Clark University, and USAID. *Nakuru: District Environmental Assessment Report.* Nairobi: NEHSS, 1984.

Grandin, B. *Wealth Ranking.* London: Intermediate Technology Publications, 1988.

Greichus, Y., Greichus, A., Ammann, B., and Hopcraft, J. "Insecticides, Polychlorinated Biphenyls and Metals in African Lake Ecosystems, III. Lake Nakuru, Kenya." *Bulletin of Environmental Contamination and Toxicology* 19, no. 4 (1978).

Griffin, Keith, and Hay, Roger. "Problems of Agricultural Development in Socialist Ethiopia: An Overview and a Suggested Strategy." *The Journal of Peasant Studies* 13, no. 1 (1985): 37–66.

Guyer, Jane. "Women in the Rural Economy: Contemporary Variations." In *African Women South of the Sahara,* edited by M. Hay and S. Stichter. London: Longman, 1984.

Haddad, Lawrence, and Reardon, Thomas. "Gender Bias in the Allocation of Resources within Households in Burkina Faso: A Disaggregated Outlay Equivalent Analysis." *The Journal of Development Studies* 29, no. 2. London: Frank Cass, 1993.

Haila, Yrjo, and Levins, Richard. *Humanity and Nature: Ecology, Science, and Society.* London: Pluto Press, 1992.

Hanson, Susan, and Pratt, C., eds. *Gender, Place, and Culture.* New York: Routledge, 1994.

Hardinge, A. "Report on the British East Africa Protectorate for the Year 1897–1898." In *British Parliamentary Papers*. Vol. 69, *Reports and Correspondence on British Protectorates in East and Central Africa, 1890–1899*, pp. 399–427. Shannon: Irish University Press, 1899/1971.

Harrison, P. *The Greening of Africa*. New York and London: Penguin and Paladin, 1987.

Hart, Gillian. "Engendering Everyday Resistance: Gender, Patronage and Production Politics in Rural Malaysia." *The Journal of Peasant Studies* 19, no. 1 (1991): 93–121.

Hartmann, Betsy. *Reproductive Rights and Wrongs: The Global Politics of Population Control and Contraceptive Choice*. New York: Harper and Row, 1987.

Hay, M., and Stichter, S., eds. *African Women South of the Sahara*. London: Longman, 1984.

Hecht, R. "The Transformation of Lineage Production in Southern Ivory Coast, 1920–1980." *Ethnology* 23, no. 4 (1984): 261–277.

Hecht, Susanna, and Cockburn, Alexander. *The Fate of the Forest: Developers, Destroyers and Defenders of the Amazon*. New York: Verso, 1989.

Hellinger, Doug. "NGOs and the Large Aid Donors. Changing the Terms of Engagement." *World Development* 15, supplement (Autumn 1987): 135–143.

Henn, Jeanne Koopman. "Feeding the Cities and Feeding the Peasants: What Role for Africa's Women Farmers?" *World Development* 11, no. 2 (1983): 1043–1055.

Herbst, Jeffrey. "The Politics of Sustained Agricultural Reform." In *Hemmed In: Responses to Africa's Economic Decline*, edited by Thomas Callaghy and John Ravenhill. New York: Columbia University Press, 1993.

Hetherington, Penelope. "Explaining the Crisis of Capitalism in Kenya." *African Affairs* 92 (1993): 89–103.

Heyzer, N. "Asian Women Wage Earners: Their Situation and Possibilities for Donor Intervention." *World Development* 17 (1989): 1109–1123.

Hoek, Annet van der. "Landscape Planning and Design of Watersheds in the Kathama Agroforestry Project, Kenya." Master's project report. Wageningen, The Netherlands: Department of Landscape Architecture and Planning, 1983.

Hoekstra, D. A. *Agroforestry Systems for the Semi-Arid Areas of Machakos District, Kenya*. Working paper no. 19, ICRAF. Nairobi: ICRAF, 1984.

Holmberg, Johan, ed. *Making Development Sustainable: Redefining Sustainability, Policy, and Economics*. Washington, DC: Island Press, 1992.

Holmquist, F. "Self-Help: The State and Peasant Leverage in Kenya." *Africa* 54, no. 3 (1984): 72–91.

Holmquist, Frank, and Ford, Michael. "Kenya: Slouching Toward Democracy." *Africa Rights Monitor* (1992): 97–111.

Hoskins, Marilyn. "Social Forestry in West Africa: Myths and Realities." Paper presented at the annual meeting of the American Association for the Advancement of Science, Washington, DC, 1982.

———. *Rural Women, Forest Outputs and Forestry Products*. Rome: Food and Agriculture Organization, 1983.

Hunt, Diana. *The Impending Crisis in Kenya: The Case for Land Reform*. Hampshire, England: Gower Publishing, 1984.

Hunter, G., and Jiggins, J. "Farmer and Community Groups." Agricultural Administration Unit, Local Diagnosis, Farmer Groups and Coordination of Services Network, Paper IV. London: Overseas Development Institute, 1976.

Hyden, Goran. *Beyond Ujamaa in Tanzania: Underdevelopment and the Uncaptured Peasantry.* London: Heinemann, 1980.

———. *No Shortcuts to Progress: African Development Management in Perspective.* Berkeley: University of California Press, 1983.

———. "The Invisible Economy of Smallholder Agriculture in Africa." In *Understanding Africa's Rural Households and Farming Systems,* edited by J. Moock. Boulder, CO: Westview Press, 1986.

———. "Food Security, Local Institutions and the State: Two Tanzanian Case Studies." Paper presented at the Second Annual Hunger Research and Exchange, Providence, RI, Brown University, April 7, 1989.

———. "The Changing Context of Institutional Development in Sub-Saharan Africa." In *The Long-Term Perspective Study of Sub-Saharan Africa.* Vol. 3, *Institutional and Sociopolitical Issues.* Washington, DC: World Bank, 1990.

Institute for Low External Input Agriculture. "Participative Technology Development." *ILEIA Newsletter* 4, no. 3 (October 1988).

Jaetzold, Ralph, and Schmidt, Helmut. *Farm Management Handbook of Kenya.* Vol. 2, Part C, *East Kenya.* Nairobi: Government of Kenya, Ministry of Agriculture, 1983.

Jama, M., and Malaret, L. "Farmer/Researcher Collaborative Approach to Rural Development." Final project report to the International Development Research Centre. Nairobi, 1992.

Jama, Mahamud, Malaret, Luis, Rocheleau, Dianne, and Jandiko, Isaac. *Farmer Participatory Research on Farming Systems in Mbiuni Sublocation.* Report submitted to the International Development Research Centre. Nairobi, 1992.

Jiggins, J. "Women and Seasonality: Coping with Crisis and Calamity." *Seasonality and Poverty; IDS Bulletin* 17, no. 3, edited by R. Longhurst, pp. 9–18. Nairobi: Institute for Development Studies, University of Nairobi, 1986.

———. "Problems of Understanding and Communication at the Interface of Knowledge Systems." In *Gender Issues in Farming Research and Extension,* edited by S. Poats, M. Schmink, and A. Spring. Boulder, CO: Westview Press, 1988.

———. "An Examination of the Impact of Colonialism in Establishing Negative Values and Attitudes Towards Indigenous Agricultural Knowledge." In *Indigenous Knowledge Systems: Implications for Agriculture and International Development,* edited by Warren D. Michael, L. Jan Slikkerveer, and S. Oguntinji Titilola. Studies in Technology and Social Change Series, no. 11. Ames: Iowa State University, 1989a.

———. "How Poor Women Earn Income in Sub-Saharan Africa and What Works Against Them." *World Development* 17, no. 7 (1989b): 953–963.

Jiggins, Janice, and Feldstein, Hilary Sims, eds. *Tools for the Field: Methodologies for Gender Analysis in Agriculture.* West Hartford, CT: Kumarian Press, 1994.

Joekes, Susan, Heyzer, Noeleen, Oniang'o, Ruth, and Salles, Vania. "Gender, Environment and Population." *Development and Change* 25 (1994): 149–179.

Johnson, Steven L. "Social Investment in a Developing Economy: Position-Holding in Western Kenya." *Human Organization* 42, no. 4 (Winter 1983): 340–345.

Kabeer, N. "Gender Dimensions of Rural Poverty: Analysis from Bangladesh." *The Journal of Peasant Studies* 18, no. 21 (1991): 241–261.

Kabira, Wanjiku Mukabi, and Nzioki, Elizabeth Akinyi. *Celebrating Women's Resistance.* Nairobi: African Women's Perspective, 1993.

Kabutha, Charity, Ford, Richard, and Thomas-Slayter, Barbara. *Participatory Rural Appraisal Handbook.* Washington, DC: World Resources Institute, 1990.

Kameri-Mbote, Patricia, ed. *African Women as Environmental Managers.* Nairobi: African Centre for Technology Studies, 1992.

Kang, B. T., and Wilson, G. F. "The Development of Alley Cropping as a Promising Agroforestry Technology." In *Agroforestry: A Decade of Development,* edited by H. A. Steppler and P. K. R. Nair. Nairobi: International Center for Research on Agro-Forestry, 1987.

Kariuki, Florence. "Integrating Conservation and Development: Lessons from Lake Nakuru Park and Pwani." Master's thesis, Clark University, 1993.

Kates, R. "Hunger, Poverty, and the Human Environment." Paper presented to Michigan State University's Center for Advanced Study of International Development Distinguished Speaker Series, 1990.

Kates, Robert W., and Haarman, Viola. "Where the Poor Live: Are the Assumptions Correct?" *Environment* 34, no. 4 (May 1992): 9–12.

Kennedy, Eileen, and Cogill, Bruce. "The Case of Sugarcane in Kenya: Effects of Cash Crop Production on Women's Income, Time Allocation, and Child Care Practices." Working paper series, no. 167. East Lansing: Michigan State University, 1988.

Kenyatta, Jomo. *Facing Mt. Kenya.* New York: Random House, 1965.

Kerkvliet, Benedict. *Everyday Politics in the Philippines.* Berkeley: University of California Press, 1990.

Khasiani, Shanyisa A., ed. *Groundwork: African Women as Environmental Managers.* Nairobi: African Centre for Technology Institute, 1992.

Kilewe, K., Kealey, K. M., and Kebaara, K. K., eds. *Agroforestry Development in Kenya.* Nairobi: International Center for Research on Agro-Forestry, 1989.

King, Ynesta. "The Ecology of Feminism and the Feminism of Ecology." In *Healing the Wounds,* edited by Judith Plant. Philadelphia: New Society Publishers, 1989.

Kinuthia-Njenga, Cecilia. "The Population Debate: Whose Agenda?" Mimeograph. Nairobi: Dutch Aid, May 20, 1994.

Knight, Virginia C. "Growing Opposition in Zimbabwe." *Issue* 20, no. 1 (Winter 1991): 23–30.

Koeman, J., et al. "A Preliminary Survey of the Possible Contamination of Lake Nakuru in Kenya with Some Metals and Chlorinated Hydrocarbon Pesticides." *Journal of Applied Ecology* 9, no. 2 (1972).

Korten, David. *People-Centered Development.* West Hartford, CT: Kumarian Press, 1984.
———. *Getting to the 21st Century.* West Hartford, CT: Kumarian Press, 1989.

Kottak, Conrad P., and Costa, Alberto C. G. "Ecological Awareness, Environmentalist Action, and International Conservation Strategy." *Human Organization* 52, no. 4 (1993): 335–343.

Krapf, Ludwig. *Travels, Researches, and Missionary Labors During an Eighteen Years' Residence in Eastern Africa.* London: Trubnee, 1986.

Kuria, G. K. "KANU Not Serious on Multi-Partyism." *Daily Nation* May 26, 1994, p. 8.

Lagemann, Johannes. *Traditional African Farming Systems in Eastern Nigeria: An Analysis of Reaction to Increasing Population Pressure.* Munich: Weltforum Verlag, 1977.

Lamb, Geoff. *Peasant Politics.* Dorset: Davison Publishing, 1975.

Lambert, H. E. *Kikuyu Social and Political Institutions.* London: Oxford University Press, 1956.

Leo, Christopher. *Land and Class in Kenya.* Toronto: University of Toronto Press, 1984.

Leonard, David K., and Marshall, Dale Rogers, eds. *Institutions of Rural Development for the Poor.* Berkeley: University of California Press, 1982.

Leonard, J. *Environment and the Poor: Development Strategies for a Common Agenda.* Washington, DC: Overseas Development Council, 1989.

Levins, Richard, and Lewontin, Richard. *The Dialectical Biologist.* Cambridge, MA: Harvard University Press, 1985.

Leys, Colin. *Underdevelopment in Kenya: The Political Economy of Neo-Colonialism.* Berkeley and Los Angeles: University of California Press, 1975.

Lincer, J., Zalkind, D., Brown, L., and Hopcraft, J. "Organochlorine Residues in Kenya's Rift Valley Lakes." *Journal of Applied Ecology* 18 (1981): 157–171.

Lofchie, Michael F. "Trading Places: Economic Policy in Kenya and Tanzania." In *Hemmed In: Responses to Africa's Economic Decline,* edited by Thomas Callaghy and John Ravenhill. New York: Columbia University Press, 1993.

Love, Alexander R. "Participatory Development and Democracy." *The OECD Observer* 173 (1991): 4–6.

Lovelock, James. *The Ages of Gaia: A Biography of Our Living Earth.* New York: Norton, 1988.

Lovett, Margot. "Gender Relations, Class Formation, and the Colonial State in Africa." In *Women and the State in Africa,* edited by Jane Parpart and Kathleen Staudt. Boulder, CO: Lynne Rienner Publishers, 1989.

Mackenzie, Fiona. "Local Initiatives and National Policy: Gender and Agricultural Change in Murang'a District, Kenya." *Canadian Journal of African Studies* 3, no. 20 (1986): 377–401.

———. "Gender and Land Rights in Murang'a District, Kenya." *The Journal of Peasant Studies* 17, no. 4 (1990): 609–643.

March, Kathryn S., and Taqque, Rachelle. *Women's Informal Associations in Developing Countries: Catalysts for Change?* Boulder, CO: Westview Press, 1986.

Margulis, Lynn. *Early Life.* Boston: Science Books International, 1982.

Margulis, Lynn, and Lovelock, James. "Gaia and Geognosy." In *Global Ecology: Towards a Science of the Biosphere,* edited by M. Rambler, L. Margulis, and R. Fester. Boston: Academic Press, 1989.

Mbithi, Philip M., and Barnes, Carolyn. *The Spontaneous Settlement Problem in Kenya.* Kampala, Nairobi, and Dar es Salaam: East African Literature Bureau, 1975.

Mbithi, Philip, and Wisner, B. "Drought in Eastern Kenya: Comparative Observations of Nutritional Status and Farmer Activity at 17 Sites." IDS Discussion Paper, no. 167. Nairobi: Institute for Development Studies, University of Nairobi, 1972.

Mehra, Rekha. *Reinforcing the Right Links: Women, Land, and Sustainable Development.* Washington, DC: International Center for Research on Women, 1993.

Merchant, C. *The Death of Nature: Women, Ecology, and the Scientific Revolution.* San Francisco: Harper and Row, 1980.

———. *Ecological Revolutions: Nature, Gender and Science in New England.* Chapel Hill: University of North Carolina Press, 1989.

Meyerhoff, Elizabeth. "The Socio-economic and Ritual Roles of Pokot Women." Ph.D. diss., Cambridge University, 1982.

Mies, Maria. *Patriarchy and Accumulation on a World Scale.* London: Zed Books, 1986.

Monson, Jamie, and Kalb, Mario, eds. *Women as Food Producers in Developing Countries.* Berkeley: University of California Press, 1985.

Moore, Henrietta, and Vaughan, Megan. "Cutting Down Trees: Women, Nutrition and Agricultural Change in the Northern Province of Zambia, 1920–1986." *African Affairs* 86, no. 345 (1987): 523–540.

Morehouse, Ward, ed. *Building Sustainable Communities*. New York: Intermediate Technology Group of North America, 1989.

Moser, Carolyn. "Gender Planning in the Third World: Meeting Practical and Strategic Gender Needs." *World Development* 17, no. 11 (1989): 1799–1825.

Mulaa, John. "Deadly 'Aliens' Syndrome." *Daily Nation* May 29, 1994, p. 13.

Mung'ala, P., and Openshaw, K. "Estimation of Present and Future Demand for Woodfuel in Machakos District, Kenya." In *Wood, Energy and Households: Perspectives on Rural Kenya,* edited by C. Barnes, J. Ensminger, and P. O'Keefe. Stockholm and Uppsala: The Beijer Institute/Scandinavian Institute of African Studies, 1984.

Munro, J. Forbes. *Colonial Rule and the Kamba*. Oxford: Clarendon Press, 1975.

Munyao, P. "The Importance of Gathered Food and Medicinal Plant Species in Kakuyuni and Kathama Areas in Machakos." In *Women's Use of Off-Farm and Boundary Lands: Agroforestry Potentials,* edited by K. K. Wachiri. Annex 1 of Final Project Reports. Nairobi: International Center for Research on Agro-Forestry, 1987.

Muriuki, Godfrey. *A History of the Kikuyu, 1500–1900*. London: Oxford University Press, 1974.

Murphy, Yolanda, and Murphy, Robert. *Women of the Forest*. New York: Columbia University Press, 1974.

Mutero, Wycliffe, Thomas-Slayter, B., and Ford, R. *Water Choices for Mbusyani: A Case Study in Rural Resources Management in Machakos, Kenya*. Cambridge, MA: Coolidge Center for Environmental Leadership, 1990.

Muthiani, L. *Akamba from Within: Egalitarianism in Social Relations*. New York: Exposition Books, 1973.

Mwaniki, N. "Against Many Odds: The Dilemmas of Women's Self-Help Groups in Mbeere, Kenya." *Africa* 56, no. 2 (1986): 210–226.

Ndi, Ni John Fru. "Cameroon: Democracy at Bay." In *Africa Demos* 3, no. 1 (February 1993): 7–18.

Nduati, Samuel. "Kenya's Economic Recovery Real." *Daily Nation* May 31, 1994.

Nelson, N. *African Women in the Development Process*. London: Frank Cass, 1981.

Ngugi, Patrick. "What It Takes for SAPs to Succeed." *Daily Nation* May 27, 1994, p. 12.

Ngugi wa Thiong'o. *Devil on the Cross*. London: Heinneman, 1982.

Ng'weno, Hilary. "Making Education Meaningful." *The Weekly Review* May 27, 1994, pp. 26–29.

Nijssen, O. "Nutrient Cycle Study of the Cultivated Area and a Study on the Use of Manure in the Kathama Research Areas." Master's thesis, Department of Soil Fertility and Plant Nutrition, Wageningen Agricultural University, 1983.

Norem, R., Yoder, R., and Martin, Y. "Indigenous Agricultural Knowledge and Gender Issues in Third World Agricultural Development." In *Indigenous Knowledge Systems: Implications for Agricultural and International Development*, edited by Warren D. Michael, L. Jan Slikkerveer, and S. Oguntinji Titilola. Studies in Technology and Social Change Series, no. 11. Ames: Iowa State University, 1989.

Nyong'o, P. Angang. "State and Society in Kenya: The Disintegration of the Nationalist Coalitions and the Use of Presidential Authoritarianism." *African Affairs* 88 (1989): 229–252.

Nyoni, Sithembiso. "Indigenous NGOs: Liberation, Self-Reliance and Development." *World Development* 15, supplement (Autumn 1987): 51–56.

Nzioki, Elizabeth. "Effects of Land Tenure Reform on Women's Access to and Control of Land for Food Production: A Case Study in Mbiuni Location, Machakos District, Kenya." Provisional report presented to the International Development Research Centre, Nairobi, 1990.

Nzomo, Maria. "Policy Impacts on Women and Environment." In *Groundwork, African Women as Environmental Managers*, edited by Shanyisa Khasiani. Nairobi: African Centre for Technology Studies, 1992.

———. "Gender Question and the South African Elections." *Daily Nation* June 4, 1994, p. 6.

Obeng, L. *Population and Environment*. Population Impact Project. Accra: University of Ghana, 1990.

———. "The Right to Health in Tropical Agriculture." Reprint from Distinguished African Scientist Lecture Series. Ibadan, Nigeria: International Institute of Tropical Agriculture, 1991.

Oboler, Regina Smith. *Women, Power, and Economic Change: The Nandi of Kenya*. Palo Alto, CA: Stanford University Press, 1985.

Odum, Eugene Pleasants. *Basic Ecology*. Philadelphia: Saunders College Publishers, 1983.

Odum, H. *Environment, Power, and Society*. New York: Wiley-Interscience, 1971.

Oduol, Peter Allan. "The Shamba System: An Indigenous System of Food Production from Forest Areas in Kenya." In *Agroforestry Systems in the Tropics*, edited by P. K. R. Nyer. Dordrecht: Kluwer Academic Publishers, 1989.

O'Keefe, P., and Wisner, B., eds. *Land Use and Development*. African Environment Special Report 5. London: International African Insititute.

Okoth-Ogendo, H. W. O. "Some Issues of Theory in the Study of Tenure Relations in African Agriculture." *Africa* 59, no. 1 (1989): 7–17.

———. *Tenants of the Crown*. Nairobi: African Centre for Technology Studies, 1991.

Olenja, Joyce. "Gender and Agricultural Production in Samia, Kenya: Strategies and Constraints." *Journal of Asian and African Studies* 26, no. 3/4 (July 1, 1991).

Olowu, Dele. "Local Institutes and Development." *Canadian Journal of African Studies* 23, no. 2 (1989): 201–231.

Ondiege, Peter O. "Local Coping Strategies in Machakos District, Kenya." In *Development from Within: Survival in Rural Africa*, edited by Fraser D. R. Taylor and Fiona Mackenzie. London: Routledge. 1992.

Opala, Ken. "CPA Meeting Censures Anti-Democracy Leaders." *Daily Nation* June 3, 1994, p. 6.

Opanga, W. R. "Are We So Reckless as to Invite a Genocide Here?" *Daily Nation* May 29, 1994, p. 6.

Owuor, George. "Rich Nations Urged to Scrap Third World Debts." *Daily Nation* June 3, 1994, p. 8.

Pala Okeyo, Achola. "Daughters of the Lakes and Rivers: Colonization and the Land Rights of Luo Women." In *Women and Colonization: Anthropological Perspectives*, edited by M. Etienne and E. Leacock. New York: Praeger, 1980.

Paolisso, Michael, and Yudelman, Sally W. *Women, Poverty and the Environment in Latin America*. Washington, DC: International Centre for Research on Women (ICRW), 1991.

Parajuli, Pramod. "Power and Knowledge in Development Discourse: New Social Movements and the State in India." *International Conflict Research* 127 (February 1991): 173–190.

Parpart, Jane L., and Staudt, Kathleen A. *Women and the State in Africa*. Boulder, CO: Lynne Rienner Publishers, 1989.

Peters, Pauline. "Struggles Over Water, Struggles Over Meaning: Cattle, Water, and the State in Botswana." Boston University Working Paper, no. 88. Boston: Boston University, African Studies Center, 1984.

Potash, Betty. *Female Farmers, Mothers-in-Law and Extension Agents: Development Planning and a Rural Luo Community.* Working paper, no. 90. East Lansing: Michigan State University, 1985.

Pretty, J. A., and Scoones, I., eds. *Rapid Rural Appraisal for Economics: Exploring Incentives for Tree Management in Sudan.* London: International Institute for Environment and Development, 1989.

Rahman, M. A., ed. "The Small Farmer Development Programme of Nepal." In *Grass-Roots Participation and Self-Reliance: Experience in South and East Asia.* New Delhi: Oxford University Press, 1984.

Raintree, J. B. "A Diagnostic Approach to Agroforestry Design." In *Strategies and Designs for Afforestation, Reforestation and Tree Planting,* edited by K. F. Wiersum. Wageningen, The Netherlands: PUDOC, 1984.

Ravenhill, John. "A Second Decade of Adjustment: Greater Complexity, Greater Uncertainty." In *Hemmed In: Responses to Africa's Economic Decline,* edited by Thomas Callaghy and John Ravenhill. New York: Columbia University Press, 1993.

Redclift, Michael. *Sustainable Development: Exploring the Contradictions.* New York: Methuen Press, 1987.

Redfern, Paul. "Kenya Tops in Development." *Daily Nation* June 2, 1994, p. 12.

Repetto, R., ed. *The Global Possible: Resources, Development, and the New Century.* New Haven and London: Yale University, 1985.

Richards, P. *Indigenous Agricultural Revolution: Ecology and Food Production in West Africa.* London: Hutchinson, 1985.

Riddell, Barry. "The Ever-Changing Land: Adaptation and Tenure in Africa." *Canadian Journal of African Studies* 26, no. 2 (1992): 337–341.

Rocheleau, D. *The Application of Ecosystems and Landscape in Agroforestry Diagnosis and Design: A Case Study from Kathama Sub-location, Machakos District, Kenya.* Working paper, no. 11, ICRAF. Nairobi: ICRAF, 1984.

———. "Criteria for Re-appraisal and Re-design: Intra-Household and Between-Household Aspects of FSRE in Three Kenyan Agroforestry Projects." Working paper, no. 37. Nairobi: International Center for Research on Agro-Forestry, November 1985a.

———. *Land Use Planning with Rural Farm Households and Communities: Participatory Agroforestry Research.* Nairobi: ICRAF, 1985b.

———. "A Land User Perspective for Agroforestry Research and Action." In *Agroforestry: Realities, Possibilities, and Potentials,* edited by H. Gholz. Dordrecht: Martinus Nijhoff, 1987a.

———. "Women, Trees, and Tenure: Implications for Agroforestry Research and Development." In *Land, Trees and Tenure,* edited by J.B. Raintree. Madison: Land Tenure Center, University of Wisconsin, 1987b.

———. "Gender, Resource Management and the Rural Landscape: Implications for Agroforestry and Farming Systems Research." In *Gender Issues in Farming Systems Research and Extension,* edited by S. Poats, M. Schmink, and A. Spring. Boulder, CO: Westview Press, 1988.

———. "The Gender Division of Work, Resources and Rewards in Agroforestry Systems." In *Agroforestry Development in Kenya,* edited by A. E. Kilewe, K. M. Kealey, and K. K. Kebaara. Nairobi: ICRAF, 1989.

————. "Gender, Conflict and Complementarity in Sustainable Forestry Development: A Multiple User Approach." *IUFRO: Congress Report,* Vol. B, pp. 432–448. Montreal: International Union of Forest Research Organizations, August 5–11, 1990.

————. "Gender, Ecology, and the Science of Survival: Stories and Lessons from Kenya." *Agriculture and Human Values* (1991a): 156–165.

————. "Participatory Research in Agroforestry: Learning from Experience and Expanding Our Repertoire." *Agroforestry Systems* 9, no. 2 (1991b).

————. *Gender, Ecology, and Agroforestry: Science and Survival in Kathama.* ECOGEN Case Study Series. Worcester, MA: Program for International Development, Clark University, 1992.

Rocheleau, D., and Fortmann, L. "Women's Spaces and Women's Places in Rural Food Production Systems: The Spatial Distribution of Women's Rights, Responsibilities and Activities." Paper presented to the 7th World Congress of Rural Sociology, Bologna, Italy, June 25–July 1, 1988.

Rocheleau, D., and van der Hoek, A. "The Application of Ecosystems and Landscape Analysis in Agroforestry Diagnosis and Design: A Case Study from Kathama Sublocation, Machakos District, Kenya." Working paper, no. 11. Nairobi: International Center for Research on Agro-Forestry, 1984.

Rocheleau, D., and Jama, M. "Annual Report of Farming Systems and Ethnoecology Research Project." Summary of interview with elders at Kathama. Mimeograph. Nairobi: Institute of Development Studies, 1989.

Rocheleau, D., Ross, L., Monobel, J., and Hernandez, R. *Farming the Forests, Gardening with Trees: Landscapes and Livelihoods in Zambrana-Chacuey, Dominican Republic.* ECOGEN Project Case Study. Worcester: Clark University, 1995.

Rocheleau, D., Benjamin, P., and Diang'a, A. "The Ukambani Region of Kenya." In *Regions at Risk: Comparisons of Threatened Environments,* edited by Jeanne X. Kasperson, E. K. Roger, and B. L. Turner. Tokyo: UN University Press, 1994.

Rocheleau, D., Khasiala, P., Munyao, M., Mutiso, M., Opala, E., Wanjohi, B., and Wanjuana, A. "Women's Use of Off-Farm Lands: Implications for Agroforestry Research." Project report to the Ford Foundation. Mimeograph. Nairobi: International Center for Research on Agro-Forestry, 1985.

Rocheleau, D., Steinberg, P., and Benjamin, P. "Environment, Development, Crisis and Crusade: Ukambani, Kenya 1890–1990." *World Development.* 1995, forthcoming.

Rocheleau, D., Thomas-Slaytor, B., and Wangari, E. (eds.). *Toward a Feminist Political Ecology: Global Perspectives from Local Experience.* London: Routledge (forthcoming).

Rocheleau, D., Wachira, K. K., Malaret, L., and Wanjohi, B. "Ethnoecological Methods to Complement Local Knowledge and Farmer Innovations in Agroforestry." In *Farmer First,* edited by A. Pacey, R. Chambers, and L. Thrupp. London: Intermediate Technology, 1989.

Rocheleau, D., Weber, F., and Juma, A. Field. *Agroforestry in Dryland Africa.* Nairobi: International Center for Research on Agro-Forestry, 1988.

Roe, Emory, and Fortmann, Louise. *Season and Strategy: Water Management in Botswana.* Ithaca, NY: Cornell University Press, 1981.

Ronderos, Ana. "Towards an Understanding of Project Impact on Gender Negotiation: Forestry, Community Organization and Women's Groups in Guanacaste, Costa Rica." Master's thesis, Clark University, 1992.

Rosberg, Carl, and Nottingham, John. *The Myth of Mau Mau: Nationalism in Kenya.* Palo Alto, CA: Stanford University, Hoover Institution Press, 1966.

Rothchild, Donald, and Chazan, Naomi, eds. *The Precarious Balance: State and Society in Africa.* Boulder, CO: Westview Press, 1988.

Rukandema, M. J. K. Mavua, and Audi, P. O. *The Farming System of Lowland Machakos: Farm Survey Results from Mwala.* FAO Dryland Agricultural Project. Katumani, 1981.

Sachs, Ignacy. *The Discovery of the Third World.* Translated by Michael Fineberg. Cambridge, MA: MIT Press, 1976.

Safilios-Rothschild, C. "The Persistance of Women's Invisibility in Agriculture: Theoretical and Policy Lessons from Lesotho and Sierra Leone." *Economic Development and Cultural Change* 33 (1985): 299–317.

Sandbrook, Richard. *The Politics of Africa's Economic Stagnation.* Cambridge: Cambridge University Press, 1985.

Schmink, Marianne, and Wood, Charles. *Contested Frontiers in Amazonia.* Center for Latin American Studies. Gainesville: University of Florida, 1990.

Schroeder, R. "Shady Practice: Gender and the Politcal Ecology of Resource Stabilization in Gambian Garden Orchards." *Economic Geography* 69, no. 4 (1993): 349–365.

Schumacher, E. F. *Small Is Beautiful: Economics as If People Mattered.* New York: Perennial Library, 1973.

Scoones, I., ed. *Participatory Research for Rural Development in Zimbabwe: A Report of a Training Workshop for ENDA—Zimbabwe Trees Project.* London: International Institute for Environment and Development, 1989.

Scott, James. *The Moral Economy of the Peasant.* New Haven, CT, and London: Yale University Press, 1976.

———. *Weapons of the Weak: Everyday Forms of Peasant Resistance.* New Haven, CT: Yale University Press, 1985.

Sen, Amartya. "Gender and Cooperative Conflicts." In *Persistent Inequalities: Women and World Development,* edited by Irene Tinker. Oxford: Oxford University Press, 1990.

Sen, G., and Grown, C. *Development, Crises, and Alternative Visions.* New York: Monthly Review Press, 1987.

Settlement Study Centre. "Planning Project for the Nakuru–Nyandarua Region, Kenya." Rehovot, Israel: David Foundation Publications on Integrated Rural Development, 1982.

Sharp, Robin. "Organizing for Changes: People-Power and the Role of Institutions." In *Making Development Sustainable: Redefining Sustainability, Policy, and Economics,* edited by Johan Holmberg. Washington, DC: Island Press, 1992.

Shaw, Robert. "Little-Understood SAPs Are Blamed for All Our Failures." *Daily Nation* May 29, 1994, p. 7.

Shaw, Timothy M. "Beyond Any New World Order: The South in the 21st Century." *Third World Quarterly* 15, no. 1 (1994): 139–146.

Shields, Dale, and Thomas-Slayter, Barbara. *Gender, Class, Ecological Decline, and Livelihood Strategies: A Case Study of Siquijor Island, The Philippines.* ECOGEN Case Study Series. Worcester, MA: Program for International Development, Clark University, 1993.

Shipton, Parker. "Lineage and Locality as Antithetical Principles in East African Systems of Land Tenure." *Ethnology* 23 (1984): 117–132.

———. *Bitter Money, Cultural Economy and Some African Meanings of Forbidden Commodities.* American Ethnological Society Monograph Series, no. 1. Washington, DC: American Anthropological Association, 1989.

Shiva, Vandana. *Staying Alive.* London: Zed Books, 1989.

Silberfein, Marilyn. "Differential Development in Machakos District, Kenya." In *Life Before the Drought,* edited by Earl Scott. Boston: Allen and Unwin, 1984.

Sithole, Masipula. "Is Zimbabwe Poised on a Liberal Path? The State and Prospects of the Parties." *Issue* 21, no. 1–2 (1993): 35–43.

Smoke, Paul. "Rural Local Government Finance in Kenya: The Case of Murang'a County Council." *Public Administration and Development* 12 (1992): 87–96.

Soja, Edward W. *The Geography of Modernization in Kenya: A Spatial Analysis of Social, Economic, and Political Change.* Syracuse Geographical Series, no. 2. Syracuse, NY: Syracuse University Press, 1968.

Sorrenson, M. P. K. *Land Reform in the Kikuyu Country.* Nairobi: Oxford University Press, 1967.

Stamp, Patricia. "Kikuyu Women's Self-Help Groups." In *Women and Class in Africa,* edited by Claire Robertson and Iris Berger. New York: Holmes and Meier, 1986a.

———. "Local Government in Kenya: Ideology and Political Practice, 1895–1974." *African Studies Review* 4, no. 29 (1986b): 17–42.

———. *Technology, Gender and Power in Africa.* Ottawa, Ontario: International Development Research Centre, 1989.

Staudt, Kathleen. "Stratification: Implications for Women's Politics." In *Women and Class in Africa,* edited by C. Robertson and I. Berger. New York: Holmes and Meier, 1986a.

———. "Women, Development and the State: On the Theoretical Impasse." *Development and Change* 17 (1986b): 325–333.

———. "Uncaptured or Unmotivated? Women and the Food Crisis in Africa." *Rural Sociology* 52, no. 1 (1987): 37–55.

Stichter, Sharon, and Parpart, Jane, eds. *Patriarchy and Class: African Women in the Home and the Workforce.* Boulder, CO: Westview Press, 1988.

Stonich, Susan. "Struggling with Honduran Poverty: The Environmental Consequences of Natural Resource-Based Development and Rural Transformations." *World Development* 20, no. 3 (1992): 385–399.

Talle, A. *Women at a Loss: Changes in Maasai Pastoralism and Their Effects on Gender Relations.* Stockholm: University of Stockholm, 1988.

Taylor, F. D. R., ed. "Development from Within and Survival in Rural Africa: A Synthesis of Theory and Practice." In *Development from Within: Survival in Rural Africa,* edited by Fraser D. R. Taylor and Fiona Mackenzie. London: Routledge, 1992.

Taylor, Fraser D. R., and Mackenzie, Fiona, eds. *Development from Within: Survival in Rural Africa.* London: Routledge, 1992.

Teel, Wayne. *A Pocket Directory of Trees and Seeds in Kenya.* Nairobi: Kenya Energy Non-Governmental Organisations, 1984.

Thomas, B. *Politics, Participation and Poverty: Development Through Self-Help in Kenya.* Boulder, CO: Westview Press, 1985.

———. "Household Strategies for Adaptation and Change: Participation in Kenyan Rural Women's Associations." *Africa* 58, no. 4 (1988): 401–422.

Thomas-Slayter, B. "Class, Ethnicity, and the Kenyan State: Community Mobilization in the Context of Global Politics." *International Journal of Politics, Culture and Society* 4, no. 3 (1991): 301–321.

———. "Implementing Effective Local Management of Natural Resources: New Roles for NGOs in Africa." *Human Organization* 51, no. 2 (Summer 1992a): 136–143.

————. "Politics, Class and Gender in African Resource Management: The Case of Rural Kenya." *Economic Development and Cultural Change* 40, no. 4 (July 1992b): 809–828.

————. "Structural Change, Power Politics, and Community Organizations in Africa: Challenging the Patterns, Puzzles, and Paradoxes." *World Development* 22, no. 10 (October 1994): 1479–1490.

Thomas-Slayter, B., and Ford, R. "Water, Soils, Food, and Rural Development: Examining Institutional Frameworks in Katheka Sublocation." *Canadian Journal of African Studies* 23, no. 2 (1989): 250–271.

Thomas-Slayter, Barbara, and Rocheleau, Dianne. "Essential Connections: Linking Gender to Effective Natural Resource Management and Sustainable Development." Working paper, no. 242. East Lansing: Michigan State University, April 1994.

————. "Research Frontiers at the Nexus of Gender, Environment and Development: Linking Household, Community, and Ecosystem." In *The Women and International Development Annual,* edited by Rita S. Gallin and Anne Ferguson. Westview Press, 1995.

Thomas-Slayter, Barbara, Rocheleau, Dianne, Shields, Dale, and Rojas, Mary. "Concepts and Issues Linking Gender, Natural Resources Management, and Sustainable Development." Working paper. Worcester, MA: Clark University, 1991.

————. *Introducing the ECOGEN Approach to Gender, Natural Resource Management, and Sustainable Development.* Worcester, MA: Clark University, n. d.

Thrupp, L. A. "Legitimizing Local Knowledge: From Displacement to Empowerment for Third World People." *Agriculture and Human Values* 6, no. 3 (1989): 13–24.

Tibaijuka, Anna Kajumulo. "Strategies for Smallholder Agriculture Development in West Lake Region, Tanzania." From Ph.D. diss. Uppsala: Sveriges Lantbruksuniversitate Institutionen for Ekonomi och Statistik, 1979.

Tiffen, Mary. "Productivity and Environmental Conservation Under Rapid Population Growth: A Case Study of Machakos District." *Journal of International Development* 5, no. 2 (1993): 207–223.

Tiffen, Mary, ed. *Environmental Change and Dryland Management in Machakos District, Kenya, 1930–90.* Working paper, no. 62. London: Overseas Development Institute, 1992.

Tiffen, Mary, and Mortimore, Michael. "Environment, Population Growth and Productivity in Kenya: A Case Study of Machakos District. *Development Policy Review* 10 (1992): 359–387.

Tiffen, Mary, Mortimore, Michael, and Gichuki, Francis. *More People, Less Erosion: Environmental Recovery in Kenya.* Chichester: John Wiley and Sons, 1994.

Timberlake, Lloyd. *Africa in Crisis.* Washington, DC, and London: International Institute for Environment and Development, 1985.

Tisdell, C. "Sustainable Development: Differing Perspectives of Ecologists and Economists, and Relevance to LDCs." *World Development* 16, no. 3 (1988): 373–384.

Toledo, Victor M. "Patzquaro's Lesson: Nature Production and Culture in an Indigenous Region of Mexico." In *Biodiversity: Culture, Conservation, and Ecodevelopment,* edited by Margery L. Oldfield and Janis B. Alcorn. Boulder, CO: Westview Press, 1991.

Trager, Lillian. "Local-Level Development in Nigeria: Institutions and Impact." Paper presented at African Studies Association meeting, Atlanta, GA, November 4, 1989.

Tripp, R. "Farmer Participation in Agricultural Research: New Directions or Old Problems?" Discussion paper, no. 256. Sussex: Institute of Development Studies, 1989.

Turner, Billie Lee, ed. *The Earth as Transformed by Human Action: Global and Regional Changes in the Biosphere Over the Past 300 Years.* New York: Cambridge University Press, 1990.

Turner, B. L. II, Hyden, G., and Kates, R. W., eds. *Population Growth and Agricultural Change in Africa.* Gainesville: University of Florida Press, 1993.

UN Children's Fund. *The State of the World's Children 1990.* Oxford: Oxford University Press, 1990.

UN Conference on Environment and Development. "Global Action for Women Towards Sustainable and Equitable Development." In *Agenda 21.* New York: UN Publications, 1993.

UN Development Program. *1994 Human Development Report.* New York: UN Publications, 1994.

Uphoff, N. *Local Institutional Development: An Analytical Sourcebook with Cases.* West Hartford, CT: Kumarian Press, 1986.

Uphoff, N., and Esman, M. *Local Organization for Rural Development: Analysis of Asian Experience.* Ithaca, NY: Rural Development Committee, Center for International Studies, Cornell University, 1974.

Uphoff, N., Cohen, J., and Goldsmith, A. "Feasibility and Application of Rural Development Participation: A State of the Art Paper." Ithaca, NY: Rural Development Committee, Center for International Studies, Cornell University, 1979.

Vonk, R. B. *Report on a Methodology and Technology Generating Exercise.* Wageningen, The Netherlands: Wageningen Agricultural University, 1983a.

———. "A Study of Possible Agroforestry Tree Species for the Kathama Area." Master's thesis, Department of Silviculture, Wageningen Agricultural University, 1983b.

Wachira, K. K. "Women's Use of Off-Farm and Boundary Lands: Agroforestry Potentials." Project report to the Ford Foundation. Mimeograph. Nairobi: International Center for Research on Agro-Forestry, 1987.

Wamalwa, B. N. "Indigenous Knowledge and Natural Resources." In *Gaining Ground: Institutional Innovations in Land Use Management in Kenya,* edited by A. Kiriro and C. Juma. Nairobi: ACTS Press.

Wangari, Esther. "Effects of Land Registration on Small-Scale Farming in Kenya: The Case of Mbeere in Embu District." Ph.D. diss., New School for Social Research, New York, 1991.

Wanjohi, B. "Women's Groups' Gathered Plants and Their Potentials in the Kathama Area." Final project report, Annex 1. In *Women's Use of Off-Farm and Boundary Lands: Agroforestry Potentials,* edited by K. K. Wachira. Nairobi: International Center for Research on Agro-Forestry, 1987.

Watts, M. *Silent Violence: Food, Famine, and Peasantry in Northern Nigeria.* Los Angeles: University of California Press, 1983.

———. "Struggles Over Land, Struggles Over Meaning: Some Thoughts on Naming, Peasant Resistance and the Politics of Place." In *A Ground for Common Search,* edited by R. Golledge, H. Coucelis, and P. Gould. Santa Barbara, CA: Geographical Press, 1988.

———. "The Agrarian Crisis in Africa: Debating the Crisis." *Progress in Human Geography* 13, no. 1 (1991): 1–42.

Weatherly, W. Paul. "NGO Outreach Project." *New York Times* January 7, 1990, p. 7.

Were, G. *Women and Development in Kenya, Siaya District.* Nairobi: Institute for African Studies, 1991.

Wijngaarden, L. van. "Patterns of Fuel Gathering and Use." Master's thesis, Wageningen Agricultural University, Department of Forestry Management, 1983.

Williams, Paula. *The Social Organization of Firewood Procurement and Use in Africa: A Study of the Division of Labor by Sex.* Ph.D. diss., College of Forest Resources, University of Washington, 1983.

Wilson, Ken. "Trees in Fields in Southern Zimbabwe." *Journal of Southern African Studies* 15, no. 2 (January 1989): 369–383.

Wipper, A. "Women's Voluntary Associations." In *African Women South of the Sahara,* edited by Margaret Jean Hay and Sharon Stichter. London: Longman, 1984.

Wisner, B. *Power and Need in Africa: Basic Human Needs and Development Policies.* London: Earthscan Publications, 1988.

Woods, Bernard. "Altering the Present Paradigm: A Different Path to Sustainable Development in the Rural Sector." Mimeograph. Washington, DC: World Bank, 1983.

World Bank. *Kenya: The Role of Women in Economic Development.* Washington, DC: IBRD, 1989a.

———. *Social Indicators of World Development.* Washington, DC: IBRD, 1989b.

———. *Sub-Saharan Africa: From Crisis to Sustainable Growth.* Washington, DC: IBRD, 1989c.

———. *World Development Report 1989.* New York: Oxford University Press, 1989d.

———. *The Long-Term Perspective Study of Sub-Saharan Africa.* Vol. 3, *Institutional and Sociopolitical Issues.* Washington, DC: IBRD, 1990a.

———. "The Population, Agriculture and Environment Nexus in Sub-Saharan Africa." Mimeograph. Washington, DC: IBRD, 1990b.

World Resources Institute. *World Resources 1994–95: A Guide to the Global Environment.* Oxford: Oxford University Press, 1994.

Wunsch, J. S., and Olowu, Dele, eds. *The Failure of the Centralized State: Institutions and Self-Governance in Africa.* Boulder, CO: Westview Press, 1989.

Young, Crawford. "Beyond Patrimonial Autocracy: The African Challenge." In *Beyond Autocracy in Africa,* compiled by the Governance in Africa Program. Atlanta, GA: The Carter Center of Emory University, February 17–18, 1989.

Youri, Pat. *South Nyanza District Health Situation.* Mimeograph. Nairobi: African Medical and Research Foundation, August 1989.

Zebralink Communications. *If Women Counted.* Video sponsored by The Netherlands Ministry of Foreign Affairs, 1993.

The Authors

Isabella Asamba has served in a research and training capacity with the government of Kenya's National Environment Secretariat and is currently a community training and development adviser with an NGO from The Netherlands. In this capacity she is part of the Programme Advisory Team advising the Lake Basin Development Authority on the implementation of the water, sanitation, and health program in Nyanza Province in Western Kenya using participatory approaches. She is coauthor of *Implementing PRAs,* a handbook to facilitate Participatory Rural Appraisals.

Mohamud Jama is a senior research fellow at the Institute for Development Studies of the University of Nairobi. He undertook a two-year leave of absence from IDS in late 1994 to coordinate the Environmental Economics Network for Eastern and Southern Africa, sponsored by the International Development Research Council of Canada (IDRC) and the Swedish Agency for Research and Economic Cooperation (SAREC).

Charity Kabutha is the regional coordinator for the African Women Leaders in Agriculture and the Environment (AWLAE) of Winrock International. She has been involved professionally with environment, health, and gender issues for a number of years as a research and training officer for Kenya's National Environment Secretariat and as a program officer in Kenya for UNICEF. Ms. Kabutha is the author or coauthor of numerous articles and manuals on Participatory Rural Appraisal and other participatory methods for community action, including "Participatory Rural Appraisal: A Case Study from Kenya," in *Participatory Methodologies in Development,* edited by Krishna Kumar.

Njoki Mbuthi is a researcher with Kenya's National Environment Secretariat, currently on academic leave. Her work pertains to women and fuelwood in Kenya.

Elizabeth Oduor-Noah is a senior environment officer with the National Environment Secretariat of the government of Kenya. Ms. Oduor-Noah has been involved in the preparatory process and follow-up activities for Kenya for the UN Conference on Environment and Development (UNCED). She is currently a member of the Task Force for the Review of Laws related to women under the Law Reform Commission of Kenya as a joint secretary; chair of the National Selection Committee of Africa 2000 Network, a project of UNDP; and vice-chair of the National Executive Committee for African Women Leaders in Agriculture and Environment (AWLAE), a program of Winrock International. She is coauthor of the second in a series of Participatory Rural Appraisal (PRA) handbooks, *Implementing PRAs.*

Dianne Rocheleau is assistant professor of geography in the Graduate School of Geography at Clark University. She has engaged in long-term field research and applied work on environment and development issues in the United States, Kenya, and the Dominican Republic. She served as a program officer with the Ford Foundation in Eastern and Southern Africa and as a senior scientist with the International Center for Research in Agro-Forestry (ICRAF) in Nairobi. She is author of *Agroforestry in Dryland Africa* with F. Weber and A. Field-Juma and "A Hundred Years of Crisis? Environmental and Development Narratives in Ukambani, Kenya" with P. Steinberg and P. Benjamin. She currently serves on the board of the Land Tenure Center, University of Wisconsin, Madison.

Karen Schofield-Leca has research experience in both Kenya and Mozambique. Ms. Schofield assisted with three of the case studies included in this volume and coauthored one of them. She is currently working with the Washington Hospital Center in Washington, D.C.

Barbara Thomas-Slayter is an associate professor in international development at Clark University and director of the International Development Program. Her work focuses on NGOs; issues in state, class, and ethnic relations; changing roles of community institutions in managing renewable resources; and the role of gender in shaping responsibilities in rural livelihood systems. She is author of articles and papers on these topics, including *Politics, Participation and Poverty: Development Through Self-Help in Kenya* and "Politics, Class and Gender in African Resource Management: The Case of Rural Kenya." She is currently a member of the board of directors of Oxfam America.

Betty Wamalwa-Muragori is currently Kenya national coordinator of the Africa 2000 Network of the UN Development Program. A recipient of several international fellowships, she has been a NORAD Fellow at the Institute of Women's Law in Oslo, an Africa-Caribbean Institute Fellow in Nairobi, and a Ford Fellow at a Women and Development certificate course at the University of Wisconsin. She is author of "Indigenous Knowledge and Natural Resources," in A. Kiriro and C. Juma, *Gaining Ground.* Ms. Wamalwa-Muragori is currently a member of the Executive Committee for the Pan-African NGO, Women in Law and Development in Africa (WILDAF).

Leah Wanjama, a lecturer in the Department of Development Studies at Kenyatta University, serves as the coordinator of the Gender Issues Action Team for Kenyatta University and is a member of the Executive Committee of the Kenya Red Cross Society, where she serves on its committee for Women in Development Disaster Preparedness. Ms. Wanjama works internationally as a gender trainer with FEMNET, the African Women's Development and Communication Network.

Index

Africa: agriculture, 25–26; Berlin Conference of 1884, 23; ecology, 2, 27–30; economy, 2, 23–27; environment, 23, 27, 28, 29; ethnicity, 33, 40; export commodities, 23–26, 27, 28; foreign debt, 25, 36; leadership, 31; politics, 23–30; trade, 30

Agenda 21, 209

Agriculture, 26, 27, 36; bananas, 93–96, 172; cash crops, 26–27; coffee, 35, 75, 92–93, 110–115, 117–118, 122, 125–127, 174; extension services, 152, 156; French beans, 93–94; grains, 35–36; groundnuts, 172, 174, 176; high potential, 78, 166; intensification, 47–49, 54, 55, 143–145; low potential, 107–109; policies, 26; prices, 26, 28; smallholders, 26, 40; sugar cane, 170, 173–176, 185; trends, 166–167; women, 26. *See also* Gikarangu; Kathama; Kyevaluki; Mbusyani; Pwani; South Kamwango

Agroecological zones: description, 137; map, 134

Agroforestry, 149; alley cropping, 59–62; experiments, 59–62; project, 50–51, 61–65

Agropastoralism, 55

Akamba (also Wakamba, Kamba), 47, 109–111. *See also* Kathama; Kyevaluki; Machakos; Mbusyani

Assistant chiefs: Gikarangu, 78, 82; Kathama, Mbusyani and Kyevaluki, 123–124; South Kamwango, 177

Associations. *See* Community organizations and institutions; Groups

Attitudinal changes in: Gikarangu 98–101; Mbusyani and Kyevaluki, 127–129

Bananas, 93–96; long-distance trade, 93–96; male intrusion, 94–95; small-scale/local trade, 94–95, 172

Beijing Conference (1995), 210

Berlin Conference of 1884, 23

Biodiversity, 47, 65–68; wildlife protection, 37

Capitalism, 75–80

CARE (Cooperative for American Relief Everywhere), 177–178, 197

Church: Apostolic Faith, 138; Catholic, 138, 177; Free Mission, 138; Full Gospel, 137; Presbyterian (PCEA), 100, 197; of the Province of Kenya (CPK), 137, 152, 197; Seventh Day Adventist, 177

Clark University, 1, 163

Class, 83–86, 140–142; in Kathama, 49–50, 55, 65–68; rich/poor gap, 33, 38. *See also* Household, differentiation; Stratification issues

Coffee, 28, 32; in Gikarangu, 75, 84–86, 92–93; largeholders, 29; in Mbusyani-Kyevaluki, 110–115, 117–118, 125–127. *See also* Agriculture

Colonial Government, 80–81, 98–99, 109–110

Commercial crops. *See* Agriculture; Bananas; Coffee

Commodity production, 75–77, 173–174

Commonwealth Parliamentary Association, 31

Community, conceptualizing. *See* South Kamwango

Community organizations and institutions, 9–18; in Gikarangu, 96–102; in Kathama, 49–50, 58, 62–63, 67–68; in Mbusyani and Kyevaluki, 120–124; in Pwani, 152–153; in South Kamwango, 163, 176–179, 186–187

Conceptual framework, 2; ecological perspectives, 8–9; institutional perspectives, 9–10

Conflict: ethnic, 77, 133; resource, 67–68

Conservation, by smallholders and communities, 29

Co-wife. *See* Polygamy

CPK (Church of the Province of Kenya). *See* Church

Debt burden, 75, 192

Decisionmaking in: Gikarangu, 77–78, 80–83, 91–92; Mbusyani and Kyevaluki, 116–120, 122, 127; Pwani, 145–151, 157; South Kamwango, 169–171, 175

Deforestation, 27, 29, 49, 56–57, 59, 80–81. *See also* Reforestation

Democratic Party in Kenya, 34
Democratization, 31, 210
District Focus for Rural Develoment policy, 176
Draught, 105–108, 110, 137

Earth Summit. *See* United Nations Conference on Environment and Development (UNCED)
East Africa, 47
Ecology, 7, 10–20, 27–30, 47, 50, 51, 66, 70, 105–110, 136–137; and economy, 10–11; issues of, 37–38
Economic Survey for 1994, 36, 38
Economy, 35–37; employment, 143–145; growth of, 35; inflation in Kenya, 35–37; international impact on national, 7, 75, 111–112, 125–127; social expenditures, 37; structural adjustment, 35–36, 37; unemployment, 77, 94–96, 116 110. See Gikarangu, Kathama, Kyevaluki; Mbusyani; Pwani; South Kamwango
Education, 39–40; in Gikarangu, 79; in Kathama, 50, 54–57; in Mubsyani and Kyevaluki, 115, 116, 118–120, 124, 127–128; in Pwani, 137, 153; in South Kamwango, 178–179, 184–185; of women, 39, 200–201
Egerton University, 112, 149, 152
"Emergency" (1952–1953), 81
Environmental issues, 7–14, 180–183; degradation, 14, 27–29; policies, 38; sustainability, 18
Environmental Liaison Centre International (ELCI), 37
Ethnicity, 23–24, 30–32; in Kenya, 34. *See also* Conflict
Ethnoscience, 47. *See also* Kathama; Local knowledge
Exchange, 108
Expectations, changing, 127
Extension services, 152, 156

Famine. *See* Food, deficits
Farming systems. *See* Gikarangu; Kathama; Kyevaluki; Mbusyani; Pwani; South Kamwango
Focus group discussions: Gikarangu, 78; Kathama 69; Mbusyani and Kyevaluki, 112; Pwani, 135–136, 145–151
Food: deficits, 166; imports, 25; production, 29; security, 115–118, 149; wild foods (famine foods), 65–71
FORD (Forum for Restoration of Democracy): -Asili, 34; -Kenya, 34
French beans. *See* Agriculture; Gikarangu

Fuelwood, 27–29; Gikarangu, 87–91; Kathama 49, 56, 57, 61–68; Pwani, 147–148; shortage, 87–91; South Kamwango, 166

Gender, 8; and building local capacities, 18–20; and division of labor, 13; in Gikarangu, 91–92; in Kathama, 49–51, 55–67; in Mbusyani/Kyevaluki, 116–118; in Pwani, 135; in South Kamwango, knowledge and practice, 149, 150
Gender-based opportunities, constraints, 192; why it matters, 145, 192–194
Gendered knowledge: changing boundaries of gendered knowledge, 63–71, 150, 206–207; education, 208–209; government policies, 156–157, 207–208; health, 208; perception and practice, 63–71, 157, 206–209; promoting livelihood security, 68–71, 149, 207
Gendered labor and livelihoods, 61–65, 135, 156–157, 204–206; impact on women's rights, 204–206; male out-migration, 55, 204; men's groups, 205–206; policies to promote food security, 206; utilization of male labor, 144, 205; women's farm management, 49–51, 55, 135, 204–205
Gendered land and property relations, 64–68, 70, 154–155, 201–204; class and gender interactions, 49–50, 64–68, 143–145, 200–201; customary law, 203; elders, 204; NGO roles, 152–153, 203–204; ownership issues, 142–143, 201; policy interventions, 155, 202–204; title deeds, 204
Gender roles, 13, 40–41; in Gikarangu, 91–92; in Kathama, 61–65; in Mbusyani/Kyevaluki, 116–118; in Pwani, 144; in South Kamwango, 171–176; and the state, 11–14
Gikarangu, 75–104; agricultural trends, 2, 92–94; colonial government, 80–81, 98–99; communications, 78; community institutions, 96–102; community profile, 78–80; ecology, 78–79; employment/unemployment, 77, 94–96; governance, 80–81; household division of labor, 91–92; impact of national economy, 75–80; land, access and control, 80–86; livelihood strategies, 91–96; map, 76; out-migration, 96–97; population, 78; stratification patterns, 83–86; trees, current use, 88–91; trees, history of, 87–88; women and land, 81–83; women's organizations, 99–101. *See also* Groups, women's
Gikuyu people, 138. *See also* Kikuyu
Global Assembly (1992), 210
Global Forum (1992), 209
Government. *See* Colonial Government; Government of Kenya

Government of Kenya, 34–41; current issues and debates, 38–39; democratization, 34; District Focus, 176; ecological issues, 37–38; economy, 35–37; education, 39–40; forest service, 134, 135, 138; Kenya Africa National Union (KANU), 121; Lake Basin Development Authority, 177; National Environment Secretariat, 37, 39–40, 112; National Environmental Action Plan, 38; National Development Plan (NDP), 1979–1983, 39; NDP, 1984–1988, 39; NDP, 1989–1993, 39; NDP 1994–1996, 200; politics and the state, 34–35; sugarcane policy, 173–176, 185–187; and women, 39–41
Greenbelt Movement, 88
Gross domestic product (GDP), 35
Gross national product (GNP), 38
Group interviews: in Mbusyani and Kyevaluki, 112; in Pwani, 135–136, 145–151
Groups, women's, 13–17; advantages/accomplishments of, 99–101, 124, 127–129, 152–153; in Gikarangu, 99–101; in Kathama, 58, 62–63, 67–68, 99; in Mbusyani and Kyevaluki, 124, 127–129; in Pwani, 152–153; rotating credit, 99–101; scaling-up, 101; South Kamwango, 178–179

Harambee, 16
Health, 164, 184–185; and sanitation, 180–183
Household, 14–18; composition, 54, 142–143; decisionmaking, 174–176; differentiation in Gikarangu, 83–86; division of labor in, 14–15; female-headed, 116–120, 122, 142; female-managed, 116–120, 122, 142–143; gender division of income, 32; in Kathama, 54–57; in Mbusyani and Kyevaluki, 113–116; in Pwani, 140–142; in South Kamwango, 169–171, 174–176
Human Development Report, 192, 208

Imports: food, 25; sugar, 173
Income, 94–96, 113–116, 124, 141–145
Independence: Kikuyu role in, 80–81, 98–99
Indigenous knowledge. *See* Ethnoscience; Kathama; Local knowledge
Institutional processes, 196–199; community empowerment, 197; enabling participatory setting, 197–198; participatory methods, 198–199; stakeholders, 197; the user of, 196–197; women's responsibilities in community resource management, 198–199
Institutional structures, 194–196; gender and the state, 195–196; local communities, 194–195
Institutions, 9, 31–32, 194–199; formal associations, 9; informal networks, 10, 15–18. *See also* Community organizations and institutions

International Council for Research in Agroforestry, 50
International economy, 2, 23–27; commodity prices, 75–78; on Gikarangu, 75–78; impact on Mbusyani and Kyevaluki, 111–112, 121–122, 125–127; structural adjustment, 8, 35–37
Irigiro Training Center for Girls, 100

Jaggary, 173, 176

Kamba. *See* Akamba
KANU. *See* Kenya Africa National Union
Kathama, 47–74; agroforestry, 59, 61–65; Athi River, 48; crops, 55; division of labor, 61–63; draught, 49, 51; ecology, 2, 47, 70; economy, 50, 54–57; environment, 51–53; ethnobotany, 65–67, 70; famine, 47, 49, 65, 67–69; farming systems, 53–57, 59–61; geographic location, 48, 49; gender division, 65–66, 68–70; government organizations, 58–59; landscape, 49, 51, 53; land use, 55–57; local knowledge, 47, 63–70; livestock, 57, 60; migration, 49, 50, 55; people, 53–55; population, 54–55; plant domestication, 66; tenure, 57–58, 64, 67–68; tree planting, 63–65; water, 57–58; wild plants, 65–67; women's groups, 58, 62–63, 67–68. *See also* Agroforestry; Tenure
Kenya Africa National Union (KANU), 34, 121
Kenya election (1992), 11, 39
Kenya Water and Health Organization (KWAHO), 197
Kenyatta, Jomo, 34
Kikuyu, 75–77, 80–83, 89, 96–99, 138–140
Kyevaluki, 105–132; community institutions, 120–121; community profile, 110–112; division of labor in, 116–118; economy, 105–109, 111, 126–127; education in, 115–116; environment, 105–109; external links, 125; farming systems, 109–111, 113–116; gendered responsibilities in, 116–118, 129–130; group activity, 121–124; land, access, and control, 118–120; livelihood systems, 116–120; livestock, 110–111, 121–122; population pressures, 125; stratification, 113–116, 122; transformation, 111–112; trends, 125–129

Labor, collective. 16–18. *See also* Groups, women's; Women
Lake Basin Development Authority (LBDA), 177
Land: -buying companies, 133, 138; common, 2, 29; degradation, 49, 50, 51, 56, 59; demarcation, 138; fragmentation of, 82–86, 138;

inheritance, 81, 118–120, 165; -use intensification, 54, 55, 82–83, 105–109; Machakos, 118–120; Murang'a history, 80–81; ownership, 81–83, 165–167; parcelization, 82–86; park periphery, 3; privatization, 8, 12, 15, 33, 81–83, 111, 126–128; Pwani history, 138; social stratification, 83–86, 113–116; tenure, customary, 82, 165; tenure, individual, 82, 138; and women, Murang'a, 81–83. *See also* Gikarangu; Kathama; Kyevaluki; Mbusyani; Pwani; South Kamwango; Tenure

Landlessness, 8, 32–33, 80–86, 108–110

Landscape, 49, 51, 53, 136–137

Land use history: in Gikarangu, 80–83; in Kathama 49–51; in Pwani, 138

Leadership, 177. *See also* Assistant chiefs

Life expectancy, 37

Livelihood, 11–14; changes in Gikarangu, 91–96; in Kathama, 49–50, 55–57; in Kyevaluki and Mbusyani, 116–120; multiple strategies, 171–173; options in Gikarangu, 77; Pwani, 143–145; South Kamwango, 164–165, 171–176; trade strategies, 94–96, 174–176. *See also* Agriculture; Kyevaluki; Mbusyani

Livestock in: Gikarangu, 83; Kathama, 57, 60; Mbusyani and Kyevaluki, 110–111, 121–122; Pwani, 150; South Kamwango, 167, 178

Local knowledge, 3, 63–70, 150, 185–187

Luo, 164–171. *See also* South Kamwango

Maasai people, 133

Machakos District, 47–50, 105–110; Boserupian model, 47–49, 105–107; ecotragedy *vs.* recovery narrative, 47–49, 105–109; maps, 52, 106; scenarios, 105–109. *See also* Kathama; Kyevaluki; Mbusyani

Maendeleo ya Wanawake, 178

Malnutrition, 182

Manufacturing, 36

Marginalization, 32–34, 77, 107–109; class, 32–33, 38, 40; ethnicity, 33–34, 40; gender, 32, 40

Markets, 31–32

Mbusyani, 105–132; community institutions, 120–121; community profile, 110–112; division of labor, 116–118; economy, 105–109, 111, 126–127; education, 115–116; environment, 105–109; external links, 125; farming systems, 109–111, 113–116; gendered responsibilities, 116–118, 129–130; group activity, 121–124; land, access and control, 118–120; livelihood system, 116–120; livestock, 110–111, 121–122; population pressures, 125; rural-urban, 110–113; stratification, 113–116, 122; transformation, 111–112; trends, 125–129

Medicine: herbal, 65–66; veterinary, 150

Members of Parliament, 178

Men: knowledge of indigenous plants, 66–70; migration of, 49, 55, 96, 116–118, 139; property resources, 64, 65, 67–68; responsibilities, 50, 61–62, 65, 90–91, 138–139, 175–176; status, 91–92; trees, 61–62, 64, 88–91, 138–139

Meru District, 28

Migori District, 161, 164–165; South Kamwango, 161–188

Migration, 12, 13, 14, 28, 38; in Gikarangu, 96–98; in Kathama, 49–50, 55; in Mbusyani and Kyevaluki, 116–118; in Pwani, 133; in South Kamwango, 171

Moi, Daniel Arap, 34

Murang'a, 75–80; map, 76. *See also* Gikarangu

Mutukanio Land Buying Company, 138–139

Mwangano Women's Group, 210

Mwethya groups: in Kathama, 58, 62–63, 67–68, in Mbusyani and Kyevaluki, 120–121, 124, 127–130. *See also* Community organizations; Women, groups

Nairobi: proximity to Gikarangu, 79. *See also* Migration

Nairobi Conference 1985, 209

Nakuru District, 133–136; map, 134. *See also* Pwani

Nakuru National Park: conflict with people and, 133, 136–137, 139, 140, 145, 150–151; ecology of, 136–137

National Environmental Action Plan (NEAP), 38

National Environment Secretariat (NES), 1, 37, 39–40, 112

Nongovernmental organizations (NGOs), 177–178, 197–199, 201, 203–204; action research, 208; promoting livelihood security, 207

North-South context, 29–30

Nutrient cycling, 60–62

Nutrition and health, 180–183

Ofwanga Women's Group, 178, 184

Park: boundaries, 1; periphery, 134

Participatory and Learning Method (PALM), 198

Participatory Rural Appraisal (PRA), 3; in Mbusyani, 112, 127; in Kyevaluki, 112, 127; in Pwani, 135

Patriarchy, 80–83, 167–169

Policy, 34–38; District Focus for Rural Development, 176; implications in Kathama, 70–71; in Pwani, 153–158

Policy options, 4, 38–39; and gendered labor and livelihoods, 70–71, 205–206; and gendered land and property relations, 70–71, 202–204; and women's status, 38–41, 200–201

Polygamy, 167–169

Population and land use, 29–30, 105–109, 116–120, 125–126, 140; Gikarangu, 78; growth, 29, 30, 35, 55, 133, 139; and migration, 116–118, 133, 139; South Kamwango, 165–167, 172, 179–180

Presbyterian Church of East Africa (PCEA). *See* Church

Pwani, 133–160; community profile, 136–140; community responses, 151–153; crops, 143; farming systems, 136, 143–145; fuelwood, 147–148; history, 133–134, 138–139; household composition, 42–45; livelihood, 143–145; livestock health, 150; local institutions, 152–153; Participatory Rural Appraisal, 135–136, 145–151; policy implications, 153–158. *See also* Nakuru National Park

Reciprocity, 63, 67–68

Reforestation, 58, 59, 61–65, 149–150

Research methods in: Gikarangu, 78; Kathama, 61–63; Mbusyani and Kyevaluki, 112–113; Pwani, 135, 136; South Kamwango, 161–188

Resettlement, 133. *See also* Settlement communities

Residents of: Gikarangu, 83–86; Kathama, 54–55; Mbusyani and Kyevaluki, 113–116; Pwani, 133; South Kamwango, 161–171

Resources, 7–20, 163; access to and control of, 11–14, 77–78, 81–83, 91, 94–95, 102, 111–112, 118–120, 140–142, 145–151, 174–176; management, 14–20, 40–41, 120–124, 144; and population, 179–180. *See also* Tenure

Rift Valley Province, 34, 35, 133

Rongo Division, 163, 171

Rural communities, 31; and the state, 31–32

School fees, 115, 127, 144

Seed banks, 149

Sessional Paper no. 1, 36

Settlement communities, 133, 138, 139, 154–156

Smallholders, 53–55, 113–116. *See also* Land; Livelihood

Soil: conditions in Gikarangu, 79; erosion, 107–111; management, 109, 120–122; in Mbusyani and Kyevaluki, 107–111

Southern Africa Development Coordinating Committee (SADCC), 25

South Kamwango, 3, 161–188; agriculture, 166–167, 171–176; births, 168; child mortality, 180–183; coffee, 174; community profile, 165–167; conceptualizing the community, 183–184; education, 179, 184–185; family planning, 179–180; forests, 166; fuelwood, 166; geography, 164–167; health, 180–183; household stratification, 169–171; infant mortality, 169; land rights, 167–171; livelihoods, 171–176; livestock, 167; local institutions, 176–179, 186; map, 162; men's productive activities, 175–176; pocket of poverty, 185–188; polygamy, 165–166; population, 165, 179–180; sugar cane, 173–174; trade, 172, 174–175, 185–186; trends, 179–185; water, 166, 171, 180–183, 187; women's groups, 178–179; women's productive activities, 174–175

South Nyanza District. *See* Migori District

States and communities, 31–32; and gender, 11–14, 16; Kenya, 34–35

Stratification (class) issues: in Gikarangu, 83–86; in Kathama, 51, 55–57; in Mbusyani and Kyevaluki, 113–116; in Pwani, 140–145; in South Kamwango, 169–171

Structural adjustment, 8, 35–36, 37; effects of, 36, 75

Sugarcane. *See* Agriculture; Government of Kenya; South Kamwango

Survey: of Gikarangu, 78; of Kathama, 57; of Mbusyani and Kyevaluki, 112; of Pwani, 138; of South Kamwango, 163–164. *See also* Research methods in

Survival. *See* Livelihood

Sustainable agriculture, 149

Sustainable development, 37–38, 47, 71

Technology "packages," 59–62

Tenure (also property), 54, 57–58, 64, 67–68; land, 54, 57, 67–68; livestock, 54, 57; trees and plants, 56, 64, 67–68; water, 57–58

Tonye Women's Group, 178

Trade, 174, 176; bananas, 94–96, 172, 175; fish, 172; international, 78, 92–94, 125; local, 94–95; long distance, 95–96; sugarcane, 174

Trees: clearing, 139; exotic, 59–62, 64–65, 87; indigenous, 51, 64–66, 87; in landscape, 50, 56, 68, 137; Murang'a, 87–88; planting, 149, 150; woodlots, 56, 64, 88–91

Trends: in Gikarangu, 77–78, 96–102; in Kathama, 170–171; in Mbusyani and Kyevaluki, 125–129; in Pwani, 158; in South Kamwango, 179–185

United Nations Conference on Environment and Development (UNCED), 29–30, 209

United Nations Decade for Women, 39, 209

United Nations Development Programme (UNDP), 38

United Nations Environment Program (UNEP), 37

Village Resource Management Plan in Pwani (VRMP), 135

Water, 166, 171, 180–183, 184, 187; access to, 57–58, 61, 107, 110, 116–117; quality, 146–147; scarcity, 146–147; tanks, 146–147; as wealth indicator, 141

"Weapons of the weak," 197

Women, agriculture, 26, 27; collective labor, 16; common property, 12; as community managers, 2, 50, 58, 101, 124, 127–130; conservation, 12–13; declining authority of, 81–83, 101, 102, 115, 119, as fun / head of household, 12, 14, 16, 40, 55, 144; education, 39–40, 79, 115, 119, 144–145; employment, 94–96, 143–

145; environmental agencies, 12–13; erosion social networks, 12; groups, 13, 14–18, 39, 58, 62–63, 67–68; and access to government, 17; informal networks, 14–15; invisibility, 47; knowledge legal rights, 80–83; land tenure, 40; legal structures, 13; marginalization, 107–109; migration, 107, 113; politics, 70; poverty and, 115, 141–145; resource managers, 40; redefining roles, 1, 50, 61–70, 91–92, 144; single mothers, 96, 100–101, 115; and the state, 35; trees, 61–65, 68, 87–91; workloads, 116–118

Women's Bureau 1991 survey, 39

Women's status, 199–201; education for women, 200–201; entitlements, 200

World Plan of Action (1975), 39

World Resources Institute, 27

Youth, 144, 145

Zero grazing, 178

The Book

Linkages among poverty, gender roles, resource decline, and ecological degradation challenge development policy and practice in many parts of the world. This book provides an analytical framework for understanding these linkages, then examines them empirically in six very different communities in rural Kenya.

The authors explore the ways that community institutions—specifically women and their organizations—respond to changing resource conditions. Looking at gender-based strategies for controlling such critical resources as soil, water, and woodlands, they consider the effects of these strategies on local decisionmaking, changing gender roles, rural stratification, and community relations within the broader social and political environment.

Barbara Thomas-Slayter is associate professor in international development and director of the International Development Program at Clark University. Her publications include *Politics, Participation and Poverty: Development Through Self-Help in Kenya.*

Dianne Rocheleau is assistant professor of geography at Clark University. She has published extensively on gender and environment, land-use changes, and agroforestry.

Coauthors include Isabella Asamba, Mohamud Jama, Charity Kabutha, Njoki Mbuthi, Elizabeth Oduor-Noah, Karen Schofield-Leca, Betty Wamalwa-Muragori, and Leah Wanjama.